DERBY WORKS
AND
MIDLAND LOCOMOTIVES

DERBY WORKS
AND
MIDLAND LOCOMOTIVES

*The story of
the works, its men, and
the locomotives they built*

J. B. RADFORD
CEng, MIMechE

LONDON

IAN ALLAN

First published 1971

SBN 7110 0185 5

© J. B. Radford 1971

*Published by Ian Allan Ltd, Shepperton, Surrey and printed in the
United Kingdom by Balding + Mansell Ltd, London and Wisbech.*

Contents

Unless otherwise stated all photographs in this book are by courtesy of British Railways.

Preface

THIS BOOK is not intended to be a completely detailed history of all the steam locomotives built in the Derby Works, for such a history would leave no room for the rest of the story. Every locomotive built is, however, mentioned in the text together with main dimensions and other features of interest.

Rather it is an attempt to draw together the loose threads of the fascinating story of the Derby Locomotive Works, and to discuss the men of great character who moulded the original complex of workshops into a great manufacturing and repair centre, and who left behind them a legacy of craftsmanship in the arts of locomotive engineering which still survives today, although perhaps the noonday of these arts is now past.

Such a story could not have been written were it not for the assistance given, not only by the chroniclers of old, but by a number of friends and colleagues whose valued assistance has made the task not only easier but very rewarding. For special thanks I would like to single out David Tee, who not only read the manuscript and pointed out a number of errors, but who made many helpful suggestions. My thanks also to Harry Daventry, Peter Rowledge and Fred Clarke for checking and supplying some information in Appendix IV, and to Oliver Carter, Andrew Haynes, Reg Clarke, Sam Shaw, the late Bill Steel and A. B. Longbottom for supplying additional information. In particular special thanks to my two typists Lorraine Pegg and Susan Adams who deciphered my rough manuscript and rendered it into a readable form.

Appendix IV, as prepared, listed all steam and diesel locomotives built at Derby with first and subsequent running numbers, date of building, renumbering and withdrawl, and type and order numbers. Owing to pressure of space, this Appendix has had to be largely omitted. It is my intention to reproduce this list separately, and interested readers should contact me at 21 Cobthorne Drive, Allestree, Derby.

Finally my grateful thanks to the Chief Mechanical & Electrical Engineer (BRB), for permission to publish the line diagrams and to quote from official records, and to Mr R. G. Jarvis, Locomotive Design

Engineer, for carefully reading the manuscript and offering his valued comments on certain aspects of the story. My especial thanks to the Archivist of the British Transport Historical Archives and his staff for their co-operation and assistance in the research for the book.

J. B. RADFORD

Allestree, Derby
January, 1971

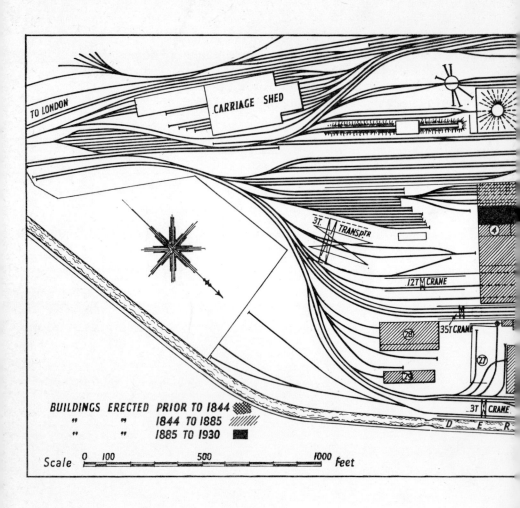

Plan of Derby Works

Showing different stages of development

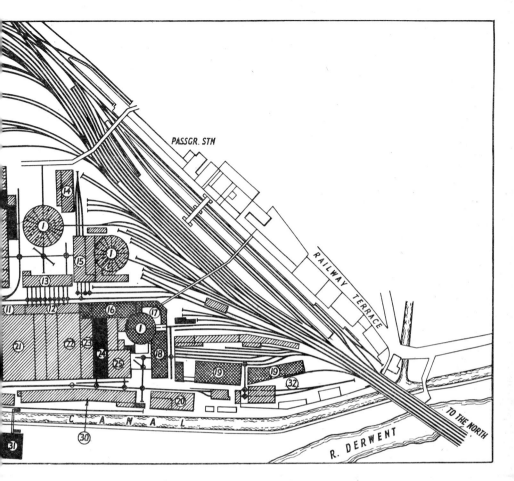

1 Old Engine Sheds 1, 2 & 3	**18** Millwrights (Former NM Carriage Shop)
2 Paint Shop	
3 Tool Shop	**19** General Stores (Former MC Engine Shop, Machine Shop & Shed)
4 Brass Fitting Shop	
5 Tool Room	**20** Works Canteen
6 Grinding Shop	**21** Boiler Shop
7 Tool and Fitting Shop	**22** Wheel and Tyre Shop
8 Erecting Shop	**23** Turning Shop
9 Offices (Later Met. Lab.)	**24** Press Shop
10 Brass Foundry	**25** Wheel Turning Shop
11 Coppersmiths	**26** Forge
12 Electric Shop (Former Erecting Shop)	**27** Concentration Depot
13 Tender Shop (Former Erecting Shop)	**28** Iron Foundry
14 Pattern Shop (Former Paint Shop)	**29** Chair Foundry
15 Lagging Shop (Former Tender Shop)	**30** Smiths Shop
16 Loco Stores (Former NM Engine Shop)	**31** Power Station
17 Main Offices	**32** Saw Mill and Timber Yard

CHAPTER ONE

Genesis

(1839-1844)

HISTORICALLY SPEAKING the establishment of the Derby Locomotive Works was closely linked with the negotiations between the North Midland, Midland Counties and Birmingham and Derby Junction Railway Companies together with the Derby Town Council concerning a suitable site for a station or stations at Derby.

By November, 1834, the details of a scheme to link three towns in the Midlands by rail with the London and Birmingham Railway, then under construction, had been drawn up by committees based in Derby, Leicester and Nottingham, and the project was tentatively christened the "Midland Counties Railway". Derby was to be a terminus, and the proposed station was to be in Derwent Street on the site of what was then Darby's Yard, with a bridge to be constructed for carrying the line over the River Derwent near to the present Exeter Bridge. This explains why the old Midland Counties line into Derby enters the present station via a violent curve, after approaching the town through what is now Chaddesden sidings. Its line would have entered the proposed station by means of an easy curve.

However this first scheme was to be much modified in the light of proposals put forward by a different group of railway promoters, who raised a scheme in October, 1835, to construct a line from Derby to Birmingham which, with the proposed North Midland line from Derby to Leeds would, as the *Derby Mercury* newspaper observed "make Derby a centre of communication and must, we imagine, increase the trade and importance of the town".

Now the promoters of the North Midland line had already arranged for their terminus to be near the Nottingham road, and the Directors of the Birmingham and Derby, seeing the importance of a link with this line, resolved to continue their route over the Derwent to connect with the North Midland at their terminus, and thus establish a direct route for through traffic.

This scheme was duly approved at a public meeting held in the Town Hall, Derby in December, 1835. However the Town Council had rather different ideas, and the following February suggested that a joint station for all three companies should be built on the Holmes, an area of low-lying pastureland to the south of the town. A deputation was sent to meet the chairman of the two principal companies together with George Stephenson and others, but the Council's proposals were dismissed, since it was considered that the site was very prone to flooding, and a request was made for an alternative site to be provided on the nearest available high ground in the Castle Fields.

The first evidence of the combined tripartite station scheme which was eventually agreed upon appears in a letter which predates the above meeting by one month, and which was sent by John Fox Bell, secretary to the Midland Counties Company, to Henry Patterson, a director of the North Midland Company. It is dated November 13, 1835, and the text reads as follows:

"I am directed by our board to send you, according to your request the inclosed tracing of our proposed terminations at Derby. Which will be adopted is not yet decided.
I remain Sir,
Yours faithfully,
J. F. Bell
Secretary"

This letter and accompanying plan are now preserved in the British Transport Historical Archives, and the plan shows the two alternative sites for the station, ie the one near the town centre, and the other in the Old Meadows.

The Derby Corporation agreed to make a better roadway to the site on the Holmes, and agreement was at last reached that this was to be the spot in June, 1838. Several plots of land were purchased in the adjacent Castle Fields, and by March, 1839, the plans were published for the building of the station and the polygonal engine shed of the North Midland Company. These were soon followed by the comprehensive plans showing the proposed workshops of all three companies.

Initially a temporary station of wood was constructed adjacent to the permanent site, and it was from this that Doctor Granville departed in the first public train on the opening day of the Birmingham and Derby Junction line on August 12, 1839, proudly holding the ticket No 1. He records the state of general confusion, and also that upon reaching Stonebridge the connecting train on the London and Birmingham line "flew by without stopping", so that his journey of 135 miles eventually took seven hours and he "inwardly thanked his stars" to find himself again upon his legs.

Of the other two lines the Midland Counties Railway between Derby and Nottingham was opened on June 4, 1839, and the North Midland line from Derby to Masborough on May 11, 1840.

The beautiful permanent station for the three companies was commenced in 1839, to the designs of Francis Thompson, the architect for the North Midland Company, and merits a particular mention, for at the time it was thought to be "too large for any possible future requirements" (*see Plate 2*).

On April 9, 1839, the North Midland Committee agreed that the Derby Station Contract be advertised, tenders to be in by May 21 following. Five tenders were received, and at a further meeting on June 12 it was agreed that the contract be let to Thomas Jackson, builder, of Pimlico, London and this was signed and sealed on July 30, 1839. His contract price was £39,986, of which the Birmingham and Derby and Midland Counties Companies agreed to contribute £4,796 and £4,923 respectively towards the cost. These two companies also agreed to pay rent at the rate of 6 per cent per annum on the proportion of the cost which was for their accommodation. The Midland Counties Company paid for the bridge over the Derby Canal, north of the station.

Seventeen drawings accompanied the station contract which included four detailing the North Midland engine house, soon to become the focal point of the Derby Works. This engine house will be described in detail later, but as to the station itself, this had a façade 1,050ft long, dominated by a boldly projecting central block, with a Venetian window above the entrance. The main two-storied office block was 14 windows wide, those on the ground-floor level being semi-circular headed and those on the first-floor level being square headed with corbelled sills. The elevation tailed off symmetrically in an arcaded screen wall punctuated by subsidiary entrances for goods vehicles.

The three-bay glazed train shed, 34ft high at the apexes was supported on 60 graceful reeded and bonded cast-iron columns 22ft high which also served as rainwater drop pipes. The single platform ran the entire length of the façade, but a number of turn-tables were provided to permit the transfer of vehicles from the platform to any of the other seven through lines. There were also two short lengths of line fronting the B&DJR and MCR platforms which were inset into the main platform face to allow the NMR platform line to be a through line, thereby not being blocked in by a train of either of the other two companies which might be at their platform faces.

A shareholders meeting room was added to the station buildings in 1856, and in 1872 both a new Board Room and a covered entrance porch and booking hall were added. Thus, though enveloped in much additional work, the most important of which was the new individual roofs for the platform islands completed in 1954, much of the original brick station building still remains. (See also Chapter 15.)

It seems that Derby can take pride in the fact that it was there that the idea of a station and hotel as joint parts of a railway complex was first thought of, for a plan of 1839 shows an L-shaped hotel building sited where the "Midland" Hotel eventually came to be built. Part of the present building was already completed by 1842, and features in a Russell lithograph of that date, but unfortunately no details of cost or of the contract have been found in the BRB archives, save in the minutes of the North Midland Company where at a meeting held on December 17, 1839, "Mr Jackson's offer to erect an hotel adjoining Derby station was accepted". Old records indicate that the original hotel was privately owned, and was not purchased by the Midland Company until several years later when they extended it considerably.

On August 14, 1860, the Midland Directors discussed the necessity for having good hotels at some of the principal stations, and since the Midland Hotel at Derby had been advertised for sale the Directors entered into a contract for its purchase from Mrs Julia Ann Blunt and others through Alpheus H. Robotham, as Trustee for the Midland Company, for £10,050. He later transferred the hotel to the MR Company by indenture on March 1, 1862.

Additional wings were added in 1874 and 1884, and in 1877 the company obtained powers by an Act of that year, to work and maintain the hotel as part of their undertaking.

The two three-storied blocks of the altered buildings were originally linked only on the ground floor, and are 100ft long, 40ft wide and 38ft high set 60ft apart. The legs have terminal blocks at each of the four corners giving dominance to the elevations. The style of both hotel and station is late Georgian in character.

In the 1930s the hotel was further extended by the provision of additional bedrooms and bathrooms and by the extension of the dining rooms, a lounge also being added between the two wings. About the same time central heating was added, running hot and cold water in 50 bedrooms and three new bathrooms were provided at a cost of some £9,400. In more recent years additional private bathrooms have been provided.

Regarding royal visits, Queen Victoria stayed in the hotel during a local visit in 1849.

We turn now to the Locomotive Works. Before the erection of the three companies' workshops the few engines on hand were stabled in the open, but a start on building operations was made in the autumn of 1839.

Part of the site for the works had been purchased as early as November 12, 1838, from J. C. B. Burrough, a local dignitary and landowner, but as a site for workshops it was a poor proposition until thousands of tons of earth and gravel had been tipped upon it, raising the level by some

8ft. The evidence of this work still survives as the difference in levels between the top and bottom yards. This infilling levelled off the works site with the station site, and only the wharves of the three companies, situated on the Derby Canal, were initially sited on the lower level.

Twelve months later the workshops and offices of the North Midland Company, also to the designs of Francis Thompson, were ready for occupation. The central feature was two large workshops and an engine house polygonal in shape with 16 sides, and 130ft in diameter lit from a pointed domed roof 48ft 10in high including a lantern top and having 48 windows. Cast-iron columns 18ft high supported the lower roof beams, the roof itself being 23ft high and the lantern 7ft 10in high. The roof covering was of slate laid on boards secured to the wooden beams.

The 16 lines of rails radiated from a central turntable and there was space for two of that days' engines on each line. To the right of the engine house were the engine workshops, 184ft 6in long and 70ft 6in wide, having a roof supported on 20 massive cast-iron columns and attached was a smithy 42ft square. To the left of the engine house was erected the carriage workshops, 191ft 6in long and 70ft 6in wide, the roof beams being supported on 16 cast-iron columns. These two main workshops formed oblique wings to the roundhouse and the total cost for the whole complex was in the region of £62,000. A second floor was added to the single storey offices fronting the roundhouse in 1859–60.*

The Birmingham and Derby Junction and Midland Counties Railway Companies also arranged for workshops to be erected, although not on the same grand scale as the North Midland.

The B&DJR had a three-road, brick-built engine shed, 150ft long and 48ft wide, erected by Messrs T. & W. Cooper at a cost of some £4,000. This was lit by 36 semi-circular headed windows, and alongside was a blacksmith's shop and a small amount of office accommodation. Three small interconnected turntables were provided outside the shed entrance. These premises were on the east side of the present Derby–Bristol line approximately where the junction of the line into the present Carriage and Wagon Works now lies.

The engine shed of the Midland Counties Company was at the north end of the station, quite near to the canal bridge. It was 134ft long and 52ft wide and the adjacent workshops were 200ft × 93ft with a repair shop 93ft × 88ft adjoining, all built substantially in brick. Alongside these shops was a large water tank 48ft 6in long × 27ft wide which supplied water for all three companies.

The Midland Counties engine shed was for many years used for shareholders' meetings, until one person was killed by a train whilst crossing the line and these gatherings were then subsequently trans-

*BTHR Mid 1/169.

ferred to the ground floor of the cheese warehouse. In 1857 the handsome new shareholders' room, by the station front entrance, came into use, and was thenceforth used for the meetings.

The old engine shed was subsequently used as a wagon shop, and later relegated to less important uses, but it still stands today, as do many of the old shops of two of the three pre-grouping companies.

Both the workshops and station were gas lit from the beginning on a system installed under the supervision of Mr Thomas Crump of Derby, involving in all 747 lamps supplied by over 1,000yd of 4in iron gas main.

Regarding staff in these early days there are some figures available for the North Midland line, covering the six months from January to the end of June, 1842. At that time the total mileage worked was 73, and the number of engines in steam daily (except Sundays) was 16.* The total engine stock was at this time 40. Weekly mileages were 5,694 on passenger trains, 4,925 on goods trains and 938 by "assistant and pilot trains".

Chief Assistant to Robert Stephenson was William Prime Marshall, who had been involved with architect Francis Thompson on the plans for the NMR stations, and in charge on the repair shops at Derby was a Mr Dobson.

There was a total Locomotive Department staff of 197, mostly located at Derby, including 2 boiler makers, 1 brass founder, 1 coppersmith, 20 enginemen, 4 engine turners, 20 firemen, 26 fitters, erectors and millwrights, 5 foremen, 3 clerks, 2 timekeepers, 2 store keepers, 4 joiners, 2 pattern makers, 14 labourers, 1 painter, 1 planer, 2 drillers, 10 smiths, 5 smiths fitters, 1 spring maker, 8 stationary enginemen and pumpers, 14 strikers, 5 turners, 11 boys "paid at 2s per day and under", 20 cleaners, 9 cokemen and 4 labourers on traffic. The total weekly wage bill amounted to only £261. 13s 10d!

On the matter of locomotive stock, the North Midland had at this time, as previously stated, 40 locomotives, mostly of the 2-2-2 type, including the famous Stephenson "mail" engines, the outstanding feature of which was the haystack firebox designed to reduce the amount of priming. These were turned out by a variety of firms, as were the other main type, the 0-4-2s, designed mainly for goods working.

Later still the company purchased a number of the famous Stephenson "long boiler" 2-4-0s on which all wheels were placed in front of the firebox which, coupled with outside cylinders and a complete lack of any attempt at balancing the reciprocating masses, made for a most uncomfortable swaying motion along the track and earned for the engines the nickname of "Polkas", after a dance craze of that period.

By the time that amalgamation with the other two companies came,

*BTHR Nom 5/2

the number of engines owned by this company had grown to 49, comprising 34 passenger singles, and 15 goods, 10 of which were 0-4-2s, four 2-4-0s and one long boilered 0-6-0.

In general command of this stock was Robert Stephenson who was appointed to the "Management of Locomotive Power" in February, 1839, and who continued in this office until August, 1842. There was also a Superintendent of the Locomotive Department from the initial opening of the line and this office was filled by W. P. Marshall, at a salary of £200 per annum until he resigned on April 4, 1843, when he was succeeded by Thomas Kirtley, brother of the later famous Matthew. Marshall went on to become the Locomotive Superintendent of the Norfolk Railway at Norwich, and in 1848 the first secretary of the newly formed Institution of Mechanical Engineers, which position he held until his retirement in 1877. He died in 1906.

Thomas Kirtley remained in the position of Locomotive and Carriage Superintendent at a salary of £250 per annum until May, 1844, when Matthew became the first Locomotive Superintendent for the new Midland Railway. Thomas was born at Tanfield, County Durham being the eldest boy in the family, and began his working life as an engine driver on the Liverpool and Manchester Railway. He then founded the firm of Thomas Kirtley & Co in Warrington, his works, the Dallam Foundry, being in Jockey Lane. There he built a few locomotives between 1837 and 1841, reportedly being the contractor for the Warrington & Newton Railway, but the firm failed during the slump in 1841, and was disbanded.

The Midland Counties engines were a rather more motley collection there being 37 Bury type 2-2-0s, three of the 2-2-2 type, six 0-4-0s and one 0-4-2 at amalgamation.

The other company, the Birmingham and Derby Junction, had but 12 engines, 10 of which were the ordinary 2-2-2 type supplied variously by Messrs Tayleur, Mather Dixon, Hawthorns and Sharp Roberts, the other two being 0-4-2 goods engines supplied by Messrs Thompson, Cole & Co. of Bolton.

These early types of locomotives suffered from many deficiencies in design, some inevitably more so than others. Many were underpowered for the heavier loads being imposed upon them, and were mechanically unsound into the bargain. Steam was not used expansively at this period in the development of the locomotive, and many were the troubles associated with the poor steaming of the early boilers.

Early in 1842 Robert Stephenson focused his attention on one particular problem, that of the rapid destruction of smokeboxes and chimneys by the very hot gases leaving the boiler tubes. He made some experiments with North Midland engines at Derby to ascertain the heat losses and found, by suspending conical cups of various metals inside the smokebox, that a temperature of 773degF was reached in the chimney, proving great waste of useful heat. To overcome this the locomotive boilers on his next designs were lengthened from 9ft to 13 or 14ft, and all axles were placed in front of the firebox. These engines were patented under the name "long boiler" and further experiments the following year proved that this new design had reduced the temperature in the chimney to about 442degF, although, as mentioned a little earlier, they were unsteady on the track.

One of these long boiler locomotives, No 71, was the first to be fitted with Howe's link motion, this being developed by one of Robert Stephenson's fitters, William Howe, but later becoming universally known as "Stephenson's link motion", although Robert himself always referred to it by the former name.

Regarding the introduction of this type of valve gear it is recorded that on December 15, 1841, Robert Stephenson called into the North Midland locomotive offices at the Derby Works after a visit to Newcastle and remarked "There is no occasion to try any further at scheming valve motions for one of our people has now hit on a plan that beats all the others" and he then explained the slotted link, developed by Howe from an idea by another member of Stephenson's staff, a man called Williams.

Two new long boiler engines arrived at Derby within the space of five weeks, the first being Stephenson's 358 delivered on September 9, 1842, fitted with Isaac Dodd's wedge motion, and numbered 70 by the Company and the second, Stephenson's 359, delivered on October 15 following, having the new link gear.

David Joy recall's seeing the wedge motion at Masborough and wrote "the bridge, links, clamps, etc, then struck me as complicated".

Despite numerous seizures in the wedges the Midland continued to persevere with this type of valve motion for quite a number of years, until the value of the Stephenson type valve gear, both in design and maintenance, became too obvious to ignore any longer, and it became adopted as a virtual standard for the future.

Thus the long series of early experiment with various types of valve gear, some extremely ingenious but expensive, some fundamentally simple but unsound in operation and others downright hopeless mechanical constructions, was effectively terminated, and many design headaches lifted from the shoulders of the locomotive designer.

Other experiments were also going on at this time, and one in particular merits mention. This was the first sustained effort to produce a locomotive consuming its own smoke, thereby enabling coal to be used instead of coke, and was applied in 1841 to Midland Counties engine

No 1 *Bee* (formerly *Ariel*) which was a 2-2-0 outside-cylindered engine supplied by the Butterley Company of Ripley, Derby in May, 1839. It had sandwich frames only partly concealing the 11in diameter × 16in stroke cylinders, and 5ft diameter driving wheels with outside bearings and cranks.

Samuel Hall of Nottingham designed the apparatus which consisted of extending 16 of the lower boiler tubes to the outside of the smokebox where they were finished with bell mouth openings.*

Eight additional air tubes were provided through the sides of the casing and firebox, and a steam jet, or "blower", was provided in the chimney for use when the engine was stationary.

Several other minor modifications were added as the trials progressed, including a form of brick arch in the firebox, probably the first application of what was to become a standard feature on locomotives some 15 years later, but the grave disadvantage of this equipment was that the inrush of air into the firebox as the locomotive proceeded along the track caused the smokebox to become red hot, the heat being "so great that the whole smokebox end of the engine was a mass of fire intense enough to ignite the adjacent sandboxes". Mr Birkinshaw, the company's engineer of the Birmingham and Derby Junction line, was instructed to inspect the apparatus and report his findings to the Directors of the line.

In addition to this, all complications in the structure of a locomotive were frowned upon, as simplicity was thought to be the essence of good practice, and the experiment was thus concluded. The engine was sold back to its makers in December, 1844 for the small sum of £150, little more than its scrap value.

---

*Markham, Proc. of the Institution of Mechanical Engineers (1860).

CHAPTER TWO

Amalgamation and Expansion
(1845-1854)

On May 10, 1844, the three companies, the North Midland, Midland Counties and Birmingham and Derby Junction were amalgamated to form the new Midland Railway Company, at that time the largest in England under single management, with a total main line route mileage of 179. This was the first great merger of smaller lines to take place, preceding the link-up which created the giant London and North Western Company by some two years.

On the locomotive side there were therefore now three contenders for the one new post of superintendent of the Locomotive and Carriage Departments: Josiah Kearsley of the Midland Counties line, who it must be said, fully expected to be offered the position: Thomas Kirtley of the North Midland line, and his brother Matthew of the comparatively small Birmingham and Derby Junction Company.

Somewhat surprisingly, and thanks no doubt to strong recommendations by the Stephensons, under whom he had served as a pupil, it was young Matthew who was appointed, at the age of 31, receiving a commencing salary of £250 per annum some £50 more than his salary on the B&DJR*. Brother Thomas accepted the choice, but Kearsley became very embittered by the decision. He still had 2½ years of his contract to run, and was bought out for the sum of £750. He refused to serve under Matthew, and removed his affections to Messrs Rothwell & Co, locomotive builders, of Union Foundry, Bolton-le-Moors.

Thomas Kirtley stayed on with the Midland Railway for a time working under his brother Matthew as an inspector, from March, 1845, until May of the same year when he was paid £100 and went to work under Thomas Brassey on the Trent Valley Railway. In February, 1847 he was appointed as Locomotive Superintendent of the LB&SCR but in November of the same year he died of a tumour on the brain.

His son, William, was to become the Workshop Superintendent at Derby some years later, and thus continue the family connections with Derby which was brought to an end by the death of his uncle Matthew.

Also from May, 1844 arrangements were made for the locomotive stock of the Sheffield and Rotherham Railway to be repaired in the Derby shops, and the belt-driven 2-2-2 *Sheffield* was sent to Derby

*BTHR Mid 1/329.

"forthwith, to be put into thorough repair." The Midland assumed control in October, 1844, and took over charge of the Holmes Works, 4¼ miles from Sheffield, at that time in charge of a Mr G. Bartholomew. The locomotive stock was in a very run-down condition and also in May, 1844, arrangements were made for a locomotive to be hired from the Midland Company to work the traffic.

The state of this company with regard to motive power well illustrates the difficulties that many of the early lines got into when using new and largely untried designs of locomotives.

Matthew Kirtley was faced immediately with the problem of bringing some kind of order and standardisation to the great miscellany of loco-motive types which he had inherited from the three old companies. Of the 90 odd engines available, a considerable number were even then not fit for further use and were immediately laid up, either for sale or breaking up. Of those fit for traffic, several were daily being stretched in capacity hauling the heavier and heavier trains.

Kirtley weighed up the various arguments concerning the most suit-able number of wheels to be provided on a locomotive and came out in favour of the six-wheeled type, having previously had first hand ex-perience of the unsteadiness of the four-wheeled, single-driver machines whilst working with them on the London and Birmingham Railway. These latter types he quickly relegated to unimportant work, and all further orders were for six-wheeled locomotives. Kirtley also became aware of the restrictions placed on the use of his stock of locomotives by the fact that when the frequent breakdowns occurred the engine was not only immobilised for a long period while spare parts were obtained from the makers, but often the cost of repairs was considerably inflated by the need to send those locomotives requiring repairs of a more serious nature back to their makers. Often these makers were extremely busy with new orders and long delays occurred, especially if that particular firm was not supplying any further locomotives to the Mid-land, as was often the case.

A sidelight on the state of the locomotive stock in these early days is provided by a minute of the Locomotive and Stores Committee dated November 5, 1850, which authorised Kirtley to accept the offer of Henry Wright of Saltley Works, Birmingham to provide 10 or 12 engines complete with drivers, firemen and cleaners to work trains between Derby and Birmingham at 1s per mile the Midland Company to pro-vide only the coke, Wright providing all other stores.*

All these factors convinced Kirtley that the existing complex of workshops at Derby should be further developed into an organisation capable not only of dealing with all repairs, but of also building the new

*BTHR Mid 1/167.

locomotives he so urgently required. In the short term he tried to ensure that all new locomotives delivered were either to his own designs or that he had approved the makers' plans for new contract-built engines.

Expansion of the workshop facilities began almost immediately. His first request was for more covered engine accommodation, and in his report of December 2, 1845 he recommended that a second round-house be erected to house 16 locomotives allocated to the Derby depot. for which no shed was available, pointing out that they were being adversely affected by standing out in all weathers during the winter time. This new roundhouse, together with additional repair facilities, was completed and brought into use in mid-February, 1847.

At the half year ending December 31, 1846, Kirtley reported a total locomotive stock of 122, including 10 new engines received in the previous six months. Ninety-five of these were in good working order, and there were 23 engines awaiting repairs, the remaining four engines being laid up for sale. Five new fireboxes, ten complete sets of tubes and nine cranked axles had been supplied in the half year.

Further workshop improvements were put in hand, and provision for warming the workshops "either by steam or hot water under the inspection of Mr Barwell and Mr Kirtley" was also made in December, 1849. The work of the various departments set up for each of the three old companies was rationalised until, by the year 1851, Kirtley was in a position to build his first new locomotive.*

Prior to this, since 1848, the major rebuilding of about ten locomotives had been undertaken in conjunction with Messrs E. B. Wilson & Co of the Railway Foundry, Leeds, who became temporary partners with the Midland for work of this nature, and the products of this union were officially regarded as built by "MR Co & Wilson".

Some of the major parts for this and other work were of course still supplied by private firms, and a number of local firms suddenly discovered this vast new outlet for their products established on their doorstep.

Local ironworks were expanded in capacity to supply the multitude of forgings and castings now required in large numbers by the railways. New techniques in iron and steel bridge making were evolved and methods of perfecting the manufacture of malleable iron were developed. Firms such as Andrew Handysides of the Britannia Foundry, Derby, later to become famous the world over, were drawn in by the Midland Company, and existing founding artistry was turned towards the production of such intricate work as cylinder blocks. These and other firms thus became close co-workers with Kirtley in the vast building and rebuilding programmes he was forced into in order to bring his engine

*BTHR Mid 1/167.

stock up to the standard needed for the traffic requirements, so that Robert Stephenson was able to report in August, 1849, that "many engines have been so extensively repaired as to make them fully equal to new engines."

Ordinary rolling stock required was largely ordered from outside contractors, and much major repair work was also undertaken by them. Soon after the amalgamation a decision was taken in July, 1844, "that in future all the carriages of the company shall be painted claret".

All this time, Kirtley, had been expanding the shops, and from early in 1849, a considerably larger proportion of both repair work and new construction of locomotives and rolling stock together with work for the Civil Engineers Department and outstations was undertaken.

It should be realised that apart from locomotive work, carriages and wagons were being constructed and repaired under the Coaching Superintendent Mr Charles Mills working under Kirtley. Robert Harland was the Chief Foreman of the carriage and wagon side, having been transferred from the same position on the North Midland line to which he was appointed in February, 1840 upon joining that company. He had been born on June 24, 1804 and served both companies well for many years.

Other carriage and wagon leading hands at the time included William Humber, foreman painter off the North Midland; John Stableford inspector of private wagons who had been in railway service as early as October, 1833 (presumably on the Leicester and Swannington line), and William Jones, foreman of the carriage and wagon smiths, an old Leicester and Swannington man, who was taken on by the Midland in August, 1847. The two carriage-shop foremen were John Goodwin, ex-NMR who joined the service on May 11, 1840, and his counterpart William Goodall who began work on the Midland Counties line in March, 1837. The wagon side was run by two purely Midland men Thomas Tomlinson and William Bartlett taken on in 1846 and 1847 respectively.

The old Midland Counties Carriage and Wagon Workshops at Leicester continued repairing vehicles for only a relatively short period, for even before the amalgamation the Midland Counties Directors had directed that all work be transferred to Derby as early as December, 1842.

Some examples of the prices paid for smiths, fitters and painters work in these early days throws an interesting light on the level of remuneration, and the figures given apply to December, 1849.
For

Turning engine and tender axles	3s 6d each
,, new eccentrics	4s each

Turning new wheels 3ft 6in to 4ft 6in   5s   per pair

     ,,   new wheels 4ft 9in to 7ft 0in   7s 6d per pair

For

Re-turning old wheels 3ft 6in to 4ft 6in   4s   per pair

   ,,   ,,   ,,   ,,   4ft 9in to 7ft 0in   5s   per pair

Hooping wheels (contract prices for labour)

To cutting and taking off tyres (all sizes)   1s 6d per tyre

To bending, welding, blocking and putting
on tyres 4ft 6in to 6ft 6in   15s   per tyre

Smiths work

To new drawbars complete for carriages
and wagons   1s 4d each

Altering side chains (carriages)   1s 8d per set

Carriage steps   1½d   per lb or

     3s 4d per set

Piecing buffer rods, and putting them
in shoes with cotters   10d   each or

     3s 4d per set

Turners work

To repairing No 210 engine   £15. 0s 0d

   ,,   ,,   ,, 206   ,,   £12. 0s 0d

   ,,   ,,   ,, 195   ,,   £10. 0s 0d

One boy to each engine paid by the company.

Boiler smith's work

To two fireboxes, putting in and staying
complete Nos 98 and 99   £18. 0s 0d each

To one boiler, new smokebox and firebox
putting in complete No 122   £22. 0s 0d

To one boiler in shop, complete No 93   £26. 0s 0d

Contract to coke tenders, clean out the
engine pits and part of the yard, at per week   £9. 2s 0d

Other work

Taking wheels off   6d   per pair

Straightening axles   6d   each

Adjusting wheels on axles   6d   per pair

Putting wheels on axles   1s   per pair

Keying wheels   1s   per pair

Painting, contract price for labour

Coupé with four compartments   £12. 0s 0d

First class   £11. 0s 0d

Composite   £11. 0s 0d

Second class   £9. 10s 0d

Enclosed third class	£9. 10s 0d
Open ,, ,,	£7. 0s 0d
Van	£9. 0s 0d
Carriage trucks	£2. 12s 0d
,, ,, (if new)	£3. 0s 0d
Horse boxes	£2. 0s 0d
,, ,, (if new)	£4. 0s 0d
Engines	£2. 0s 0d
Tenders	£1. 10s 0d

It will be understood that these contract prices for many jobs were paid to the leader of a gang, whether he be a smith, painter or a turner. The smith himself was responsible for setting on his own staff, and he it was who decided how much each person in the team should receive out of the price paid by the company. In certain trades, of course, there was no question of a team being involved, the workmen receiving the whole payment for the work done himself.

Weekly wages bills in 1849 for the Locomotive, Carriage and Wagon Departments amounted to some £1,442, the cost of working engines being £814. 16s 11d, repairing engines £419. 2s 6d, and repairing carriages £204. 8s 2d.

A month's work load (September, 1849) for the works was as follows:

Repairs

Locomotive engines	28
First carriages	18
Composite carriages	6
Second carriages	21
Third carriages	7
Post Office carriages	1
Guards' Vans	42
Horseboxes	6
Carriage trucks	2
Wagons	414
Wagons painted	184

New construction

Second class carriages	3
Replacement Enclosed Third Class Carriages	1
New goods wagons (with spring buffers)	12
Replacement new goods wagons (with spring buffers)	3

The first new locomotive turned out by the Derby shops appeared in September, 1851, and was a six-wheel coupled goods tender engine bearing the number 147. It had 5ft driving wheels* on an 8ft + 8ft wheelbase and 15in diameter × 24in stroke inside cylinders. It was re-numbered 166 in 1852, 322 in 1862, and 158 in 1866 when it was with-drawn and replaced by a Derby-built 2-4-0 passenger engine.

A sister engine, No 146 was turned out in December, 1851, but she was subsequently rebuilt in 1862 as a six-wheel coupled tank engine with 4ft diameter driving wheels and 16in × 24in cylinders and with-drawn from service as No 217 in 1867. Few other details have survived of these two early engines.

Further 0-6-0s, Nos 148 and 149 were turned out in February and June, 1852, respectively, having the same dimensions as the first two, and these were the last of this type to come out of the Derby Works until 1857.

The first passenger engine turned out solely by the Derby shops appears to have been No 96 which appeared also in December, 1851, having 6ft driving wheels and inside cylinders 15in diameter × 20in stroke. However this early single did not last 10 years, being broken up in 1860 and replaced

She was one of a batch of four new locomotives, Nos 94 and 96–8, turned out between December, 1851 and June, 1852 and followed the almost complete renewal of an earlier locomotive No 95 which appeared in December, 1850, and which was a similar engine except that her cylinders were 15in diameter × 22in stroke. The "class" was completed by a further locomotive No 93, which was of the same dimensions as 95, and was also an almost complete renewal of an earlier locomotive.

Two further singles, Nos 91 and 92, originally turned out by R. B. Longridge & Co of Bedlington, in February and June, 1847 respectively, were also extensively rebuilt in October, 1849 and January, 1851, making up a small class of "up to date" passenger engines.

Fortunately there is a drawing extant of this class, one of the very few Kirtley drawings to survive the ravages of time and non-historically minded officialdom. This shows the class to have had inside frames stayed to and terminating at the front of the firebox and rear of the smokebox, and full-length outside frames, both 1¼in thick, with tie bars from the front buffer beam to the leading wheel horns and another to the trailing horns. This latter tie bar was stayed adjacent to the driving wheel by a Y-shaped forked bar. The driving wheels of 6ft diameter, had inside bearings and underhung springs and the 4ft diameter leading and trailing wheels had outside axleboxes and overhung springs sup-

*Throughout this book the Derby term "driving wheels", as opposed to the more correct description "coupled wheels", will be used.

porting the axlebox by means of a rod passing through the horns. The wheelbase was 7ft 6in + 7ft and the length over the engine buffer beams was 21ft 7½in.

The boiler barrel, of 3ft 9in outside diameter, was 10ft 6in long and the firebox 4ft 2½in long × 4ft 5½in wide at the top and 4ft 2½in at the bottom, the boiler being stayed to the outside frame at the firebox, and between the leading and driving wheels. The firebox was of the raised round-top type.

Quadrant type reversing gear was provided, and the feed pump was driven mechanically from a small crank pin placed off centre on the end of the driving crank axle.

These first passenger engines were in fact basically Derby versions of the "Jenny Lind" class, many of which had been supplied by E. B. Wilson not only to the Midland but also to the LB&SCR and others. David Joy is given a large slice of credit for the neat and successful original design. The secret of its success is stated to be the then relatively high pressure of 120psi to which the boiler was pressed.

The first one turned out, for the LB&SCR, bore the name *Jenny Lind*. She did trials on the North Midland line, greatly impressing Kirtley, who immediately put in an initial order for six at £2,350 each, the total quantity eventually delivered being 20. There is even a story that the original engine, with name removed, was bought by the Midland as a result of the trials, but this is not true.

There is a drawing of an engine bearing the name *Jenny Lind* carrying a builder's plate showing it to have been Wilson's 132nd of 1848 and which hung for very many years in the works Managers office at Derby. However the first engine delivered to the Midland Company in September, 1847, was given the running number 45. Driving wheels were 6ft diameter and the leading and trailing wheels 4ft diameter on a total wheelbase of 13ft 6in (7ft + 6ft 6in). The boiler pitched 5ft 9in above rail level carried 124 2in diameter tubes 11ft long, giving a heating surface of 720sq ft to which the firebox added a further 80sq ft. The inside cylinders were 15in diameter × 20in stroke providing a calculated tractive force, at 65 per cent boiler pressure, of 4,876lb. Working weights were: engine 24tons 1cwt (of which 10tons were on the driver) and tender, carrying 800gal of water and 2½tons of coke, 15tons 13cwt, totalling 39tons 14cwt.

Coke consumption was officially rated at 36.2lb per mile at tests carried out in May, 1848, between two of these engines and two Sharp Bros 2-2-2 engines on the route from Derby to Masborough, at which both Matthew Kirtley and William Marlow were present and apparently very impressed by the "Jenny Lind's" performance.

More of these passenger engines, nine of which were joint products of

Derby and E. B. Wilson & Co, were turned out from the Derby Works up to the beginning of 1854, all of the same basic "Jenny Lind" type.

These were Nos 5, 12, 13 and 101 with 14in × 20in cylinders and 5ft 6in driving wheels, No 105 with 15in × 20in cylinders and 6ft driving wheels and Nos 116–9 with 14½in × 20in cylinders and 6ft driving wheels together with an odd couple of Derby-built singles Nos 102 and 103 with dimensions the same as No 5. A considerable number of parts for these particular engines were supplied by the contractor to the Derby Works where erection was carried out. Obviously in these early years the capacity of the works to produce new parts for batches of new locomotives was not sufficiently well developed.

In seven years the class acquitted themselves so well that, with a few of his own modifications, Kirtley began to turn them out as a basic design from Derby in 1854, starting with No 3 in August. These continued with Nos 4, 7, 8, 10, 14, 16, 104, 106–9 in 1855 and 110–15 in 1856, the last (115) emerging in June (*see Plate 5*). These Derby engines all had 6ft driving wheels and 15in × 20in cylinders, and later in life some of the engines of this class still running were to go through a strange metamorphosis, becoming 0-6-0WTs and one, No 8, lasted in this form until September, 1920 carrying 10 different numbers and emerging in final form as nothing at all like the original locomotive!

By the end of 1855 Kirtley was able to report that 33 new engines had been completed in the companies' shops during the previous four years, and 16 supplied by contract with outside firms, leaving 14 new engines to be completed during the next year, and 8 engines the following year. This total includes all engines previously mentioned in this chapter, and excluded only the rebuilding of a Fenton 2-2-2 of March, 1841, which was turned out from Derby in October, 1855 under its old No 17, using only the firebox of the old engine. This was former North Midland No 35, and had cylinders 14in × 20in and 5ft 6in driving wheels. She was withdrawn from service in December, 1859.

At Derby the Works had a large increase in expenditure and labour on locomotive and carriage and wagon repairs in 1855, when part of the absorbed Birmingham and Gloucester stock was converted from broad to narrow gauge, as much as could be adapted being so treated and the cost charged to revenue.

Kirtley had reported in July, 1849 that he had 120 engines on hand and of that number one half were required to be in perfect condition to meet all contingencies, leaving 60 for repairs. At that time 58 wanted repairs including those light engines laid up for sale. He had previously had 60 engines considered too light for use on his hands and of these 37 had by then been sold or otherwise disposed of, leaving a further 23 still on hand of no further use.

He gave some interesting figures regarding engine repair costs, and in the six months ending in June, 1849, £21,796 had been spent of which £2,490 had been expended on new tubes, fireboxes and boilers and £19,306 on general repairs.

A fair estimate of the length of time the following items would last had been arrived at over the previous years. Boiler tubes gave an average 75,000 miles run in service, fireboxes 150,000 miles and boilers 300,000 miles, this working out at ¾d per mile depreciation to cover the deterioration of these components.

An unfortunate accident was reported by the Midland chairman on February 26, 1856, when he recorded the exploding of the boiler of an old ex-Midland Counties four-wheel coupled engine at Kegworth. As a result all were immediately taken out of service to be "renewed" (as was the Midland phrase for practically brand new locomotives at that time) as passenger locomotives of a modern type for use on the Leicester to Hitchin line. The term "renewed" in Midland parlance generally referred to a new locomotive built to replace an old one and charged to revenue account.

It is perhaps worthwhile recording here that early in 1857 the first length of steel track ever used commercially was laid down at the north end of Derby station at a place where heavy traffic had formerly required the replacement of the iron rails every six months or so.* It was produced as a casting, with manganese introduced into the melt to act as a de-oxidiser, to a modified Bessemer process invented by R. F. Mushet. This length of rail remained in use for 16 years when it was considered worn out and removed for scrap. The Midland Company were therefore yet again pioneers in a new field, for it was not until five years later that the LNWR and the NER introduced them for use in similarly arduous conditions.

On the other hand the Midland were somewhat tardy in introducing "steel tires" for their locomotives, for it was not until 1861, some two years after the LNWR, that they were tentatively used. They soon showed their merits for on heavy engines they lasted 120,000–150,000 miles as against 50,000–60,000 for the iron types, being 2⅜in thick as new.

Misdemeanours were rather uncommon in these early days, but those who offended were sternly disciplined and frequently lost their jobs. On October 16, 1849, Kirtley reported that he had discharged 12 painters, and there are other records with instances of both driver and fireman being discharged for fighting and using bad language on the footplate.

* *The Centenary of the Steel Rail* by J. Dearden, "Railway Steel Topics", Vol. IV, No. 1 (Spring 1957)

Disciplinary action was also taken against those committing breaches of the working regulations and one driver in particular became quite famous by having the locomotive pit in front of the locomotive works offices named after him. He was Joseph Pickering, who was taken off main-line duties following a collision at Knighton Junction on November 25, 1854, for which he was held to be responsible. He was demoted to shunting duties and it was "Old Joe", as he came to be known, who used to run ex-works locomotives on trial trips to Willington and back, putting such locomotives as the Stephenson long boilers through their paces after repairs.

These were days when engines were not particularly well balanced, there being no weighbridge, and "Pickerings Pit" was where Old Joe attended to the weight distribution and other maladjustments and defects prior to the trial run, usually undertaken without the boiler or cylinder clothing. Having been on the Midland since 1845, Joe wrote to the Midland Director's following his retirement on July 22, 1882 at the age of 79, asking that some "pecuniary assistance" should be granted to him in consequence of his long service, but this was denied him.*

On the subject of nicknames, other parts of the works have had names bestowed upon them by the workmen, but the origins are lost in the mists of time. "Stone pit" south of the erecting shop, where the fireboxes and smokeboxes etc were cleared of ash and soot before the engines were shopped, is of more recent construction, and no doubt is so called because of its method of construction. But others such as "Spike island", the area of rough ground well to the south of all the shops and adjacent to the Derby Canal and the gas works boundary, and "Klondyke" where engines awaited the call into the shops, defy all attempts to discover their origin.

In the works a new wheel repair shop, costing £5,500, including tools and plant, was proposed in 1856, together with a new repair and painting shop costing £2,000. Engine and store sheds costing £1,179 had already been built, and by the end of the year alterations to the works and offices costing £7,950 and £760 respectively had been done. Travelling cranes were installed in the tender and No 1 fitting shops, and new boiler shops, to replace the sheds erected on the bottom yard in 1855, were put in hand in the summer of 1857. Machines and tools for the new shops, including steam hammers, a tyre cutting machine, anvils, a wheel slotting machine and hydraulic press, boiler makers and tyre hooping furnaces, and a wheel blocking press were all installed, and an amount of £5,000 was set aside for their provision.

A brass foundry and a mess room were provided, to cost £2,500, in 1859. In addition a footbridge was erected to provide access from the

*BTHR Mid 1/168.

station platform, across the running lines, to the locomotive offices, at a cost of £1,000, and this was completed by the end of 1860.

A new fitting shop (No 3) was provided, and the space between turning and boiler shops on the bottom yard roofed over in 1860. By way of explanation the bottom yard refers to the lower of the two workshop levels adjacent to the Derby Canal.

Messrs Handyside's of Derby supplied most of the castings, not only for the new workshops but also those required for locomotives, carriages and wagons as previously noted.

The third roundhouse known as No 3 shed was added in 1852. This was larger than No 1 and 2 sheds, having 24 roads (four with access from outside) with accommodation for that amount of engines. This new roundhouse was 170ft in diameter with a 90ft diameter clear central area. Height to top of the lantern was 51ft 6in and the design was drawn up by the Midland architect John H. Sanders. The contractor was George Thompson, and the contract was signed on May 27, 1851, the shed being brought into use the following year at a cost of some £6,500.

As a footnote the North Stafford Company at that time occupied the old Birmingham and Derby Junction shed at the south end of the station, and continued to do so until a new two-road shed was constructed for their use by agreement upon the demolition of the old shed to permit rail access to the new Carriage and Wagon Works about 1873.

An additional mess room was provided in 1862, and the following year a new saw shed, coppersmiths and tinsmiths shops were erected. By this time the area of the works had increased four-fold and the number of managers, superintendents, clerks, foremen, guards, engine drivers, firemen, porters, labourers and "mechanics of every description" exceeded 2,000.

The year 1864 saw the erection of a new millwright's shop and a set of new carriage shops. Also erected was a new time office, and a 42ft turntable was put in. Travelling cranes were provided for the millwrights and fitting shops and a new smith's shop built in 1865, during which time also a new roof was erected over the space between boiler and fitting shops to give more space for this work.

It will be realised from the foregoing that Kirtley had set about expanding the capacity of the works with vigour, ably backed initially in his exertions by the chairman of the Midland Company, George Hudson who had instigated a policy of rapid expansion over the system as a whole, fully realising that a bold fight for existence was the only way of defending their precarious position, in the light of the many schemes for similar expansion by their opponents.

Absorbed by the Midland Company, following the initial 1844 amalgamation, had been further small companies.

The Sheffield and Rotherham was absorbed in 1845, followed by the Leeds and Bradford, Leicester and Swannington and Bristol and Birmingham the following year, and later the "Little" North Western was leased to the Midland in May, 1852. Actual working of the line commenced on June 1, and the line finally purchased in January, 1871.

In the mid 1850s certain efforts were made to substitute bituminous coal for more expensive coke, as fuel for locomotives, and many experiments were carried out, in particular by Joseph Beattie of the London and South Western Railway, who also sought to perfect some form of feed water heating at the same time. At Derby in 1856, Kirtley associated with Charles Markham in his experiments to this end, and three years later they produced as the answer a divided firebox obtained by fixing an inclined brick arch under the tube plate and adding a deflector plate sloping downwards fixed inside the firedoor. Primary combustion took place on the firebars and secondary combustion was achieved by mixing the hot gases from the firebed with secondary air entering through the firedoor. Thus a simple arrangement achieved what Beattie had had to use combustion chambers and other intricate details to achieve.

A new Derby 2-2-2 passenger tender engine No 39, turned out in the autumn of 1859, was one of the engines chosen to take part in these experiments along with Stephenson singles Nos 131 and 135. No 39 was driven for the trials by one of the old school engine drivers, Frederick Leopold Smith, attended by the first regular locomotive inspector William Atha. Smith was later promoted to locomotive inspector, and Atha became running forman at Derby.

One of the major difficulties was to teach the drivers of coal burning engines to produce only the absolute minimum quantity of smoke, since the emission of this was forbidden by Act of Parliament.

Also involved were two interesting double framed 0-6-0 goods engines built by Messrs Beyer-Peacock & Co in December, 1858, being makers Nos 89 and 90 and carrying MR Nos 428 and 429. These were of the firms own design, and employed Joseph Beattie's patent firebox and feed water heater, originating in 1853 and as used on the LSWR, the water being heated by some of the exhaust steam from the cylinders. The firebox was designed for burning coal and was divided laterally into two parts, there being a combustion chamber in the boiler.

Driving wheels were 5ft and cylinders 16in × 24in the wheelbase being the usual 8ft + 8ft 3in. The 396 tubes were $1\frac{3}{16}$in outside diameter × 5ft $6\frac{3}{4}$in long, giving 722sq ft of heating surface. The combustion chamber provided 74sq ft and the firebox 114sq ft making a total of 910sq ft. Grate area was 17sq ft and the engine weight in working order was 33tons 3cwt. The double frames were both of full length, and no cab was provided, merely the usual spectacle plate. Both were rebuilt in June, 1860 with the normal type of boiler (*see Plate 7*), their trials not proving successful enough for general adoption of this type of boiler, the simplicity of Markham's device having won the day.

Charles Markham at the time of these experiments was Assistant or "Outdoor" Locomotive Superintendent. He was a tall and massive man, who went by the nickname of "long-stockings". He had come to Derby in June, 1851 and succeeded Joseph Tomlinson in this important post at a salary of £250 per annum, staying until the end of March, 1864, when he left to take control of the Staveley Iron Works for Richard ("Dicky") Barrow, where in the development of this extensive plant his great ability and influence were brought to bear. He always remained a great friend of the Midland. He was succeeded in his position on the Midland by Henry Burn, the former foreman at Sheffield, at £350 per annum.

As a matter of interest the Joseph Tomlinson referred to above went to the Taff Vale Railway and in 1858 made trails on his own locomotives using Welsh steam coal as fuel, which was a much better proposition owing to its high carbon content. No doubt with his connections he was well aware of the experiments of Markham with his old company.

CHAPTER THREE

Towards Standard Classes
(1855-1865)

As A SUCCESSOR to the "Jenny Lind" class Kirtley designed a larger version of the 2-2-2, with 6ft 6in driving wheels and 15in diameter × 22in stroke cylinders (later 16in × 22in). It had the usual sandwich frames and the raised firebox casing associated with Kirtley, with a wide polished brass band, or "cleading", at the junction of firebox and boiler barrel. Weight of engines was 28tons 9cwt of which 12tons 4cwt was on the driving wheels.

The first two Nos 136 and 137 emerged in December, 1856. The boiler carried 151 tubes of 2in diameter, leading and trailing wheels were 4ft in diameter and the total wheelbase of 15ft 3in was divided 7ft 6in + 7ft 9in. Boiler barrel was 11ft long × 3ft 11in outside diameter, and the firebox shell was 4ft 6in long. The ¾in thick inside frames extended from the front buffer beam as far as the firebox front plate and the outside sandwich frames were full length, comprising two ⅜in plates +3in wood "sandwich". The springing for the driving wheels was double in form, that on the outside frame being overhung and that of the inside frames underhung. The leading and trailing wheels had outside axleboxes only, whilst the driving wheels had inside and outside axleboxes. Length over framing and 6in thick buffer beams was 22ft 6in.

Here was an important step in the development of Midland locomotive design, for the old type of inside framing, fastened to the smokebox at the front and the firebox frontplate at the rear imposed severe stresses on the boiler shell, and caused not a few boiler explosions in these early days. In the new sandwich frame configuration both inside and outside frames ran from the front buffer beam to back of the engine and after cross staying and the mounting of the cylinders at the front end, the boiler merely sat in place on expansion brackets at the rear, with the firebox sandwiched between the inside frameplates, and was connected by means of bolts or rivets to the smokebox, itself attached to the main frames. Thus at last boiler and chassis were separate units, and could therefore be easily parted in the works for the necessary repairs at shoppings.

Further singles of the same class emerged from the works in the autumn of 1857 in the shape of Nos 138–144 followed by 145–149 the following year. It will be observed that the wheelbase of this class was 3in shorter

34

between driving and trailing wheels, than engines 136 and 137 previously mentioned. The frames were similar, but had a tie bar between the leading horns and the front buffer beam. They had slightly larger 16½in × 24in cylinders and carried a varying number of tubes, but No 140 had a total heating surface of 1,039sq ft comprising 959 sq ft (tubes) and 80 sq ft (firebox). All tubes were 2in diameter. One of these engines, No 141, was rebuilt with new plate frames in December, 1880 and replaced the 30 class single No 100 on Directors saloon duties in February, 1881, by then carrying the number 33

For main line express goods work Kirtley turned out his first Derby built 2–4–0s in 1856, the first one being No 300 in September, followed by Nos 307–9, 334 and 337 later in the year.

The driving wheels were 5ft 6in diameter and the leading wheels 4ft diameter, the total wheelbase being 14ft 9in divided thus:- 7ft 3in leading to driving and 7ft 6in driving to trailing. The firebox was 4ft 2½in square, and the boiler was typical Kirtley with raised firebox casing. The inside plate frames, which extended to the front of the firebox only, were ¾in thick and the distance between them 3ft 11in. The outside frames were also rather unusual for the period made of plain plate, being 1in thick and having tie bars between the horns and to the front buffer beam. The distance between inside and outside frames was 1ft 0⅝in. The distance from the leading wheel to the end of the frame was 4ft 0½in with a 6in buffer beam and from the trailing wheels to the frame end was 6ft 0½in also with a 6in buffer beam.

The driving axle was supplied with inside and outside bearings to each wheel, the inside springs being suspended below the axlebox and the outside springs overhung supporting the axlebox on a guided bar. The outside cranks were of 1ft radius.

In 1862 this class were renumbered 160–5 in order of building. They went through a series of renumberings and were scrapped between 1866 and 1876, the first built being withdrawn in October of that year.

These were joined in the second half of the following year by a further batch of larger 2–4–0s numbered 311–314 and 327 and having 6ft diameter driving wheels and 15in × 22in cylinders. This particular class were renumbered 90–95 in that order in 1859 and all were rebuilt in 1861–2 as 2–2–2s. They were for use on the new Midland branch to Kings Cross via Hitchin, but on the heavily graded line, especially the Wigston-Bedford portion they were not a great success, and thus came the rebuilding to singles. Their principal defect was that they bent and sometimes lost their coupling rods, supposedly due to uneven wear of both iron tyres and iron rails, accentuated by the more rapid wear taking place on the driving wheels. Nos 90, 93 and 95 were scrapped in 1871. No 92 was scrapped in 1872, whilst No 91 lasted until August, 1873, having run up a total of 403,431 miles in the 16 years since it was built.

For other freight work Kirtley retained his preference for the six wheeled coupled goods tender engine, and in 1857 he turned out from the Derby Works five of what are believed to have been inside framed engines Nos 171–3 and 175–6, having 5ft diameter driving wheels and 15in × 24in cylinders. Of these five Nos 171, 173 and 176 went as early as 1867, whilst both Nos 172 and 175 were rebuilt as 0-6-0WT the latter outlasting the rest until February, 1906. No 172 was reconverted to a 0-6-0 tender engine in October, 1879, and lasted until September, 1899.

The gap in the sequence is due to another old Rothwell 0-6-0 of August, 1846 which had come from the Birmingham and Bristol Committee stock and which was not replaced until 1862.

There might have been a gap of two in the sequence but for the timely yet tragic explosion of old No 175's boiler at Birmingham on March 5, 1857 which put an end to her career. She was an old Rothwell 0-6-0, delivered in May, 1846, which had belonged to the Birmingham and Bristol Managing Committee, and one of the boiler plates was blown through the roof of Messrs Adams & Co's factory nearby, killing a workman. She had been retubed in December, 1853, and had since that date run 76,268 miles as a local shunter in use 12 hours a day, her boiler pressure being limited to 85psi.

Further goods engines but of the double framed type were built in the works during 1857–8 commencing with No 187, believed to be the first of this type, constructed at Derby in June, 1857, the remainder all being outshopped the following year, these being numbered 180, 182, 185, 189, 200, 211, 220, 294, 338 and 424–7. These were known as the 180 class and had 16in diameter × 24in stroke cylinders and 5ft 2in diameter driving wheels (5ft nominal). Those in the 400 number range were considered as additions to capital stock. These engines all carried boilers with flush fireboxes, which had been introduced on Derby built engines about a year earlier by Kirtley in preference to the old raised type. They were to become the new standard for goods engines although passenger engines continued to carry the boiler with the raised firebox until 1869.

The locomotives mentioned above were followed by a further 20 standard 0-6-0 goods engines with a somewhat different appearance, having hornplates solid with the frame and not bolted on as before (*see Plate 16*). Tie bars were still rivetted on, a standard feature, and there was again a variety in the number of tubes carried by the boilers but a number had 168 tubes of 2in diameter giving 1,025sq ft of heating surface which, with 84sq ft of firebox heating surface gave an

1,109sq ft total. Driving wheels were 5ft 2in diameter on an 8ft+8ft 6in standard wheelbase and the inside cylinders were 16in diameter × 24in stroke. Nos. 160, 178, 198, 215, 216, 302, 311, 316, 317, 319, 321, 328, 339 were added to revenue stock, and Nos 430-6 to capital stock during 1859. Of these 311 and 436 were sold as new to the Oxford, Worcester and Wolverhampton Railway for £2,500 each in April 1860, as their Nos 54 and 55, later becoming GWR 280 and 281 in 1863. Neither of these locomotives is recorded in the official figures of locomotives turned out from Derby Works for the Midland, presumably because they never become part of MR stock, and after running trials went straight to their new owners. Incidentally No, 316 was the first MR goods engine to be fitted with an enclosed cab; this being done in 1872.

On the subject of wheelbase for Kirtley's 0-6-0 goods engines Ahrons* records that in 1850–2 this was 16ft equally divided, changed to 16ft 3in in 1853–7 the extra 3in being between middle and trailing axles. This was further changed from 1858 to what was to become a virtual standard for all future engines, 8ft+8ft 6in totalling 16ft 6in to be followed in 1863 by the change from straight to curved framed engines.

Also worth mentioning is the adoption of 140psi working pressure for boilers of goods engines from 1860 onwards which coincided with the introduction of boilers with welded longitudinal seams to be described in Chapter 4 later.

The following year (1860) a further batch of 20 engines was turned out, similar to the above and numbered 179, 202, 203, 204, 310–314, 327, 332, these being revenue account replacements, and Nos 436–444 (capital account additions) (see Plate 8). Messrs Fairbairn & Sons built a further ten locomotives of the same general design and it should be mentioned here that large numbers of Kirtley goods engines were supplied to the Midland by outside manufacturers over the years.

Returning now to passenger locomotives, a new class of heavier 2-4-0s for main line work, Nos 150–155, emerged from the Derby shops during 1859. Up to this time the 2-4-0s had been rather diminutive, being used only for branch and ordinary passenger services, leaving the express work to the faster singles. This new class had inside cylinders which were 16in diameter × 22in stroke, and driving wheels of 6ft diameter. They lasted only until 1873 however, when they were put down to be "renewed and rebuilt", a peculiar phrase often used on the Midland to denote a completely new locomotive apart from a few odd items "rescued" from the old one. The only one which can be said to have been "rebuilt", in the true meaning of the word, was 150, which was dealt with in June, 1873, and emerged with 16½in × 22in cylinders,

* The British Steam Railway Locomotive From 1825–1925 by E. L. Ahrons.

and carrying a boiler having 148 tubes of 2in outside diameter giving 871sq ft of heating surface. The firebox added 85sq ft giving a total of 956, the firebox shell being 5ft long. This locomotive became part of Class 6 at Johnsons 1873 classification. Nos 151 and 152 were broken up in 1873, and Nos 153–5 were renewed early in 1874, as smaller 2-4-0s with 6ft 2in driving wheels and $16\frac{1}{2}$in $\times$ 22in cylinders, retaining parts of the motion and the wheels of the older locomotives. These were to become part of the 156 class, and will be dealt with in more detail later. The tenders for the 150 class were originally 1,600gal.

No 156 turned out in the latter part of 1859 was a 2-2-2 generally similar to the class described above, but having larger 6ft 6in diameter driving wheels and 4ft leading and trailing wheels on a wheelbase of 7ft 9in + 7ft 9in. As with the former class, the outside frames were of the full-length sandwich pattern and the inside frame plates extended only as far as the front of the firebox where they terminated in sliding joints to allow for the expansion of the boiler.

In the express passenger engine field a further range of 6ft 6in dia-meter single driving-wheel engines, with 16in $\times$ 22in cylinders and weighing $28\frac{1}{2}$ tons were built as a continuation of the 136 class of 1856 (see Plate 4). The leading and trailing wheels were 4ft diameter and the total wheelbase was 15ft 6in, equally divided. The outside sandwich frames were of 3in thick wood between two $\frac{3}{8}$in plates, and the inside frame plates were $\frac{3}{4}$in thick, 4ft 1in between.

The leading and trailing axles had outside axleboxes whilst the driving wheels had both inside and outside axleboxes. Rail to centre-line of boiler was 6ft $7\frac{1}{2}$in and height to top of chimney was 13ft $5\frac{7}{8}$in to top of bell-mouth which was 2ft $2\frac{1}{2}$in diameter. The firebox was 4ft 9in long (outside) and 1ft $9\frac{1}{4}$in wide (inside).

There were 24 locomotives in all, and they were built as follows: Nos 1, 2, 6, 22 and 39 in 1859; Nos 9, 11, 13, 15, 17–19, 72, 88, 89, and 96 in 1860; Nos 12, 20, 23, 24, 33, 54 and 102 in 1861 and No 103 in 1862.

Following the building of No 103 the whole class were renumbered that same year, into the range 1–24, and of these numbers 1–10 were initially stationed at Derby and 11–20 at Leeds for working the first passenger trains between Rugby and Leeds via Derby. They were withdrawn between 1871 and 1894.

One of the class, No 54, was so substantially rebuilt in April, 1869, that Johnson considered it to be "equal to a new engine".

Two further locomotives were turned out in December, 1860, these being Nos 320 and 222. They were special large-sized outside framed 0-6-0WTs with 4ft 2in driving wheels on a wheelbase of 8ft 3in + 8ft 3in, and inside cylinders $16\frac{1}{2}$in diameter $\times$ 24in stroke (see Plate 17). Built specifically for banking trains up the Lickey incline between

Bromsgrove and Blackwell, they had no cab but merely a spectacle plate, and the dome on the second ring of the boiler had twin Salter safety valves. The boiler carried 166 tubes 2in in diameter, giving a heating surface of 1,019sq ft to which the firebox added a further 82sq ft.

No 320 was renumbered 220 in May, 1866, 220A in the duplicate list, in November, 1879 and was then rebuilt in December, 1883, as a goods tender engine with 5ft 2½in diameter driving wheels, being eventually scrapped in November, 1899. Its partner, No 222, which was a renewal of an ex-Birmingham and Bristol Management Committee 0-6-0 built by Jones and Potts in July, 1843, was renumbered 222A (duplicate stock) in March, 1890, and withdrawn from service in February, 1894.

On the subject of 0-6-0WTs about 28 of this particular type with a wide variety of dimensions were turned out by the Derby shops, a summary of these being given in Appendix II. Prior to the appearance of the above two locomotives four 0-6-0 goods engines had been rebuilt to this form in 1857, these being then Nos 217, 218, 224 and 225. The dimensions varied, and these and their subsequent history can best be drawn from Appendix II. Other well tanks will be referred to later in the text.

As was the case with all the Locomotive Superintendents of the larger companies, the purchasing of a particular type of locomotive was no longer the imprecise art which it had been in the days before the first amalgamations, but rather a deliberate policy of weeding out the worst performers leaving those designs which proved themselves well able to perform the tasks allotted to them, and then by gradual improvement, some standardisation on a small number of proved types was possible with corresponding savings in maintenance costs accruing from this policy.

There were of course departures from the general scheme of things in order that future designs could embrace new ideas for improving these basic types, and this occasionally produced both brilliant and more rarely, perhaps, decidedly mediocre classes. The former became the forerunners of new basic designs while the latter soon faded into obscurity, and were replaced or rebuilt at the earliest economic opportunity.

The goods engines were now more or less standardised, although there were still those small variations which make life more interesting for the dedicated ferro-equinologist!

Up to the end of 1862 all the Derby built 0-6-0 mineral or goods engines had been of the straight framed type, that is having a straight top to the frame giving a flat running-plate over the wheels. However from 1863 until the end of Kirtley's time a change was made, and all further engines of this type had curved frames raised above each horn-block, although there were slight variations in frame detail between the various classes. A few engines, for instance, had curved-top shallow frames with the old tie bars from the horns, but these were by outside makers.

Further o-6-os of the old standard straight framed pattern (*see Plate 9*) were turned out as follows: 1861 – Nos 196, 206, 291, 295, 325, 326, 329, 331, 333, 335, 340 (all to revenue) and 445–9 (capital); 1862 – Nos 174, 194, 315, 330, 334, 336, 337; 1863 – Nos 170, 241, 253, 270, 290, 212.

From here on the straight framed o-6-o tender engine gave way to the aforementioned curved frame type with frames slotted out of one piece of solid plate, the horn plate tie bars becoming part of the solid frame although there is still some doubt about No 246. Up to the end of 1866 these new beasts of burden were turned out as follows: 1863 – Nos 246, 251; 1864 – Nos 183, 188, 197, 245, 247, 256, 257; 1865 – Nos 181, 184, 193, 249, 254, 255, 259, 309, 323, 342, 356, 532; 1866 – Nos 531, 537, 538, 574, 577, 579, 580–3.

These had larger $16\frac{1}{2}$in × 24in cylinders and boilers pressed to 140psi but the driving wheels remained at 5ft 2in diameter on an 8ft + 8ft 6in wheelbase (*see Plate 10*). Nos 580–3 were additions to capital stock and Nos 581–3 and 537 carried 1867 building plates for domestic reasons but were actually turned out in December, 1866.

All these engines carried boilers with 168 tubes of 2in diameter as built, the fireboxes being 5ft long. The original boilers were gradually replaced by boilers with a larger heating surface supplied by 221 tubes of $1\frac{3}{4}$in diameter.

Before turning to the development of the workshops during the years up to 1866 we must cover the few remaining classes of passenger engines built up to this date. There were three main types of 2-4-0 tender engines being constructed at this time, the 80 class (these being the largest), the 70 class and the 50 class.

Dealing with the largest first, the 80 class, Nos 80–85, were built for use on the heavier passenger trains working from Kings Cross, especially the excursion traffic and for the 1862 Exhibition special trains. These had $16\frac{1}{2}$in diameter × 24in stroke cylinders inclined downwards towards the driving axle, and 6ft 2in diameter coupled driving wheels, the leading wheels being 4ft 2in diameter on tread. The wheelbase was the by now almost standard 8ft + 8ft 6in. Total working weight was 33tons 11cwt, empty 30tons 10cwt and the tender carried 1,600gal of water. These engines had outside sandwich frames with tie bars to the horns, and the inside plate-frames extended, as in the past, to the front of the firebox. The boiler barrel was 4ft 3in diameter and 11ft 6in long, and the flush firebox shell was 5ft long. The tubes varied somewhat, but the heating surface is given in the 1873 classification book as being 1,045sq ft tubes + 91sq ft firebox totalling 1,136sq ft. Three of the class were later fitted with a firebox shell 5ft 11in long, these being Nos 82–4 and Nos 80 and 81 were rebuilt with boilers from other passenger engines having a 5ft 3in firebox shell. Nos 82–84 were rebuilt between December, 1876 and December, 1881 with new Johnson boilers. Nos 80–84 worked for many years in the Birmingham area and the last one to be withdrawn was No 83, then numbered 83A in the duplicate stock, in December, 1894.

The next group of 2-4-os have usually been referred to as the 70 class, but from a consideration of all the information now available it would appear that these engines fell into two distinct classes. Both had full-length outside frames but inside frames only as far as the firebox front plate but there were two distinct sizes.

Of these numbers 70–74, built in 1862, had 16in × 22in diameter cylinders and 6ft diameter driving wheels on a 7ft 9in + 8ft 3in wheelbase. The leading wheels were 4ft diameter and the boiler had a firebox shell 4ft 9in long, the boiler barrel being 11ft long and 3ft 11in diameter at the first ring.

The remainder, numbers 75–79 and 86–89, had 16½in × 22in cylinders and 6ft 2in diameter driving wheels on an 8ft + 8ft 6in wheelbase (see Plate 14). The leading wheels in this case were 4ft 2in diameter and the boiler had a firebox shell 5ft long, the barrel length and diameter being the same as for the first five. This information is drawn from Midland Drawing No 74–144 and is partially confirmed by the Classification in detail of Engines, (Mid 5 Piece No 14) in the British Transport Historical Archives.

All had the same general appearance as the 150 class mentioned previously with the polished brass "cleading" where the raised firebox joined the boiler barrel. Heating surfaces for the first five is given as: tubes 970sq ft, firebox 81sq ft, totalling 1,051sq ft and for the remainder tubes 871sq ft, firebox 85sq ft, totalling 956sq ft although there were some minor variations between the different engines.

They were built in 1862–3, but of this first five all but No 74 had gone by October, 1876, and she only survived by virtue of the fitting of a second hand boiler in 1878, being eventually broken up in 1883. The larger, second group fared better except No 78 which was withdrawn from service in 1874, the remainder being broken up in the 1880s except for No 75, which was rebuilt to 156 class form in December, 1877, with a C class boiler built to O/686 whilst Nos 76, 87 and 88 were reboilered with second hand boilers before being withdrawn.

Tie bar pattern sandwich frames did not completely disappear until 1866 when the last four engines of the so called 70 class were built (although this description now appears to be erroneous). These were numbers 101, 118, 119 and 162, and were generally to the same dimensions as the later engines of the previous group.

From 1866 onwards all passenger engines were built with solid plate frames, rather than the mixed type of sandwich frame, and the 156 class with this type of frame, and which attained a high degree of performance will be described in Chapter 5.

The third and smallest of the three passenger classes were the ten 2-4-0s of the 50 class (*see Plate 13*) having 15in × 22in cylinders and only 5ft 8in diameter driving wheels on a short wheelbase of 14ft 6in equally divided, and having sandwich-type plate frames. These were turned out of the works as follows: 1862 – 53; 1863 – 54, 55, 56, 57, 169; 1864 – 50, 51, 52, 58.

The other main dimensions were as follows:

Tubes	800sq ft	(later 820)
Box	75sq ft	(later 69)
Total	875sq ft	(later 889)
Shell	4ft 3in	(later 4ft 2½in)
Leading wheels	4ft diameter	
Barrel	10ft 6in long × 3ft 9in outside diameter	

These were generally employed on lines west of Birmingham in their early days.

As mentioned before between 1859 and 1862 Kirtley had turned out a class of 24 singles for the Rugby to Leeds traffic, and in 1863 a further development of this class emerged from Derby shops mainly for use on the Leicester–Kings Cross via Hitchin trains. These were the famous 30 class of 6ft 8in driving wheel 2-2-2s having 16½in × 22in cylinders (*see Plate 6*). Two of these, Nos 30 and 26 were outshopped towards the end of 1863, and the rest were built as follows: 1864 – 25, 28, 31, 33, 35, 36, 38, 39, 98, 100; 1865 – 29, 32, 34, 37, 94, 97, 99; 1866 – 27.

Of these Nos 25, 26, 28, 33, 35 and 39 had the old pattern frame plate with tie bars to the horns, whereas the remainder, with the possible exception of Nos 36 and 38, had the solid plate integral frame. These locomotives had the typical Kirtley bell-mouth chimney, tall dome with Salter spring-balance safety-valves, and boilers with raised firebox, having polished brass cleading to the standard pattern. The cab consisted of a spectacle plate with the top bent over to provide some protection and the side sheets were in two panels extending about 1ft past the firebox front plate, although some 20 engines of 1863–4 had the cab top continued as an "awning" to cover the whole of the engine footplate and supported at the rear by steel rod pillars. These were said to be introduced because one driver on a particular run had a brick dropped on him by some mischievous boys on an overbridge. However the drivers disliked these cabs as the roof drummed and rattled at speed.

The tenders were of the six-wheeled 1,600gal type, with outside frames and axleboxes. On both types the injector was mounted immediately below the front of the cab side-sheeting on the outside of the frame.

The boilers had a total heating surface of 1,039sq ft comprising tubes 954sq ft and firebox 85sq ft, and the firebox shell was 5ft long. All were later altered to 5ft 3in long fireboxes except for Nos 33, 35, 36, 39, 94, 97–100 which had 5ft 6in fireboxes. Leading and trailing wheels were 4ft diameter, and the equally divided wheelbase totalled 16ft. The boiler barrel was 3ft 11in outside diameter and 11ft long. No 100 worked the Directors saloon until February, 1881 when replaced by old 141 of 1857 specially rebuilt with new plate frames for the purpose as mentioned before.

Two more of the 0-6-0 well-tank engines were "built" at Derby about this time, Nos 223 (December, 1862) and 221 (December, 1863) (*see Plate 19*). They were somewhat larger than the 1860 engines, No 222 having a longer wheelbase of 16ft 9in divided 8ft 3in + 8ft 6in, and a longer (5ft) firebox shell. These two joined the earlier locomotives banking heavy trains up the Lickey incline. No 221 was officially minuted as a further "rebuild" of J. E. McConnell's first purpose built banking engine No 38 *Great Britain*, constructed at the Bromsgrove Works of the Birmingham and Bristol Management Committee in June, 1845, specifically for banking trains up the Lickey incline. She was originally a 0-6-0ST of some 30tons, having driving wheels 3ft 9in diameter and outside cylinders 18in diameter × 26in stroke. The boiler carried 134 tubes, 12ft 6in long and 2in in diameter. She had been completely rebuilt in January, 1853 as a double-framed tank engine (it is not clear whether saddle or well type) with inside cylinders 16in diameter × 24in stroke, but retaining 3ft 9in driving wheels, having outside cranks, and emerged from the works as No 300 completely transformed. According to the minutes of the Locomotive & Stores Committee, only the boiler of this engine was broken up, so presumably the frames and parts of the motion were used in the construction of the new 221. Thus this "locomotive" theoretically had a continuity of service on the Lickey incline from June, 1845 until broken up in May, 1901, a span of 56 years of the most gruelling work any engine could be called upon to perform. Incidentally the cylinders for the 1853 rebuilding were cast at the Britannia Foundry, Derby, by one of the local firms which had developed rapidly with the coming of the railways to the town.

The other locomotive was merely, like No 222 mentioned earlier, a renewal of an older Jones & Potts 0-6-0 goods tender locomotive of July, 1843 which had come from the Birmingham and Bristol Management Committee.

To round off this survey of the locomotive classes developed by Kirtley at this period we must again mention the well tanks. Of these Nos 320 and 222 of 1860, 223 of 1862, and 221 of 1863 have already been mentioned. This class of four later became "Class 18" at Johnson's 1873 classification, and were later joined by Nos 1092, 1094 and 200.

One of the other groups of well tanks has already been mentioned as rebuilt in 1857, but added to these in 1862 were Nos 219 and 318. The former appears to have been a rebuild of one of the two Kitson, Thompson & Hewitson "Crampton" 2-2-2-0 locomotives supplied in December, 1847, and which had been rebuilt about 1851 as a 0-6-0 tender engine like its sister, now numbered 218, which had been rebuilt as a well tank in 1857. Originally Nos 101-2, they had been renumbered 230-1 before taking on their above mentioned numbers.

In 1867 five further Derby built 0-6-0 goods tender engines were converted and renumbered 213-17 with the possible exception of 216, for which certain evidence is lacking. These retained their 5ft 2in diameter driving wheels on an 8ft+8ft 3in wheelbase and also their $16\frac{1}{2}$in diameter × 24in stroke cylinders, with the possible exception of 215 which had smaller 4ft 2in diameter wheels on a 3in longer wheelbase They were all later rebuilt as 0-6-0 goods tender engines except the above mentioned 215 which lasted as No 2038A until February, 1906 (*see Plate 18*).

This type, with odd locomotives taken over from other lines and private firms, numbered 26 in 1866 and Kirtley therefore decided to have them grouped in a certain number range. In April of that year he rearranged his locomotive numbers so that all passenger engines were below 200, all these tanks were to be numbered in the range 200–239 and all goods engines were to be numbered 240 and above. A complete list of these tank engines is given in Appendix II since the author knows these to have been very much of a stumbling block in the past to locomotive historians. This list now given is based on the best possible sources of information, the majority of which is drawn from official sources.

Up to the end of 1866, 288 engines are officially supposed to have been built at Derby of which 260 were replacements to revenue account and the remainder additions to capital stock, these being Nos 424–7, 430–49 and 580–3.

The additions to capital account are straightforward but the story regarding the replacements is somewhat complicated by several factors. Firstly the engines jointly built or "rebuilt" by the Midland Company and Messrs E. B. Wilson & Co appear to have been counted as MR built. Secondly, this figure appears to include engines which were officially regarded as rebuilds, such as No 95, a single rebuilt in December, 1850, the banking engine No 300, the old Fenton No 17 and a number of the well tanks in their many vicissitudes.

The figure excludes apparently, the two new 0-6-0 goods tender engines sold to the Oxford, Worcester and Wolverhampton line.

Working to official lists and minutes the figure to the end of 1866 appears to be about 276, leaving the remaining 14 (taking account of the OWWR locomotives) to be accounted for by major rebuilds.

CHAPTER FOUR

The Works and its Personalities

(1866)

By THE YEAR 1866 the Derby Works presented a vastly changed panorama to the eye from that of 1844. From the nucleus of the North Midland shops had begun to expand to the south a great company of additional manufacturing and repair shops.

Some of the additions have already been listed, but a brief tour will perhaps be enlightening and give a more general picture of the vast changes which had taken place.

Starting by the north end of the station the former shops of the Midland Counties line had been converted for use as part of the Carriage and Wagon Department. The engine repair shops were now divided up as carriage-building and painting shops, whilst the engine shed was now one of the wagon shops, and the associated running-repair shops had become saw mills, turning shop and stores, with a new saw mill built on to the rear in 1863. Adjacent to these were the new gas works, and to the south of this the first mess room had been erected in 1854 for the use of the workmen at breakfast and dinner times.

In the North Midland camp the offices fronting the original round-house had been enlarged in 1859 by the addition of a second storey and a bridge linking the offices with the station was completed at the end of 1860 at a cost of £1,000.* The old carriage shops were now used for the repair and building of new wagons, while the engine shops had retained their use as erecting or "fitting" shops as they were then known, the engines standing side by side. Two further fitting shops, Nos 2 and 3 had been built, one adjacent to the old No 1 shop between which the old smithy of the North Midland now served as a turning shop. New smiths shops and a brass foundry had been erected at the rear of No 1 shop, together with what is now the present spring shop and smithy across the "bottom yard" by the canal.

There was a further smithy in the old Midland Counties shops adjacent to the carriage shops which had been one third demolished to make better access to the wagon shop, the other third being still in use as a spring shop.

*BTHR Mid 1/18 & Mid 1/169

Adjacent to the No 3 fitting shop, and facing No 2 shop across the "top yard", were a new tender and lagging shop, smiths shop for casual repair work, and a coppersmiths shop all adjacent to the No 2 roundhouse, slightly larger than No 1 shed and erected in 1847. Beyond these now stood the No 3 roundhouse of more generous proportions than the others (*see earlier*). Adjacent to this on the station side was the new engine painting shop (now pattern shop) and a coal stage.

On the bottom yard to the rear of the No 2 fitting shop a large covered area of shops had been constructed embracing a boiler shop, two more smiths shops and hooping, plating and turning shops, all under one roof. Beyond all these on the canal side of the bottom yard stood the new millwrights shop put up in 1864.

There were of course other minor additions too numerous to mention, but the above gives a brief picture of the works of 1866. It is interesting to note that at this stage, over 100 years ago, apart from the iron foundry and the large block comprising the present erecting and machine shops put up some 10 years later, the present day form of the major part of the works was already established, and apart from change of use, very little was to change for almost a century.

The personalities of these early days are fascinating, and, to amplify information gleaned from various official sources, I have to thank George Pratt, a clerk to the company and one time honorary secretary of the Midland Railway Institute for a series of pen portraits which he produced on these early characters.*

Matthew Kirtley has already been mentioned in some detail, and also his eldest brother Thomas, former Locomotive Superintendent of the North Midland line. He moved to Brighton with Peter Clarke, the disappointed ex-secretary of the NMR, who had hoped for a similar appointment on the Midland. Thomas became, for a short while, the Locomotive Superintendent of the LB&SCR but he died of a brain tumour in November, 1847. Later one of his sons, William, was to come from the Midland depot at Kings Cross, where he was foreman, to become the foreman of the workshops at Derby in January, 1864, at a salary of £250 per annum, and this position he retained until the arrival of Samuel Johnson on the scene in 1873. William had been entered as an apprentice at the Derby Works in April, 1854, and had been looked upon kindly by his uncle Matthew, working his way gradually up through the ranks.

Whether he got on with Johnson or not is hard to tell, but he was to leave his position within a year of Johnson's arrival to take up a new post as Locomotive Superintendent of the London, Chatham and Dover line, where he remained until his retirement in 1898.

Midland Railway Memories by G. J. Pratt. FCIS (1924)

The first recorded Works Manager or "general foreman" as he was then called, was John Fernie, a very capable manager of men, who took up his duties on April 17, 1855 at a salary of £350 per annum, the most that the Directors "felt justified in giving for the appointment".*

He had come from the local firm of Andrew Handyside & Co of the Britannia Iron Works, Derby, who had established themselves in 1818 as manufacturers of high-grade cast-iron work known as "Derby Castings". They later became world famous for such erections as Olympia, in London, Manchester Central Railway station, and bridges and other such structures as far afield as China.

Fernie was the typical dour Scot and got the very best out of his workmen. He it was who co-operated in 1868 with the then foreman of the boiler shop, George Alton to produce a welded boiler with very few rivets indeed, the patented design of which dispensed with all angle irons, longitudinal seams, lap, and plated or "battened" joints. Alton's original idea was to use thick-edged plates in a welded joint, and these were rolled by Hird, Dawson & Hardy of Low Moor, having thicker edges of from $\frac{7}{16}$in to $\frac{5}{8}$in, to allow for flanging to the smokebox tube plate and to compensate for the loss of section caused by the circular rivet holes.

The boiler was made in three sections, all about 4ft 1in diameter. each of which was welded and afterwards faced up on a lathe at the joints so that close contact was made. These three sections were united by a hoop, 10in × $\frac{5}{8}$in in section, and shrunk on like a tyre on a wheel, being secured by wide pitch double rivetting. The dome combined both itself and a hoop all in one piece, and was similarly shrunk on. After welding, each section was annealed and in final assembly of the boiler, the welds were orientated so that they were above the water line. Exceptionally qualified men were required for the welding process, the thick-edge plates were rather expensive and difficult to produce, and after the intial application on some Kitson & Co 0-6-0 goods tender engines in the range 660–9 built between May and September, 1858, the use of these boilers was discontinued.

One particular incident in the works bears repeating, and it concerned a contract which the head foreman boilermaker had for producing a certain number of new boilers, having the work done by men paid directly by himself, he receiving payment from the company for the boilers made. A junior clerk, sent to make some simple enquiries received such evasive answers that, after further questions were put, it was discovered that the foreman had no men of his own, but all were on the company's paybill. Thus they were being charged twice over for the same contract boilers!

*BTHR Mid 1/168

1 The works offices and the famous Clock Tower; a photograph taken before the clock and bell were resited when the top floor of the offices was added in 1893.

2 An engraving of Derby station *c*. 1842. The No 1 roundhouse, offices and workshops of the North Midland Company can be seen on the left.

3 No 42, a Sharpe's 2-2-2 built in November, 1847 as altered to 2-4-0 at Derby in June, 1860. Photograph taken at Kettering. [*Author's Collection*

4 Kirtley 2-2-2 1A, built as No 1 in December, 1859. One of a class of 24 locomotives built between 1859 and 1862, a development of the Sharp's single.

5 A rare early photograph of a Derby 2-2-2 No 1010, built in May, 1856. This class were developed from the "Jenny Linds" of E. B. Wilson & Company. No 1010 was built as No 112, renumbered 732 and later 1010 and scrapped in September, 1873. (One of only two known photographs of this type).

6 One of Kirtley's 30 class singles, No 28, built for use on Leicester-Kings Cross trains in 1864.

7 One of the two Beyer-Peacock 0-6-0s built originally with Beattie's patent firebox and feedwater heater. Photographed later as rebuilt to conventional form at Derby in June, 1860 but with Johnson boiler and chimney. *[Author's Collection*

8 Kirtley straight framed 0-6-0 No 312 Apparently in original condition as built at Derby in June, 1860. Photograph taken at Kettering. [*D. F. Tee Collection*

9 No 270 one of the last straight framed Kirtley 0-6-0s turned out in December, 1863 and shown as rebuilt with a Johnson boiler, chimney and cab in 1888.

10 Curved framed Kirtley 0-6-0 No 256 built in December, 1864 as reboiled by Johnson. [*Author's Collection*

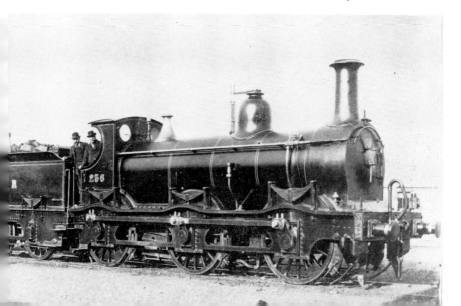

11 The earliest known photograph of Derby Works and station taken in 1860. In the foreground the No 1 roundhouse and just beyond the new clock tower and first floor offices. Beyond can be seen the original station before the addition of other platforms and right centre the old joint North Midland and Midland Counties goods warehouse burned down in 1868.

12 Kirtley curved tramed 0-6-0 No 681 built in November, 1868 and shown as reboilered by Johnson.

13 The smallest of Kirtley's early 2-4-0 passenger locomotives No 14 of the 50 class with 5ft 8in driving wheels and short 14ft 6in wheelbase built in June, 1863, and shown here as rebuilt in 1877.
[*F. Moore*

14 Kirtley 70 class 2-4-0 No 76 built in October, 1863 and shown as reboilered in 1877 with second-hand Kirtley boiler, Johnson chimney and cab.

15 Kirtley 156 class 2-4-0 No 158 as originally built at Derby in September, 1866. This locomotive is now preserved in Midland livery as 158A at Leicester.

16 Shop foremen's group *c.* 1872. Back row (left to right) D. Horton; 6th Melrose; 7th J. Weet (front row) 5th G. Leavers; 7th W. Marlow; 8th R. Chambers; 10th T. Bagley; 11th T. Jewsbury. Photographed in front of Kirtley 0-6-0 No 321 built at Derby in June, 1859.

17 A group from the Smiths shop taken in front of Bromsgrove tank engine No 220, built as 320 in December, 1860 and converted to a tender engine in December, 1883. (Photographed in 1872)

[*Author's Collection*

18 Another genus of Derby well tank converted from Derby 0-6-0 No 175 of June, 1857 in 1867. This engine lasted until February, 1906, and is shown here as reboilered by Johnson in June, 1879.

19 Bromsgrove banker No 223A, an 0-6-0WT built in December, 1862. This engine had a remarkably long life being broken up in July, 1928 and is shown here as rebuilt with a Johnson boiler.

20 0-4-2WT No 202, rebuilt from a Fairbairn 2-2-2 tank engine at Derby in 1865, and once part of the stock of the little North Western Railway, absorbed by the Midland in 1852.

21 Kirtley 0-6-0WT No 2008 built originally at Derby as a "Jenny Lind" type 2-2-2 in May, 1856 and converted to the form shown in March, 1871. This locomotive was one of a class of twelve such converted from singles in 1871–2 and later reboilered by Johnson.

22 Footplate view of Kirtley 2-4-0 No 10 built as 109 in October, 1867.

23 Footplate view of Deeley 4-4-0 No 754 built as 844 in September, 1904.

24 The Kirtley family at home. Matthew with his wife Ann in the window, and daughters Elizabeth Ann, the eldest, seated and Emily standing. Photograph taken at Litchurch Grange about 1862.

25 Thomas Clayton and Samuel Johnson. The Carriage and Wagon and Locomotive Superintendents of the Midland Company are the only gentlemen present in this delightful family group photograph taken about the turn of the century.

26 Kirtley 800 class 2-4-0 No 66A built in July, 1870 as No 66, shown here as reboilered by Johnson in July, 1895. She was broken up in April, 1922.

27 No 130, an example of Johnson's version of Kirtley's 890 class 2-4-0s with his own P type boiler, built in December, 1874. No 130 was renumbered 130A in 1899, 123 in 1907 and scrapped in December 1932.

28 Johnson 2-4-0 No 113 shown as built in November, 1880 with a P class boiler.

29 Engines off duty — a mixed batch of Kirtley and Johnson types in the sidings at Derby one weekend about 1888.

30 A view of the works and station taken from the engineers offices about 1888. Extreme left centre are the original Midland Counties engine shed and repair shops. Beyond, left to right are the North Midland carriage shops (with skylights) by now converted to mill- wrights shops, the old No 2 round shed beyond the footbridge. Judging by the angle of the sun and the time on the clock (2.30pm) the photo- graph must have been taken in either early spring or late autumn).

31 No 3 engine shed, built in 1852 to provide much needed additional stabling accommodation for locomotives. Outside are Johnson 2–4–0 No 131 and 0–6–0T No 1720. This shed was seriously damaged during a zeppelin raid on Derby on January 31, 1916.

Fernie took the staggering news to his chief, and Kirtley in his wise old way said "Leave the matter to me, and send the foreman up here". When he appeared he was told that it had been decided to terminate contract work, and strong words followed. The foreman, seeing his game was up, angrily demanded his money and left, and thus an ugly incident was quietly smoothed over, and the hierarchy presumably "never heard a whisper".

During 1858 Fernie was also responsible for the gradual introduction of a system of templates and gauges based on Whitworth's system, together with other more accurate manufacturing methods for producing castings to closer tolerances which enabled the first fully interchangeable series of locomotive components to be produced, thereby permitting replacement parts to be sent from stock to any outstation with the assurance that on arrival they would fit the locomotive in question.*

This was a great step forward in manufacturing parts, although Messrs Beyer Peacock & Co Ltd had for some years used their own methods for ensuring duplication of parts between engines in any one batch, but at that time they had no universal system of templates and gauges correct to the nearest thousandth part of an inch such as was now introduced on the Midland, and which was to spread throughout other manufacturing workshops in this country and indeed throughout the world.

Joseph Whitworth had exhibited a machine at the 1851 Exhibition in Hyde Park for obtaining minute measurements by touch and in 1857 he first advocated the use of the inch as the basis of measurement in engineering work, to be sub-divided into a thousand parts for the finer dimensions.

Fernie had noted upon his appointment as general foreman of the Derby shops that the workman's rule was the real standard and the "bare $\frac{1}{16}$in or a full $\frac{1}{32}$in" embraced a very wide field indeed, extending even to such demanding fits as the shrinking on of a tyre or the boring out of a wheel seat.

With Matthew Kirtley's approval a small machine made by Cocker of Liverpool, from Whitworth's own gauges, was used to make standards, but it was soon found to be inadequate and the system of end measurement with a gravity piece, as invented by Whitworth, was then adopted, using a machine of 12in capacity which was soon found to be insufficiently long and lengthened to 100in. This machine had a V groove planed throughout the entire length of the bed plate, was provided with a head stock and a tail stock, and was fitted with finely graduated handwheels which enabled duplicate lengths of metal up to 100in long

*Proc. Institution of Civil Engineers Vol. XXII. Session 1862–3 Paper 1095

D

to be cut and kept and from which accurate male bar and female horseshoe gauges, with hardened workfaces ground accurately to a few thousandths of an inch, could be made and held in the tool room until required.

One of the first applications of the use of the system in the workshop was to establish correct interference fits for wheels on axles, and experiments determined that the permanent set produced in the bore of any wheel boss by pressing onto an axle was minimal with an interference fit of ·003in and small with an interference fit of ·005in. Although the ·003in interference was thought to be the best this was rather beyond the ability of a normal lathe of that day, and the ·005in fit was selected. Similarly an interference fit of ·015in was fixed upon for the interference fit of outside cranks on axles, about one half of the old standard.

Using plug gauges it was now possible to determine the increase in pin sizes and decrease in hole size which took place during hardening processes on motion parts, and a considerable reduction in the amount of after-grinding and lapping was thereafter necessary in order to bring them to the correct-fit sizes.

Fernie also brought with him of course a lot of know how in the arts of founding metals, and it was under him that the first iron foundry was developed in the works. He introduced considerable improvements in plate moulding, especially with regard to the casting of locomotive cylinder blocks using accurately located moulding boxes and cylinder half patterns together with accurately made and located cores for the barrel bore, ports and steam passages, "whereby", he said, "the manufacture is brought within the grasp of any man who can throw in sand and ram it".

Another important innovation was the use of surface plates and machine fixtures on a special stand for the initial erection stages of new locomotives, and upon which the registration and final machining of the various parts, main frames, cylinder blocks, spectacle plate, cross stays, slide blocks, pistons, etc, was done. All engines erected in this manner were very accurate duplicates of one another and thus all parts were interchangeable, and quite apart from economy of manufacture and greater perfection in workmanship, it was possible to stock spares with the assurance that they would fit a locomotive on arrival at any outstation.*

Perhaps the biggest single benefit of this system was that, gradually, the old methods of manufacture, introduced with the opening of the works and in which the workman was the sole judge of his own stan-

*The use of this special stand is the most probable explanation for the wide use of a standard coupled wheelbase of 8ft + 8ft 6in centres on the Midland for many, many years.

dards, gradually gave way to the machine-tool age where one man with a machine could do the work of 10 men without, replacing large numbers of the latter. In fact it was as much in the workshops of the Midland Railway Company at Derby as anywhere, that the factory system, fully embracing the use of machine-tools in heavy engineering, was developed to a fine art and we can thank men such as John Fernie for having the foresight and courage of his convictions to introduce such revolutionary systems designed to so much improve the products of English manufacturers.

At the end of 1863 Fernie resigned and went to Leeds to become a partner in the firm of Taylor Brothers at the Clarence Foundry and Iron Works, and afterwards went to America.

A short time later, in March, 1864, the works lost Charles Markham, the Outdoor Locomotive Superintendent, famous for his coal burning experiments. He went to work for Richard Barrow as the manager of the Staveley Iron Works, as previously recorded.

Succeeding Markham came Henry Burn who hailed from Sheffield, where he was Locomotive Foreman. He had been Locomotive Foreman at Leicester in 1855–6 at the time of the Crimean War, and when the Balaklava Military Railway was laid down, Sir Joseph Paxton, MP, a Midland Director (but more famous perhaps for his designs for the Crystal Palace) was asked by the Government to find men to work the line and several Midland Railway drivers from Derby were selected and went out to the Crimea under the care of Mr Burn.

When peace there was restored he returned to Derby but at this time some Directors of the Midland had an interest in financing and constructing the Danube and Black Sea Railway from Czernavoda to Kustendjie. A number of men were released for this work under Mr Burn who was appointed Locomotive Superintendent, with Mr Rowland Steer, from the stores department, as head storekeeper. The line was also furnished with many items of Midland equipment including cranes and rolling stock.

However competition from the Varna-Rustchuck Railway caused a decline in the fortunes of the line, and, in 1862, Burn returned to England to be appointed to succeed Ralph Hope as Locomotive Foreman at Sheffield. After appointment as Assistant Locomotive Superintendent at Derby, in the spring of 1864, Burn stayed until April, 1870, when he left to found an iron works in Litchurch Lane, Derby which failed, after which he emigrated to New Zealand. As a matter of interest, he it was who returned from Germany impressed by the thin line between hour and minute figures in their timetables to distinguish pm from am, and, after consultation, this was introduced in Midland timetables from that time onwards.

Of the many other characters, space allows but mention of two more. There was Michael Bishop, messenger porter, but previously a driver, who was removed from the footplate for some indiscretion or other which he would never tell about. He deserves to be mentioned because he left behind not only writings on the early locomotives, but many "flamboyant" paintings of the earlier types, and which at one time could be seen in many homes and public houses in the locality of the station at Derby. Many of these were the only records of these locomotives built in these palmy days, but unfortunately few of these are left today. The author himself saw one at the former Midland Railway Institute, but this has now disappeared.

At the other end of the scale (almost) was James Newbould, the first Chief Draughtsman, a kindly man who had married "well" by taking the daughter of Kirtley's favourite foreman, William Marlow, as his wife. In these days Mr Newbould had the design responsibility for almost everything, from locomotives and turntables to hydraulic apparatus and water and gas installations.

Mr Newbould is said to have been "microscopical and accurate in all he did, punctilious to a fault", and he eventually became the first secretary of the Midland Railway Institute at Derby. He lived to be 94 years old, and never needed spectacles or an eyeglass, perhaps due to his habit of taking "forty winks" as soon as he got home after the days work, seated in a straight backed chair with his arms entwined round the uprights to prevent him from falling off it. Newbould retired from the post of Chief Draughtsman in January, 1898 having held this position for over 40 years, and his retirement was marked by the presentation of an illuminated address from members of his staff.

A word now about the origin of that part of the grounds known as "Etches Park", the area to the south of the workshops adjacent to the Litchurch Gas Works. This was the rather pretentious name given to quite a small area of land around a rather "unpretentious" house by the owner William Jeffrey Etches, a prosperous cheese factor in the town, whose main warehouse occupied part of the station buildings adjacent to the north end of platform No 1.

When the new more direct line to Nottingham over Deadman's Lane was constructed during 1866–7, having been authorised the year before, the Midland Railway purchased the house and grounds, and many pieces of statuary were transferred to the Derby Arboretum, which Loudon had completed as the first public park in this country in 1840. The Spondon line was opened on June 27, 1867, incidentally, but the house remained occupied for many years, first by the way and works accountant, and then by the chief storekeeper.

CHAPTER FIVE

Kirtley's Last Years
(1866-1873)

THE LAST YEARS of Matthew Kirtley were perhaps his finest. There is no doubt that the men in the Locomotive Department held him in great esteem right from his Chief Foreman down to the lowest paid messenger boy, and he demanded and got the fullest co-operation from his staff.

So far as the works was concerned, his initial reorganisation and expansion plan had been completed to a major degree by 1866 and, although there were other minor additions, it was not until shortly before his death that he masterminded the planning of yet another large extension to the workshops area, which he unfortunately never saw built in his lifetime.

The great scheme of reorganisation was prompted by the decision to separate the Locomotive Works from the Carriage and Wagon Works entirely and to establish the latter on a completely new site on the other side of the London Road.

Output from both the Locomotive and Carriage and Wagon sides had continued to expand, and it was now necessary for a great leap forward to be made to keep pace with the growing traffic demands.

Turning to locomotives, the previous section on his standard designs was rounded off by a brief mention of the one-time renowned 156 class of 2-4-0 tender engines, which began to emerge from the works in 1866. No 156 herself was the first to be completed in the September, followed by Nos 158 in the same month, 157 and 159 in October and 115 and 117 in November. The following year saw the construction of Nos 102–13, followed in 1868 by Nos 114, 116, 160, 163 and 164 (*see Plates 15 & 22*).

Five further sets of frames were constructed in Kirtley's time, but the engines were not built until after his death, and his successor Samuel Johnson, turned them out in 1873–4 as Nos 75, 150 and 153–5, although Nos 75 and 150 officially were considered as rebuilds of earlier locomotives of 1862 and 1859 respectively.

These had frames cut from solid plate in place of the older pattern with tie bars. The driving wheels were 6ft 2in diameter and 8ft 6in centres and the leading wheels were 4ft 2in diameter on the tread, the total wheelbase being 16ft 6in. Boilers with raised fireboxes were used, the barrel being 11ft long and 3ft 11in diameter. Total heating surface varied between 1,033 and 1,080sq ft and the grate area was 14.8sq ft.

Working weight, as built, was 33 tons 5cwt. The inside cylinders were 16½in diameter × 22in stroke.

No further passenger locomotives were turned out of the works until 1870, and the building programme was concentrated on the goods or mineral engines of which more and more were in demand to move the ever-increasing volume of such traffic.

In 1867 further o-6-os Nos 248, 584–9 and 670, of the now standard curved frame type, were built, followed by Nos 292, 301, 304 and 671–83 in 1868 (see Plate 12). No 304 was the first Midland locomotive to be built with bushed ends to the coupling rods. All had formerly had cottered ends with split bushes, but from this time onwards the bush was adopted as a standard fitting. The following year Nos. 210–12, 226–7, 242, 296–9, and 684–9 emerged from the works, of which the latter six were additions to capital stock, the rest being replacements. Of these Nos 684–7 had 5ft long fireboxes and a heating surface of 1,119sq ft and the remainder and all subsequent Kirtley o-6-os had longer 5ft 6in fireboxes, and these 1869 locomotives had 1,088sq ft of heating surface.

From 1869 Kirtley adopted 17in diameter cylinders as a standard, in place of the 16½in used heretofore, and the first engines to have this new size of cylinder were the six o-4-4WTs of the 690 class built by Messrs Beyer Peacock & Co for the Metropolitan "Underground" services. The first Derby-built engines with this diameter of cylinder and 24in stroke were Nos 696–9, o–6–o goods tender engines, which emerged towards the end of 1870. Also built the same year with this size of cylinders were Nos 910 and 914, whilst 228 was built with the old size of 16½in ×24in cylinders. These former two were quickly renumbered however into available spaces, as Nos 224 and 303 respectively, during the following year. A similar thing happened with No 912 built in 1871, which was renumbered 252 the same year. Also built in 1871 was No 218, followed by Nos 219, 225, 229, 243, 244, 279, 352 and 354 in 1872, and 215, 271, 272, 350, 351, 353, 355, 357 and 358 in 1873. These were to be the last of Kirtley's Derby built goods engines without cabs for starting with Nos 279, 352 and 354, built towards the end of 1872, these, and all later goods-tender locomotives, were provided with proper cabs for the protection of the driver at the time that the engines were built. Of these only No 229 had the old size 16½in × 24in cylinders as new.

By 1871 most of the earlier "Jenny Lind" type passenger singles had been withdrawn but 12 were given a further lease of life by virtue of being rebuilt as tank engines of the six-wheel coupled variety. Some of these had been out of use for some time and all were already in the duplicate list, the usual fate of the older "superannuated" locomotives.

The first duplicate numbers for the "Jenny Linds" had been 722–37, and the second 1000–1014. Three of this latter range were not rebuilt, these being Nos 1007 and 1010–11, which were scrapped.

According to F. H. Clarke, who investigated early Midland rolling stock records at the beginning of this century before many of them were scrapped, four of the rebuilds were in the form of saddle tanks, and the remainder well tanks. There are no known photographs of the saddle tanks and no records extant are available to verify this statement.

The wheelbase of the "new" tank engines was 7ft 3in +6ft 9in and the driving wheels 4ft 2in diameter. The two inside cylinders with slide valves, were 15in diameter and 22in stroke and they took numbers in the 2000-2014 range either when rebuilt or soon afterwards (see Plate 21). All 12 were later rebuilt with Johnson boilers between 1875 and 1878 and in this form lasted at least 20 years, the first being scrapped in 1897 and the last remained in service until January, 1924 being taken over by the LMS. Further details are given in Appendix II.

Turning now to a review of the few remaining passenger classes, the first locomotives to be considered are the renowned 800 class which could be considered as the finest design of express locomotive turned out in the Kirtley era, later to be further improved by Johnson (see Plate 26). They had full length double-plate frames and outside cranks and were of the 2-4-0 wheel arrangement, having 17in × 24in cylinders and 6ft 8in diameter driving wheels on a wheelbase of 8ft + 8ft 6in, the leading wheels being 4ft 2in diameter on tread. The boiler contained 168 2in diameter tubes, and carried a heating surface of 1,088sq ft, the boiler barrel being 11ft long and 4ft 2in outside diameter. First to be built were Nos 166 and 167 in February, 1870 followed by 165, 168 and 169 in March, 60 and 61 in April, 62 and 64 in May, 63 and 65 in June and 66 in July. The same year Messrs Neilson & Co Ltd, of Glasgow turned out a further 30 engines of the same class Nos 800–29, commencing with 800–802 in July, 1870, making 42 in all.

The main difference between the Derby and Neilson engines lay in the reversing gear which was of the usual lever and quadrant type on the Derby-built engines, whilst the Glasgow-built engines had screw reverse, arranged vertically on the first 10 locomotives and horizontally on the remainder. The vertical screw led to No 809 being involved in a smash near Kibworth while working the Scotch Pullman on October 9, 1880, when the driver forgot that he had stopped with the gear in reverse to assist braking and, on restarting, ran backwards in dense fog into a following ironstone train, with the loss of two lives.

When built the Derby engines were allocated to Leicester, and the Neilsons to Kentish Town (12), Leeds (8) and Bristol (10) in that order. The class as a whole was later rebuilt by Johnson to deal with the heavy traffic over the then new Settle–Carlisle route opened partly in 1876, and will be referred to again later.

Of a generally similar design were six locomotives built in 1871, these being Nos 3, 22, 23, 93, 138 and 139, which were referred to as the 96 class. These had similar general dimensions, but were 3in shorter in wheelbase from driving to trailing wheel, this giving a similar reduction in length of firebox. Heating surface for Nos 3 and 139 was 1,112sq ft of which the 232 tubes of 1½in diameter gave 1,020sq ft whilst the remainder had 148 tubes 2in in diameter giving 963sq ft of hs. They had the normal quadrant reverse and the first four were allocated to Skipton whilst Nos 138 and 139 were used on the Wennington–Carnforth line, being stationed at Carnforth. After a few years however they returned to their native Derby to work trains to Leeds and York.

An interesting story revolves around the construction of these two classes, for it is said that a deputation of main line drivers had a meeting with Kirtley and expressed their view that the old singles, and many of the coupled engines as well, were inadequate to haul the increased weights of trains over the heavy gradients on the Midland main lines. It is said that Kirtley took their criticism, and promised that they would have engines fully capable of hauling everything required of them, and thus the 800 and 96 classes were born. There are many fine recorded runs extant proving their achievements which fully bore out Kirtley's promises.

The next class were the first of a more modern design, having inside bearings only for the coupled wheels, and outside bearings for the leading wheels. These were known as the 890 class, and the first to emerge from Neilson's was No 890 herself in July, 1871, closely followed by Nos 891–909 the same year.

First to emerge from the Derby Works was No 2 in September, 1872, followed by 90, 92, 95, 125 and 148 the same year 5, 12, 19, 21, 40, 41, 43, 46, 49, 68, 123, 127 in 1873, 7, 42, 44, 45, 47, 48, 67, 69, 72, 78, 91, 120, 121, 124, 126, 128, 130–2, 151, 152 in 1874 and 134–6 in 1875. The cylinders were 17in × 24in as on the 800 class, and the leading and driving wheels were of the same size also, on the standard 8ft + 8ft 6in wheelbase. Boiler size was the same as the 96 class, the firebox shell being 5ft 3in long, and the barrel 11ft long and 4ft diameter outside. The tubes gave 871sq ft of heating surface, and the firebox 92sq ft giving a total of 963sq ft for most of the Derby built engines, whilst the 232 1½in diameter tubes on Neilson's engines gave 1,025sq ft + 92sq ft firebox equalling 1,117sq ft of total heating surface.

There was quite a number of minor variations in heating surfaces, and in particular this applied to Nos 126, 128, 130 and 134–6 which were fitted as new with a larger Johnson boiler of the P type, having 223 tubes of 1¾in diameter giving 1,216sq ft of heating surface (*see Plate 27*). Of the others the majority had 963sq ft of heating surface, made up as given above, except Nos 92, 125 and 148, and all those built in 1874 and after (except Nos 67 and 69, 91 and 121) which had 1,073sq ft.

The 1872 Derby-built engines were the last passenger engines to have Kirtley's side-hinged double-folding rectangular smokebox doors. Later engines had the more modern circular dished doors. All of these loco- motives later came to be "Class 1" when Johnson arranged a classifica- tion of all locomotives in 1873, and those without Johnson boilers were rebuilt with those of P class from 1875 onwards, and all but Nos 21, 68, 127 and 72 later carried B boilers from 1903 onwards. Some at least of this class originally had vertical reversing screws as built, these being removed after the 1880 smash.

Nos 134–6 were engaged in the Newark brake trials of 1875 before being set to work on the London–Derby–Leeds express passenger ser- vices for which they were intended. The working weights of these were leading 11 tons 18cwt, driving 13 tons 4cwt, trailing 12 tons 12cwt, total ing 38 tons 4cwt.

There was concern expressed as to the soundness of the wrought-iron axles for engines in October, 1870, and apart from boring out 50 mis- cellaneous axles to determine their soundness, the Locomotive Com- mittee agreed to order 12 steel axles from Messrs Whitworth & Co as an experiment. This eventually led to the adoption of steel as the standard material for the future.

At this point it is worth while taking a close look at the works again to bring to attention some of the lesser personalities involved in the last years of Kirtley's superintendency.

The head foreman, and Matthew's right hand man, after the Loco- motive Workshop Superintendent William Kirtley, was William Marlow, who was the oldest serving foreman on the works having, in October, 1871, a total of 32 years and 2 months service to his credit. He had served with Matthew Kirtley on the Birmingham and Derby Junction Railway, taking up employment on that line at its opening on August 12, 1839.

Regarding the other foremen there is fortunately a list surviving which gives all their names and the time each had been employed by the Mid- land or its pre-grouping constituent companies as at October, 1871, and this is given on page 58.

Records from this period of time regarding personalities are almost non-existent but a few remarks concerning some of these characters can be added.

Reuben Chambers was a well built man with long, white side whiskers, who always wore a bow tie, waistcoated suit and a flat topped bowler-type hat. He had been originally recruited by the North Midland Company in August, 1840, and was at this time yard foreman, numbering among his staff James Riley, James Mathers, Ishmael Jenkinson, Sam Wilson, and A. Haynes.

LIST OF FOREMEN IN THE LOCOMOTIVE DEPARTMENT DERBY

	Years	Months		Years	Months
Thomas Lewty	28	6	Thomas Jewsbury		9
F. Brownsword	10		David Horton	15	9
James Hunt	30	6	George Baggaley	30	6
Henry A. Cartmale	5		William Marlow	32	2
Reuben Chambers	31	2	William Kirtley	(Loco. Works	
Samuel Tetley	24	4		Supt.)	
H. Wall	19	3	James Melrose	29	8
Joseph Weet	9		(Sen)		
E. Clark	26	9	George Leavers	25	9
T. Wallis	23		Thomas Baggaley	31	
William A. Jackson	13	9	William Millar	15	8
M. Tempest	16				
James Melrose (Jun)	10				
R. Baker	26		Total Service	454	6

One of these, James Mathers, was a well known character both socially and politically, and is credited as being "one of the finest men to take charge of a breakdown crane that ever lived". He was not only a good practical mechanic, but his speed and skill in clearing the line of debris after an accident was marvellous to see. He lived at No 3, Railway Terrace, and he and his neighbours had a most dreadful experience when the cheese warehouse of Messr's Smith, Cox & Co opposite was burned to the ground on June 18, 1868. Over 200 tons of cheese was destroyed and damage to the value of £20,000 done.

This fire, added to the one which destroyed the Saw Mill, Timber Yard and some machinery which occurred a little earlier, showed up the deficiencies of both the Midland Company and the Derby Town fire brigades, and resulted in the former not only ordering a new Shand-Mason fire engine at a cost of £500, but also in them engaging Mr William Medcalf of the Metropolitan Fire Brigade as the new Fire Brigade Superintendent in October of the same year. The new fire engine served both the company and the town well for several years until replaced in 1873 by one of a better design by Merryweather's. In addition to the fire engine a new and much extended system of water mains and hydrants was laid in the works.

Returning to other characters, James Hunt was the foreman coppersmith, another old B&DJR man, and the black-bearded Joseph Weet was foreman of the brass foundry. Thomas Jewsbury, a fierce-looking well-built man with a heavy black beard, was foreman of No 18 shop, and his assistant foreman was D. Horton. George Baggaley later became assistant foreman of the new No 8 Erecting Shop, and he and his brother Thomas had come from the Midland Counties line. William A. Jackson was foreman of the press shop and Samuel Tetley foreman of the lagging shop.

William Marlow, mentioned previously, was head foreman of all the erecting shops, and the other senior foreman was James Melrose (senior) who had charge of both the smiths and wheel shops, with his son, James Melrose (junior), as his assistant. The father was an old stager, having come from the North Midland line where he was first employed in February, 1842. He is recorded as being one of the best of men, of good character and disposition and a very able engineer. His smile was regarded by some as "almost a benediction". George Leavers was foreman of the bottom stores, formerly old No 1 shop, and he had replaced William Banks, a very stout red-faced little man. William Millar was the foreman of the wheelwright's shop.

In the way of salary these foremen drew between 63s and 75s per week about 1870, small remuneration indeed by today's standards, and for their annual leave one weeks holiday with pay was allowed. The workmen's only privilege was a single weekday excursion to some popular nearby place of interest such as Buxton. An application by them for a similar "privilege" to that enjoyed by the foreman was, in July, 1870, "firmly declined".

A few other characters in the works engage our attention. Joseph Pettifor, originally station master at Nottingham, enjoyed the position of stores superintendent. He was a dapper gentleman, good at business, but who was vigorously defensive if anyone encroached on his preserves, his department being at this time part of the Locomotive Works.

Mr Richard A. Jarvis, "Dick" to his friends, was chief clerk in the Locomotive Department, of whom, in company with his close friend Hickling, the accountant, it was said they could "generally be found in the *Brunswick* public house during the day and the *Big Ship* at night!" These were days when ale was drunk by the gallon rather than by the pint!

John Mosley was chief clerk of the Carriage Department, under Robert Harland, and his "striking and venerable figure" was much in evidence at the old Temple Chapel on London Road. His son succeeded the above mentioned James Hunt as the foreman coppersmith.

Two other characters deserve mention. One was James Balderson, for many years the head timekeeper who ran a small shop at 27, High Street, and was such a lover of Shakespeare that he once offered to recite the works of the bard to his chief for 4hr without a break, a "treat" that was gently but firmly declined.

The other character was Abraham Bailey, erector, a quaint figure of a man, who had come from the North on the opening of the line. He later took to carrying a stick, which with his long frock coat, tall top hat and choker neck tie gave him an easily recognisable appearance. He was a leading man at the London Road Wesleyan Chapel and was "always willing to talk to you about your soul's welfare or sell you a mangle, sewing machine or home made medicine." His plasters, of which Burgandy pitch formed the main part, found a ready sale, their drawing power being "tremendous".

Many of these men had come from outside the county, from Yorkshire and Tyneside, and, with their "rude energy, broad outlook and ready tongue", were regarded with suspicion by the local inhabitants lest the "tenor" of the town be upset. However, they were quickly knit into the community, and were well housed by that days standards in the companies houses in the locality of the works and station, and living and working alongside the locals, these fears of lowering the tone of the town were quite quickly allayed.

Shortly before Kirtley's death in 1873, the Midland Directors decided that the Carriage and Wagon Department should be separated completely from the locomotive side, and a new site on the other side of the London Road was provided. Mr Thomas Gething Clayton was appointed as the Carriage and Wagon Superintendent at the instance of James Allport, the General Manager, who had become disturbed by the poor facilities being offered generally on railways at that time for the third-class passenger. Most of the existing carriages were small fourwheelers, with archaic roof rails for luggage and other outdated accoutrements. Allport had undertaken an extensive tour of North America in 1872, and returned impressed by the comfort and luxury of George Pullman's parlour and sleeping cars. Allport obtained the sanction of the Directors to give Clayton full rein in the layout of his new Carriage and Wagon Works, and further arranged with Pullman for the design, building and operation of his cars on the Midland, but at Pullman's own risk. Clayton took up his duties on July 1, 1873 at a salary of £700 per annum.

So began a long needed reform of coaching stock on the Midland which was to revolutionise rail travel comfort throughout the company's system. With the gradual transfer of this side of rolling stock construction and repair on the Midland to the new works between the years 1873 and 1877, the Locomotive Department was left on its own for the very first time. It was at this time that Kirtley arranged for two trains to be fitted up in the works with the Westinghouse Air Brake to enable trials to take place on May 21, 1873, with one train running between Leeds and Bradford and the other on the Metropolitan lines and the results in each case was the approximate halving of the stopping distances, even with ordinary tender and guard's brakes. Further trials with other types continued over a period to prove the findings of this first experiment.

Kirtley was already aware of pressures on the Locomotive Department for quicker turn-round of locomotives at repair, and had drawn up preliminary plans for further large extensions including more shops and a re-arrangement of the work of some of the shops to improve the efficiency of the works as a whole. These were laid before the Locomotive Committee in April, 1872, and were approved for passing forward to the general purposes committee in June of the same year.* A siding, necessary to serve the new shops to be erected, passing through the Derby Gas Company's property, at a cost of £3,500, was also agreed to.

The new paint shop was completed by the end of 1870, but the majority of the alterations were still outstanding when Kirtley's successor took over, for on May 24, 1873, Matthew Kirtley died, after a prolonged illness, at his home, Litchurch Grange, aged 60. His funeral cortège to the cemetery on Uttoxeter New Road was followed by large numbers of those who knew and loved him, among whom were Directors, engineers and workmen, all equally anxious to pay their last tribute of respect to one whose character had inspired so high a feeling of esteem in all with whom he was associated. Over his grave a stone obelisk was erected, paid for by subscriptions from the men of the Midland Railway at Derby and elsewhere, who wished to mark his passing. On the memorial are also the names of his wife and her sister, Kirtley's two daughters, Elizabeth and Emily, and Emily's husband, Sir Thomas Roe, MP, Jane the widow of George Stephenson of Liverpool, and the widow of Thomas Kirtley and three of their children.

Matthew Kirtley was indeed a veteran of the railway world, having been onetime pupil of George and Robert Stephenson, a driver on the London and Birmingham line and Locomotive Foreman at Hampton on the Birmingham and Derby Junction Railway, before his appointment as Locomotive Superintendent of that line, being specially selected by the Stephensons, which factor had ultimately led to his appointment to that position on the Midland which he occupied for the remaining part of his life.

On the amalgamation of 1844 there had been only a miscellaneous selection of about 100 odd locomotives, whereas by the time of his death 1,050 were on the books, comprising many fine classes which, through various rebuildings by his successors, were to run for the better

*BTHR Mid 1/172.

part of a century. Not only had the design of locomotives been his responsibility but also that of the carriages and wagons had been under his general supervision.

He was one of those who elevate themselves through the ranks from the workshops floor to attain the highest position in their respective department, yet in spite of, or perhaps because of this he retained an urbane manner, ever ready to advise or sympathise with both officials and workmen alike over whom he had control. Nevertheless, despite his kindly manner, his influence never lessened for want of necessary firmness and decisiveness when called for.

Behind him he left his wife Ann, and his two daughters Elizabeth and Emily, and it was to these three that two beautiful illuminated addresses were presented, one by the Officers of the Locomotive Department and the other by the enginemen and firemen of the company, in which they expressed the respect and esteem they felt for their chief.

So ended a great chapter in the story of the Derby Works, and with the advent of his successor, a new and equally great chapter was to be written.

CHAPTER SIX

Johnson Takes the Helm
(1873-1886)

AFTER MATTHEW KIRTLEY'S DEATH, as a temporary measure, his nephew William, already the Workshop Superintendent, took on the duties of Locomotive Superintendent as well, until a successor for his uncle could be found, assisted by the two District Locomotive Super-intendents, making up a three man commission.

The new Locomotive Superintendent, Samuel Waite Johnson, took office on July 1, 1873, at the same time that his opposite number, Thomas Gething Clayton took up his post as the new Carriage and Wagon Superintendent. The Midland Directors were indeed very fortunate to secure Johnson for this position. He had been the Loco-motive, Carriage and Wagon Superintendent of the Great Eastern Railway at Stratford since 1866, and a brief survey of his career before that date may be of interest. He was born at Bramley, near Leeds, in 1831, educated at Leeds Grammar School and from there he began his railway career by serving his time at E. B. Wilson's Railway Foundry, which was then building the "Jenny Lind" design in large numbers, being a pupil of James Fenton, an early railway engineer and one-time partner in a locomotive building firm. Johnson's first appointment was as manager of workshops for repairing locomotives .on the Great Northern Railway under Archibald Sturrock, where his father was an engineer.

From there he moved to Gorton as Works Manager of the Loco-motive, Carriage and Wagon Shops of the Manchester, Sheffield and Lincolnshire Company under Charles Sacre, the Superintendent. From there he became Locomotive, Carriage and Wagon Super-intendent of the Edinburgh and Glasgow Railway at Glasgow before the age of 30, where, upon absorbtion by that company into the North British Railway Company, he was retained as Locomotive Super-tendent of the Western Division of the new system, embracing Glasgow and Edinburgh. After two years in Scotland he removed to his penultimate post as Locomotive, Carriage and Wagon Superintendent of the Great Eastern Railway at Stratford in 1866, replacing Robert Sinclair. There he remained until his removal to the Midland.

Kirtley and Johnson were as different as "chalk and cheese" as the saying goes. Whilst Kirtley was a rough, jovial, homespun sort of engineer as Ellis* accurately describes him, his engines reflecting his character, being robust and substantial, Samuel Johnson was a much more genteel character, meticulous and an out and out Christian, whose engineering was much more of a fine art, and whose locomotives proved to be not only mechanically perfect, but beautiful to a degree as well.

Coming to Derby, Johnson could have begun by importing a lot of designs from the Great Eastern, bringing his favourite officials with him and ruthlessly displacing the many middle aged and older men at Derby. This he did not do for he was too good a statesman and organiser. Instead he set about moulding the existing staff to his will, getting them to work his way by degrees. He went to work improving methods all over the line as well as at Derby.

Engine sheds continued to be enlarged to accommodate the ever-increasing locomotive stock, and old cramped buildings were swept away and replaced by new ones of more spacious design. In Kirtley's time a policy of building airy and spacious roundhouse sheds had been pursued at the larger depots, and this policy was to continue through Johnson's time. Perhaps the most notable improvement during Johnson's term of office was the gradual introduction of high-level coal stages which greatly speeded up the coaling of engines. So far as locomotive design was concerned Johnson set about rebuilding and otherwise improving Kirtley's engines, reboilering where necessary. A census of engines taken on June 30, 1873 showed a total stock of 1,012 in the following condition:

General good order	894
Moderate order	97
Bad order	3
In shops rebuilding	8
Broken up for rebuilding	10
	1,012

There were also 46 engines as duplicate stock making 1,058 in all. Average age of normal stock was 6.47 years and of duplicate stock 19.3 years. Of the 97 in moderate order 37 were almost ready for breaking up for renewal with 3 in bad order, which with the duplicate stock gave 86 engines liable shortly to be unavailable for traffic purposes. He did bring in some new ideas and designs to the Midland, and in the first years his 0-4-4 tank engines and his new design of 0-6-0, based on the Sharp Stewart 0-6-0s supplied to the Great Eastern, were the fore-runners of a long line of good solid engineering workhorses. One detail change was the first use on the Midland of Mansell's fastening for

* *The Midland Railway* by C. Hamilton Ellis.

locomotive tyres, which was immediately introduced as standard for future in November, 1873, commencing with Sharp's 1070 class 2-4-os. Only a few men came with Johnson from Stratford, and one of these was John Lane, brought for the specialist job of Inspector of Boilers (*see Plate 33*). His job was to ascertain the existing condition of the company's stock and also to inspect engines under construction at the Derby Works as well as at the private locomotive builders. He was awarded a salary of £250 per annum for his efforts, and took office on August 5, 1873. Lane was later to become the Works Manager.

The staff, once they had seen the new chief, liked what they saw, and were only too ready to help and adapt themselves in any way required. Johnson was more like a father than a chief, and really lived up to one of his favourite sayings "Do everything you can for everybody, but never be an obliging fool".

Changes in the other offices were bound to follow Kirtley's death, and the following year William Kirtley left to become the Locomotive Superintendent of the London, Chatham and Dover Railway Company, in March, 1874, being replaced as Superintendent of Workshops by Francis Holt, a tall, gaunt man, somewhat peculiar in manner, having a mordant humour, but being on the whole a very capable officer, by no means disliked by the men (*see Plate 34*). His one fault perhaps was that, coming from Beyer Peacock & Co's. Gorton Foundry, Manchester, he was obsessed with the idea that everything they did was the last word in engine construction and practice. In fact to him Beyers spelt "perfection", which was somewhat irritating to the proud men of the Derby Works! He took office in May, 1874 at a salary of £700 per annum, receiving £100 more than his predecessor.

By July, 1873, the pressure of work was telling on the general drawing office, and Newbould requested the Locomotive Committee to appoint an assistant draughtsman. From 22 applicants it was James Fenton of the Great Eastern Railway, and recommended by Johnson no doubt, who was given the appointment on August 5, 1873, at the princely salary of £144 per annum, the senior draughtsman, William Green, receiving a "consolation prize" of a £10 increase in his remuneration.*

Fenton went on to become the First Inspector of Engines on October 14, 1873 at £210 per annum plus £40 per annum expenses, and remained with the company until the end of 1876 when he resigned. He died at Putney on November 8, 1893, two days before his 55th birthday. Clearly there was a policy here of expanding the design department at Derby to a capacity able to produce the drawings for all future designs, especially in view of the new engines likely to be born from Johnson's reappraisal of the state of the locomotive stock.

*BTHR Mid 1/173

E

In September of the same year Thomas Say Bloxham, a fine engineer and a most excellent draughtsman, joined the team, and in the November William Bancroft of Derby and J. C. Evans of London were added to the design staff. The following year more changes took place, and six of the leading draughtsmen were awarded a fortnight's pay in lieu of a week's holiday in consequence of extreme pressure of work.

Henry Hedley, who was responsible for assisting Johnson's detailed classification of engine stock by producing a sheet of somewhat sparse diagrams showing the main dimensions of all the types then in use, was spurred on in his efforts by having his salary raised by 6s to 30s a week.

Bloxham only remained in the drawing office until June, 1875, when he took over the position of Locomotive Superintendent at Hasland in place of W. N. Adams, who had died the previous month. F. T. Addison of Manchester took his place in the Derby office.

The first Chief Locomotive Draughtsman, appointed by Johnson, was Robert John Billinton,* who had been the Assistant Locomotive Superintendent, under William Stroudley, on the London, Brighton and South Coast Railway. Born at Wakefield on April 5, 1845, he served a part-apprenticeship from 1859–63 at the works of William Fairbairn & Sons, of Manchester, and the remaining two years of his time-serving was spent with Messrs Simpson & Co of Pimlico, London. After two years with R. Child of Wakefield, engaged in mining and civil engineering, he became Assistant Manager at Messrs Walker & Eaton of Sheffield, builders of locomotives and general machinery, in June, 1866.

In 1870 he was appointed assistant to Stroudley on the LB&SCR, in charge of the design of locomotives, carriages and wagons, and other rolling stock, where he stayed until his appointment on the Midland in November, 1874, at a salary of £225 a year, and with a promise of a further £25 the following July.

His work was, as a result of his wide field of experience, of the best class, and during his term of office many excellent types of engines were turned out as will be recounted later. It is recorded that he knew as much about old-time railwaymen as almost anyone at that period, since, owing to his father's contacts as a contractor of sorts, he had met railway engineers and managers and other figures of note, from a child upwards. The North West, Lancashire and Yorkshire were his special areas, and he seemed to be well acquainted with everyone of note from personal contact in that part of the country.

The new foreman of Derby running shed, appointed on July 26, 1875, was John Augustus Sach. He was of German origin, his real name being Sach, although he always spelt it with a "k". He was said to be clever at

*BTHR Mid 1/173 Billinton's official title was "Head Draughtsman".

his job, but his origin frequently became obvious in conversation. On one occasion, when explaining about something being pushed out of place, he is recorded as saying to a colleague "It shuft it, it shuft it, it shuft it out", and "shuft-it" became his nickname for a long time afterwards. He later became engine inspector on January 1, 1877 and foreman of templates and gauges on July 9, 1878, resigning the following September, possibly considering the latter post a demotion.

Clayton had begun to get his separated Carriage and Wagon Department under way soon after his appointment, and his staff recruitment began in August, 1873 with the transfer of three clerks from the Locomotive Department to his own. Thereafter he swelled the ranks by the transfer of certain of the workmen skilled in carriage and wagon building at the old works as leavening for the "lump" of new staff he was forced to take on as his workshops on the new site began to go into production.

On the locomotive front, Johnson was quickly made aware that with the Settle–Carlisle line under way, and other traffic increasing in volume, with heavier and heavier trains becoming the order of the day, he had to begin his term of office by providing for these with better, more powerful classes of locomotives, especially for working passenger and goods trains over the Pennines.

Johnson began his own system of works order-numbers which identified all orders put into the shops, whether for new locomotives, tenders, spare boilers or rebuilding. These orders will be referred to as "O/1" etc, in the text following, and this system of Johnson's has been retained right up to the present day. amplified by the Job Nos system for modifications and Lot Nos for new building programmes for use outside the works.

Johnson also arranged for the locomotive drawing office to commence a new numbering system for all drawings produced from 1874 onwards. The prefix to the drawing number gave the year the drawing was made, and the second part was a continuous numerical series beginning at No 1, thus the first drawing was 74/1. All the old drawings still in existence were numbered with a "K" (for "Kirtley") prefix.

Johnson also arranged in March, 1874 for Messrs Neilson & Co Ltd of Glasgow to supply the drawing office with a valve-motion-model machine at a cost of £170. This enabled those working out the valve events for any particular engine to set up the model in full-size facsimile of the actual motion and obtain all the readings required directly from the scales provided. This was a great advance on the old time-consuming method of setting out each interval of forward and backward gear to arrive at the values needed. This motion-model, with some later additions from Stoke and Crewe, was used right up until the close of the steam age for some of the British Railway's Standard locomotive valve gears. It is now to be seen in the Museum of British Transport at Clapham, London.

The first new order was for ten 0-4-4T condensing engines Nos 6 15, 18, 137, 140–4, and 147 having 17in × 24in cylinders and 5ft 3in diameter driving wheels at 8ft centres. The boiler carried 223 tubes of 1¾in diameter giving a heating surface of 1,123sq ft which, with the firebox, gave a total of 1,227sq ft. The tank held 950gal, and the bunker 20cwt, of coal, working weights being as follows: leading 13 tons 10cwt 1qtr, driving 14 tons 17cwt 3qtr, trailing bogie 14 tons 18cwt giving a total weight of 43 tons 6cwt, (with tanks ¾ full and 10cwt coal). These engines were for working the South Tottenham and City trains, and had no cabs as built, although all-over cabs, were added later. These engines were known as Class C, and this was the only case of a Midland Railway-built order of engines being given a class letter. In the future, Derby-built engines were to be referred to by order and engine numbers as previously stated and only those classes built by outside contractors were given class letters, in strict ordering of building, from "A" onwards

The original design for the first 0-4-4T on the Midland was for a much smaller locomotive, having the same size of 5ft 3in driving wheels but at only 7ft centres, and with inside cylinders only 15in × 22in diameter. The drawing for these engines shows a most unusual feature in that the steam dome was on the first ring of the two ring barrel, next to the chimney. The drawing, being dated January 30, 1874, probably represents Johnson's first thoughts on a passenger tank locomotive for Midland use, which he afterwards decided was too diminutive to provide the required power output for its duties. Further details are given below, for no mention of this design has, so far as the author knows, been made before:

Length of boiler barrel 9ft 3in
Diameter of boiler barrel (inside) 3ft 10in
Length of firebox shell 4ft 6¾in
Capacity of tanks 900 gal
Capacity of coal bunkers 20cwt
Height of centre of boiler from rail 6ft 8in
From centre of driving axle to centre of bogie 10ft
Diameter of bogie wheels 2ft 9in
Centres of bogie wheels 5ft
Outside crank 10in

The locomotive was to have had an all-over cab, with the side tanks extended to just short of the joint between first and second boiler rings, and seems to have been a scaled down version of the Great Eastern type, introduced by Johnson in 1872–3, and built by Neilson & Co and the Avonside Engine Co to his designs. This was the first use on a British railway of the inside framed 0-4-4T which was to become so popular on many other railways in later years.

The first passenger design built during Johnson's term of office was a development of Kirtley's 890 class, and had inside frames, 6ft 2in diameter driving wheels and 17in × 24in cylinders. Messrs Sharp Stewart built 20 engines of this class, Nos 1070–89, during 1874–5, beginning with 1070 in June, 1874, and 10 of these engines were built at Derby to O/97, Nos 1, 9, 10, 13, 70, 71, 73, 74, 96 and 146, the first out being Nos 1 and 9 in February, 1876. The Sharp's engines carried a Kirtley boiler pressed to 140psi, giving a total heating surface of 1,063sq ft of which the 188 tubes of 1¾in diameter provided 971sq ft and the firebox 92sq ft while the Derby engines had a Johnson P-class boiler carrying 221 tubes of the same diameter giving an increased heating surface of 1,206sq ft, of which tubes provided 1,096sq ft. One feature of this design was the leading inside axleboxes which had the sliding top of Cartazzi pattern. Height to top of chimney was 13ft 2in, and the driving wheel centres were 8ft 6in. The leading wheels were 4ft 2in diameter placed 8ft in front of the leading driving wheel. Reversing was by means of a screw and handle.

The Derby engines were allocated mostly to Skipton until later replaced by new engines, when they moved to Nottingham, with No 96 going to Kentish Town. All of these had the Westinghouse air brake fitted.

The Sharp Stewart-built engines are often considered to be the last passenger engines built to Kirtley's designs, although they are classified along with the Derby locomotives which are credited to Johnson.

With these and all future locomotives he was fighting a battle against the constrictions of the 4ft 8½in gauge. He was firmly of the opinion that 5ft 3in would be an ideal gauge, and that the use of such wider gauge would have greatly reduced the difficulties countless Locomotive Superintendents experienced in crowding all the machinery into the space between the frames. This he observed limited the boiler diameter when the driving wheels were large, cramped the firebox width and unduly reduced the dimensions of the crank bearing surfaces and webs. The remark about limited boiler and firebox dimensions became particularly relevant when he introduced his renowned single wheelers, but that is later in our story.

One of the Derby built engines, No 96, was the last Midland 2-4-0 engine running, not being withdrawn until October 28, 1950, having been renumbered 155 in 1907, and 20155 in 1937, in between this being named *Engineer South Wales* from 1933 to 1936. In all she ran a total of 1,425,151 miles in service.

The class as a whole were renumbered 127–56 in order of building in 1907. At boiler changes P boilers with different heating surfaces were put on Nos 1070–89 and all but five of the class were later rebuilt with B boilers pressed to 160psi. Four, Nos 13, 73, 96 and 146, were rebuilt with Belpaire G6 boilers between 1924 and 1927. All had their cylinders enlarged to 18in diameter between 1887 and 1902.

When built these engines were for use on the new Settle–Carlisle "road" which had been opened for goods traffic on August 2, 1875, and was due to be opened for through passenger-trains from St Pancras to Glasgow and Edinburgh on May 1, 1876.

The same year larger versions of this class emerged from the Derby Works having $17\frac{1}{2}$in × 26in cylinders. These were built to O/107 and were Nos 50–4 with 6ft 6in driving wheels and 55–9 with 6ft 8in driving wheels, the first one being turned out in August. All had Johnson's P boiler with total heating surface 1,206sq ft of which the 221 tubes of $1\frac{3}{4}$in diameter provided 1,096sq ft, and at standard working pressure of 140psi. The ten 2,800gal tenders for the Derby engines were built to O/150 and carried 5 tons of coal.

On the engine the leading wheels were 4ft 3in diameter and the driving wheels were at the standard 8ft 6in centres. The leading axle-boxes were as for O/97, and screw reverse and a Furness lubricator were provided. Working weights of a Dübs built locomotive were: engine 38 tons 8cwt 3qtr and tender 32 tons dead. Incidentally, Nos 1282–1301 were fitted with Smiths simple vacuum brake for working the London–Manchester services, and 1302–11 had Westinghouse brakes for working the expresses from St Pancras to Scotland. Of the Derby built engines Nos. 50–4 were allocated to Sheffield and 55–9 were at Skipton for a time, then later replaced by more powerful engines and moved to Sheffield, and still later came to be allocated to York in 1880.

In 1877 ten further 2-4-0s, with 7ft driving wheels and having running Nos 1347–56, were built at Derby, for use on the fastest main line passenger trains, being allocated to Skipton (1347–50) and Saltley (1351–6). The first two of these engines had Westinghouse brake equipment, and the class was built to O/179. The cylinders were $17\frac{1}{2}$in × 26in, but all were later enlarged to 18in × 26in. The leading wheels were 4ft 3in diameter, and the boiler was again the P boiler, with heating surface as before on the 50 class, pitched 7ft $3\frac{1}{2}$in from rail. The tender was 2,950gal, and, with 2 tons of coal, the working weights were: engine 38 tons 5cwt 3qtr, tender 32 tons 11cwt 1qtr. Of the engine weight 14 tons 2cwt were on the driving and 12 tons 2cwt 3qtr on the trailing wheels. The cost of each locomotive was £1,572.

The class were renumbered 1347A–56A and again 101–10 in 1879, becoming 197–206 in 1907. The first was withdrawn in April, 1924 and the last (1354) in October, 1941. All were later rebuilt with B class boilers, and three with G6 Belpaire boilers.

Briefly mentioning engines built by outside firms, Dübs built two orders of 6ft 6in 2-4-0s in 1876, all with $17\frac{1}{2}$in × 26in cylinders, Nos 1282–1301 and 1302–11 and in the same year Messrs Kitson & Co turned out the first Johnson 4-4-0s for the Midland, Nos 1312–21. These had the same driving wheel and cylinder dimensions, but the new design of B class boiler had a total heating surface of 1,223sq ft, comprising 221 tubes of $1\frac{3}{4}$in diameter totalling 1,113sq ft and firebox 110sq ft. The firegrate was standard on all classes of passenger tender engines at 17.5sq ft up to the year 1887. These engines had Smiths simple vacuum brake and were allocated to Liverpool. These were followed up in 1877 by 20 further engines by Messrs Dübs, Nos 1327–46 being Class G, and having 18in × 26in cylinders and 7ft driving wheels and with a different version of the B boiler, carrying 1,260sq ft of heating surface, of which the tubes gave 1,150sq ft, there being 246 tubes of $1\frac{5}{8}$in diameter at the smokebox end. The Kitsons had 2,760gal and the Dübs 2,950gal tenders, and the leading wheels on the Kitson engines were only 3ft 3in diameter compared to the Dübs 3ft 6in. All had screw reverse and Furness standard lubricator, but the Dübs engines had a Roscoes lubricator and jet for the cylinders. The Kitsons cost £2,750 and the Dübs £2,690 and £2,495 for the later build.

The next passenger engines built were further 2-4-0s, Nos 1400–09 to order 232, in 1878, the first of 75 such engines built up to 1881, after which no more 2-4-0s were to be made (*see Plate 28*). These are tabulated below:

Year	Order	Nos	Cyls	Dia of Driving Wheels	Leading Wheels	Cost per Engine
1879	O/232	1400–1409	18in × 26in	6ft $8\frac{1}{2}$in	4ft $2\frac{1}{2}$in	£2,205
1880	O/283	111–115	$17\frac{1}{2}$in × 26in	6ft $6\frac{1}{2}$in	4ft $2\frac{1}{2}$in	
1880	O/279	1472–81	18in × 26in	6ft $8\frac{1}{2}$in	4ft $2\frac{1}{2}$in	£2,264
1880	O/273	1482–91	18in × 26in	6ft $8\frac{1}{2}$in	4ft $2\frac{1}{2}$in	£2,337
1881	Like O/232	1502–31	18in × 26in	6ft 9in	4ft $2\frac{1}{2}$in	£2,445
1881	O/275	1492–1501	18in × 26in	7ft $0\frac{1}{2}$in	4ft $2\frac{1}{2}$in	£2,166

All the above were built at Derby, except Nos 1502–31 which were by Neilson & Co, and carried the same P boiler of 1,206sq ft total heating surface as the 50 class. Screw reversing gear was fitted, and the tenders were of 2,950gal capacity, being the first to have outside sprung axleboxes with the springs below the platform level.

Turning aside from the business of "locomotive hardware" for a moment, the subject of liveries is a most interesting one and the painting of No 1500 and nine other engines in a new red colour in September, 1881, in place of the old sombre Kirtley dark green, which had been modified by Johnson to a lighter shade in 1876, began a process of colour change which was to improve the appearance of the locomotive stock, and trains took on a new uniformity since the majority of coaching stock was already claret and was later to be turned out in the new livery.

The first red was not the "glowing" colour eventually agreed to in 1883 but a rather dull shade. This however soon gave way to the famous crimson lake or "Midland Red" as it became to be known, which was such a distinctive colour that it stood out anywhere.

The reason for the change was that the existing green livery did not last long, being labelled a "fugitive" colour, and being also more expensive to maintain in reasonable condition. The cost of painting an engine and tender varied only by a few shillings in favour of the oxide of iron paint. In a total years (1880) cost of £5,176 for painting locomotives, the saving would be of the order of £2,000–£2,500 per annum taking into account the fact that the red colour, being more durable, would outlast the green livery by twice the period. The General Purposes Committee approved the change of locomotive livery on October 18, 1883, and thereafter no further engines were painted green.* The old Kirtley livery, applied to both goods and passenger engines was, as mentioned before, a dark green, picked out in black and fine lined in white. This was applied to the boiler, frames, splashers, handrails and weather screen in two coats after the following preparation: one coat of lead colour-primer, two coats of stopping and three coats of filling-up. This was then rubbed down, and a further two coats of lead colour applied, then the whole was sand-papered. The tyre rim was painted black with a white line and the inside of frames and the axles were painted with one coat of vermilion and one coat of varnish, as were the buffer planks.

Smokebox, chimney, firebox back, platforms, steps and guards were painted black (two coats) and the inside of the cab was finished in brown and lined out. The tender was finished in the same manner as the engine. It was rather unusual on other lines for underframes to be painted the same colour as the rest of the locomotive and this was a rather distinctive feature.

The new standard livery consisted of the following: the boiler,

*BTHR Mid 1/176

frames, splashers, tanks (if fitted), coal bunker and cab had one coat of lead colour or oxide, well stopped and filled up, rubbed down, then a further two coats of lead colour or oxide, sand papered, two coats of oxide and crimson lake, picked out with black and fine lined with yellow, followed by three coats of varnish. The outside of the frames, sandboxes and wheelguards were treated in similar fashion.

The inside of the frames and axles were vermilion with two coats of varnish; the buffer planks carrying the company's initials in gilt, were also vermilion with three coats of varnish. The smokebox, firebox back, platforms, steps and brakehangers had one coat of black and one coat of black Japan. Tyre rims were black, The inside of the cab had a two-coat preparation similar to the frame, but finished in light-oak graining with three coats of varnish. For exhibition purposes the underside of the boiler barrel clothing was painted white to reflect light onto the finely finished and polished motion below although this was only done at Kentish Town locomotive depot.

The crimson lake was manufactured for a considerable period in the paint shop at Derby, the principal constituent being cochineal, a scarlet dye stuff consisting of the dried bodies of certain insects gathered from cactus plants grown on special farms for this particular purpose, in Spain, Mexico and the West Indies, which gave the Midland livery such a distinctive appearance. Latterly the paint was supplied by Messrs Leech and Neal of Derby, and the Strathclyde Paint Company of Glasgow, and was termed "Oxide of Iron and Lake", the change of name taking place about 1896.

There was also a new clause added to the directions for painting which read "Twelve hours must elapse between each coat of varnish and 24 hours after the last coat before it (the locomotive) goes out of the paint shop."

Before closing this chapter mention should be made of the appointment of the first Midland Railway official photographer, Thomas Scotton, who took up his duties on September 22, 1882, at the princely salary of £1. 12s 0d per week. He was born on June 26, 1844 and was first taken on as a painters labourer on June 11, 1860. From his interest in photography he produced many fine pictures which resulted in the appointment.

The following year his son, Thomas Albert, was appointed assistant photographer on March 26, 1883 at 5s 8d per week at the age of 23, and father and son built up a fine collection of negatives which still exists today in the care of the Curator of Historical Relics. By means of this collection we have a very fine record of the many classes of Midland engines produced not only in the Derby Works, but also by outside firms, as well as pictures of rolling stock, stations, scenes along the line etc. Thomas Scotton the elder died "in harness" on October 9, 1894, of a haemorrhage of the brain, and his son was promoted to take his place, still at the same salary of £1. 12s od per week.

Throughout 1892 and 1893 the photographers were extremely busy taking views of scenery and places of interest on the various Midland routes for the adornment of Midland carriages, and the practice of using such photographs continued throughout the remainder of the Midland's history and also through LMS days.

CHAPTER SEVEN

A Tour of the Works
(1876)

BEFORE PROCEEDING with further descriptions of the locomotives turned out by the Derby Works, some other matters command attention at this period of time, the main item being the addition of a large new complex of shops, comprising the present erecting and machine shops, the former paint shop, and new boiler and coppersmiths shops with a brass foundry. These were built to the designs of the Midland Company's architect, Mr J. H. Sanders, and their erection began shortly before Johnson's arrival being completed about the beginning of 1877.

On June 17, 1873, the Locomotive Committee had ordered "that Mr Sanders be requested to proceed with the erection of the new fitting shops at Derby with all speed", and in November of the same year it was resolved that "the whole of the land to the north of Spondon curve be appropriated for locomotive purposes, the said curve to form the south boundary."*

In detail those plans were for an extension of the smiths shop on the bottom yard, a new boiler shop, (*see Plate 69*), which incidentally retained its identity to the end of the steam era, as did the new coppersmiths shop and brass foundry. A new iron foundry was also added, (*see Plate 68*), with the large complex comprising erecting shop, tool and fitting shop, grinding shop and toolroom, and then, beyond the end of the block, and standing on its own, the new painting shop. Also added was a new grease manufactory.

With the addition of these shops came the new sidings to serve them, emanating from the Etches Park area past the new Derby Gas Works at Litchurch. This was because of the impracticability of arranging an entrance to the new shops from the direction of the station, and also to tie in with the proposed Nos 4 & 5 sheds which were to be built adjacent to the new painting shop. These were to be two twin turntable engine houses of rectangular shape, (rather than separate circular or square roundhouses), each turntable having 22 roads emanating from it, making 44 roads in all per shed. As it turned out, only No 4 shed came to be built, and this was completed, along with carriage store sheds in the Etches Park area by 1889.

*BTHR Mid 1/173

Incidentally on March 10, 1875, the old works of the Derby Gas Company were handed over to the Midland Company, who were thus able to produce all the gas necessary for their own purposes in the Derby area.

Regarding the works, an enlightening article describing a tour of Derby Locomotive Works in 1876 appeared in the *Sheffield Daily Telegraph*, under the pen name of "Strephon", and a resumé of this article is given below, since it throws an interesting light on many aspects of the works at this date. "Strephon" was the pen name of Edward Bradbury, a Derby railwayman.

After crossing the well known iron lattice footbridge, which connects the works to the station concourse, his first call was at the fire station where the "Merryweather" steam fire-engine, mounted on a railway truck, was ready with furnace prepared, for a call to any part of the system (*see Plate 66*). Adjacent to this was the reservoir of water erected over the weighbridge, for use in case of fire.

Describing the roundhouses, he then visited the No 1 erecting shop, "the oldest on the ground, now devoted entirely to the repair of goods engines". This was the old North Midland engine shop, entrance to which was gained through side doors opening at intervals to connect with the sidings outside, and by means of which the shop was connected to the running lines by traversers and turntables. He describes how the engines were shopped bodily, standing in rows of two, with about 20 engines undergoing repair at any one time. Flexible gas piping provided illumination for the white moleskin jacket craftsmen in the pit beneath each engine, whilst other workmen were "busily fixing the brass fire tubes". At the end of No 1 shop a recently erected room provided for the manufacture and storage of gauges and templates of every size, and it also housed a tensile testing machine.

Adjacent to No 1 shop, on the top yard, was the No 2 erecting shop, (now the No 4 electric shop) (*see Plate 59*) devoted then entirely to rebuilds, and supplied with a 30-ton overhead crane, where new boilers, cylinders and other such repairs, requiring engines to be stripped right down, were carried out. The figures given are interesting: new engines will run two years before general repairs; the average boiler age was 15 years with total mileage of 450,000 or 82 miles per days' run. These figures are for goods engines, the harder worked passenger engine requiring repairs after a shorter period. Also in this shop were three new passenger engines then being constructed for use on the Settle-Carlisle line, and fitted with the Westinghouse Patent Air Brake. He records that the wooden lagging for the boiler was not fitted until after the locomotives had made a trial run to enable easier detection of defects and the remedying of such as were found.

From this shop a descent was made to the "lower turnery", now the axle turning shop, which was then the major machining shop, and held lathes, shaping, drilling, slotting, boring planes and other machines. Many of these were then steam driven of course, and must have presented an impressive spectacle in those early days.

He mentions in particular the steam planing machinery "carving iron like butter", and being used to cut every description of metal part except the chilled cast-iron axlebox slides which were cut by special emery-wheels. Crank-axles were being turned on a slide-rest, using water as a coolant, and slotting machines were busy on "aperture" work.

Next the wheel turning and tyre boring shops were visited (see Plate 64) where 30 lathes were hard at work, and the large hydraulic presses for forcing wheels on axles were busily engaged. And then on to the spring shop to see the manufacture and testing of the engine and tender springs. Next he visited the Smithy, the largest, longest and loftiest of the old shops. It had the reputation of being one of the finest in all the United Kingdom. Sixty smiths fires were "aflame and sixty anvils echoed and re-echoed to the blows of the smith on the workpiece". The smiths of course would be dressed in their characteristic fisher caps and leather aprons. While the strikers, with sleeves tucked up, would be continuously swinging their heavy hammers bringing them down with unerring precision on the heated iron as the smith slowly turned it on the anvil. In the centre of the shop were half a dozen steam hammers for heavier work, and at the end of the shop a large furnace for the reclamation of scrap iron from the various departments.

"Out in the yard the fussy little tank engines with loaded wagons, are puffing in every direction, up impossible gradients and round the most extraordinary curves", he stated.

The millwrights shop was next visited; not the present one, which was at this time being converted from the old North Midland Carriage and Wagon shop at a cost of some £1,350, but what later became the gas fitters shop, and latterly the tube shop, on the canal side of the bottom yard beyond the smithy. Here, as largely today, the renewals of cranes, steam traversers, engine turntables, stationary engines, and the general maintenance of workshop machinery was being undertaken.

In discussing the present millwrights shop, then undergoing conversion, mention should be made of a most interesting example of cast-iron work. This is the original spiral staircase to the upper storey, provided for the North Midland Company by Messrs Haywood Brothers of London. It still survives today in excellent condition, a tribute to the workmanship of a century or more ago. Mention should also be made of the large one-piece cast-iron window-lights to be found in various parts of the works. These were made locally at the Britannia Foundry of Andrew Handyside and iron founders today cannot match the skills of the founders of old in equalling this feat of great craftsmanship.

No 3 erecting shop was next on the visitors list, a repetition of No 1 shop, except that it was used only for the repair of passenger engines; and then on to No 4 shop, a facsimile of No 2, followed by the "top turnery", and thence to the tender shop, where tenders were repaired and manufactured. This was adjacent to No 2 roundhouse, and was later to become reserved only for the repair of tender tanks, and later still for a "new age" use as a repair shop for diesel railcar engines. Adjacent to these was the lagging shop, tinsmiths and coppersmiths, and thence to the paint shop, adjacent to No 3 roundhouse, which is now the pattern shop, being converted on completion of the new shops then being erected. Incidentally the new paint shop was even then in use.

The next shops to be visited were the new brass foundry, and the pattern shop (later to become the coppersmiths) on the top yard, the former being the then home of the famous or infamous *Loco Bull*, described by Strephon as "that revolting railway whistle, the nerve shattering screams of which to aesthetic exquisites make day dolorous and night hideous" but to others "the never failing teller of the time on six occasions during the working day", but of this more later.

Thousands of numbered and classified patterns, painted mostly red, with the core prints black, were to be found in the pattern shop, alongside the dozen or so skilled pattern makers who produce these most accurate pieces of woodwork, assisted by still more joiners who were entrusted with the "rougher work".

On the bottom yard the visitors were able to visit the new boiler shop already in commission, being 270ft long and 150ft wide, and adjoining the old shop to which it formed a much needed extension.

The new shop was of three bays, each served by a travelling crane driven by an endless cord. Of the deafening noise in this department the author observes "a park full of artillery at practice is perfect serenity compared to the sound of these Midland Railway Titans" and he was told that all boiler-makers were as "deaf as a door nail". (Perhaps he meant "post".)

He next visited the new workshops which comprised eight distinct buildings covering several acres, and states that contracts let amounted to £120,000, apart from the expenditure involved in the purchase of plant and machinery, and in laying out the new railway connections to these shops. Of these, in the new machine shop machines costing £1,745 were ordered for the purpose of producing the turned and finished items of brasswork which had, right up until this time, been purchased

A TOUR OF THE WORKS

from outside manufacturers, but which were henceforward to be cast and machined in the Derby Works.

The largest of these new shops was the engine erecting and fitting shop, 450ft long and 325ft broad, comprising seven bays divided by iron pillars supporting a glass and iron roof (see Plate 61). The erecting portion of three bays was divided from the fitting section by partition arches of brick and contained six lines of engine pits in pairs, each pair having a central access line which was also used for repairs and gave accommodation for a total of 108 engines at a time. The original cranes for this shop were driven by a one-inch rope running at 2,000ft per min and capable of lifting a weight of 25 tons.

It is worthwhile mentioning at this time that the repair of an engine in the erecting shop was the responsibility of a gang usually comprising four men and two boys, the leading hand contracting to build the engine labour only at a fixed price, the operation taking about three weeks. Weekly wages were paid to each member of the gang, and at the end of the job the balance remaining was equitably divided.

The new painting and stores shed, standing alone, was 450ft long and 110ft broad, having room for about 40 locomotives at a time, and the other shops mentioned were a brass and copper foundry 250ft × 45ft, a smiths shop 210ft × 45ft, a wheel and turning shop 110ft × 45ft, and a new iron foundry 190ft × 110ft, (opened in 1877). The new grease manufactory and stores was 200ft × 110ft. The work of the iron foundry was further expanded when a new shop for chair making was opened in 1884, at a cost of £3,800 including machinery and permanent way. Weekly output of this new foundry was soon up to 100 tons per week including cylinder blocks, lamp posts, water pipes, signal fittings, chimneys, firebars and brakeblocks. Total men employed at this date was about 2,500 and the number of locomotives on the books was just over 1,300.

The final place visited was the mess room, there being at this time three, one for engine drivers, firemen and running department staff, and two for the workmen in the various shops. Of these two for workmen, one held accommodation for 200, the other for about 700. "Strephon" is somewhat out here in his capacities for the official figure for the old mess rooms was 550. In August, 1876 a scheme to demolish the small mess room and enlarge the existing one, which had been erected in 1862, at a cost of £2,550 was agreed to. The new one was to accommodate 1,500 men and put an end to what the management regarded as a very objectionable habit, ie workmen taking their meals in the workshops, which was however unavoidable at this time owing to lack of space in the proper mess rooms. This habit was said to encourage rats. The building of the new extension commenced the following autumn, 1877 and this was split into two at the men's request. In the latter election addresses were delivered in times of political stress, as the only diversion, but in the former the breakfast hour each morning embraced a devotional service, at which local or visiting ministers, and even distinguished visitors and Bishops on occasion, addressed the assembled company. In this place it was often impossible to gain a seat for the men had certain regular places all the year round which they regarded as much their own as their family pew in church or chapel. These men enjoyed the Bible with their bread and bacon, and many who "came to scoff remained to pray" (*see Plate 67*).

The origin of these meetings was very humble and they began, before a proper mess room was provided, as Bible and prayer meetings in the stationary engine house of one George Wilkins, member of a well known Derby religious family. They were held by the side of his out of work engine during the breakfast hour. From the original small group of supporters with similar leanings, the gatherings increased in size until when the new mess rooms were erected, the smallest of the three was, at the men's request set aside and thereafter known as the "chapel" or "religious mess room". One William Scattergood was for many years the secretary and organiser, an appropriate name, though often mischievously pronounced "Scatter guts" and he kept a small provision shop on Burton Road. There was not a parson in the district who had not been approached by this man, and pressed for his services, and eminent men from other towns, after taking services on Sundays in Derby, were also often enlisted to speak the following Monday morning at these meetings.

It is recorded that many a minister could conduct the meetings against the clatter of cutlery tins and cups, as of manner born, while others became disconcerted and faltered, or become uninteresting, the clatter from the tables then becoming "louder and more continuous than usual".

"One fledging cleric", Pratt recalls, "had been struggling in the agony of oratory for a quarter of an hour, and, as he descended the platform, one of the "old standards" called him aside. "Look here, young man," he said, "before yo' come here again, just put a bit more cotton on your bobbin, will yer'?" In connection with these services it may be mentioned that a small organ, provided by public funds, was presented to the religious mess room on 23 December, 1887 in time for the Christmas services. This was of a type imported from France by Chappel & Co of New Bond Street, London, having been awarded the "Medal of Honour" in the 1855 Paris Exhibition. It is 3ft 4in high, 4ft wide and 2ft 4in deep having 14 stops of which 10 are of the speaking variety, and was used daily at lunch times and at the weekly early morning services in the religious mess room. It was handed over to the Curator of Historical Relics for the BRB in 1955.

With the alteration in working hours and the abolishment of breakfast time in the works, this naturally put an end to these particular services, and this morning fellowship time which "gave the hearers an uplift which carried them with a modest, but beneficial example through the day, and was radiated in a silent but practical manner to those around them as they went about their daily task" disappeared completely.

After breakfast each of the men left behind his respective basket in his usual place, and the cooks prepared the mens' midday meals from the contents as required, cooking the stews, steaks, eggs and bacon, meat and potato hash, apple dumplings, soups, etc. The cooks came to know, in the course of time, exactly how each man liked his meal cooked, and prompt at 1.00pm the meals were placed on the tables ready for the men. "Eating took the best part of a half hour after which the rest of the time was spent dozing, reading aloud in groups, smoking, or arguing on every subject from politics to the ministry."

Mention was made earlier of the *Loco Bull*, the steam whistle which announced to the whole of Derby that the men in the Locomotive Works were either about to start work or leave it, and it sounded six times on a normal working day. Pratt refers to the "few timorous rivals, like poor relations at a rich man's feast" which "used to chip in, but were reckoned of no account".

No record of the actual installation of the *Bull* appears to have been made, but in March, 1864 a page of pictorial allegory to its honour and glory, drawn by Mr G. F. Smith, a local artist appeared in the press. Derby people set their clocks by the *Bull*, regarded by many as the "local representative" of Greenwich, and many imagined its operation to be free from all human agency! The truth was that a disc on the big finger of an ordinary clock "dropped", and upon this signal a man on a step ladder pulled a chain, releasing steam from a boiler thus giving the *Bull* his voice.

In 1861 the operator was one Sammy Brown, and for many many years, without a single omission, he performed the simple operation six times a day and everyone was happy until one day, as passing years had taken their toll, he started the *Bull* at twelve o'clock instead of the usual one o'clock! What an upset in the town; gossip ceased and dinners were quickly set on the table an hour too soon. Brown had performed his task for a period of 20 years, but as a result of this incident he was taken off the job, which broke his heart, and he died in December, 1881, shortly afterwards. Strange to relate, his successor had performed the task for another 20 years exactly when he too repeated the very same error that

F

led to poor Brown's downfall. Nowadays this type of time signal is not quite so common, but by the turn of the century there were so many competitors that the inhabitants of Derby had a job to tell "t'other from which".

The *Bull* today is operated in a similar manner but the disc now breaks a connection causing a solenoid to close thus operating the *Bull* without human agency, so no doubt the hour early "sound-offs" will never be heard again!

One other great "institution" was then and still is, the turret clock above the offices, which formerly occupied a somewhat lower position than now, being then surmounted by the bell hung in the housing that is now the home of the clock dials.

This timepiece was the last one to be made by the celebrated John Whitehurst the younger, of Derby, in 1840. The names "Whitehurst – Derby" appear cast onto the front barrel plate, and the date "1840" on the back barrel plate. It has been maintained in excellent working order by the various companies right up to the present day, and even now, after almost 130 years, there is very little sign of wear, the moving parts and pinions having been tempered and hardened in a coke fire by Whitehurst himself. He would retire into the rear workshop after the other employees had ceased work for the day, and would emerge later with the parts. His secret method of hardening them unfortunately died with him. The mechanism has pin wheel action with dead-beat escapement, and the pendulum rod is fully compensated. The clock is wound once per week, the weights being contained in a special trunking running down inside the tower beneath. The going side weight is 1½cwt, and the striking side 2½cwt.

The working parts are now housed in the old dial room and drive the fingers on each of the four dials by means of a double rod passing through the bell chamber into the dial chamber itself. Three of the dials date from 1878, when the old ones, cast by Whitehurst himself, were replaced at a cost of £28 by a "new more satisfactory mode of lighting the clock", saving £12 6s od per annum. The new dials were made by John Smith and Sons of Derby, successors to Whitehurst in the local business. The rear dial was also provided by Smiths when the position of the clock and dials was changed in 1893 to facilitate the addition of the third floor to the office block. At this time the dials were removed to the old bell housing on top of the tower and the bell was relegated to a lower position.

This bell, which has an hourly chime struck by means of a hammer, is believed to have been taken from the old St Pancras chapel in London, when the building was being demolished to make way for St Pancras station in 1865. It is now over 250 years old, being inscribed "William Sadler, Isaac Sadler, Trustees, 1717". Between the date and the names coins are embedded in the bell metal, and are presumably those of the reign of George I, although the passing years have rendered the markings indecipherable.

At this juncture a brief note is called for on the social atmosphere in the town as a result of the coming of the railways and the great change from small factory organisation to heavy industry coupled with the necessarily large influx of labour. Most of the increase in population took place in the "Royal Township" of Litchurch, which had a population explosion from a mere 35 people in 1801 to 1,720 by 1851, and to 6,560 ten years later. Most of the increase which took place between 1831 and 1851 was ascribed to the extension of the traditional silk and lace industries in the town, but the increase between 1851 and 1861 was clearly brought on by the extension of the Midland Railway's works.

Litchurch, on the outskirts of the borough of Derby and adjacent to the station, became the focus point of the new railway community. A new housing estate was rapidly built up which completely swamped the ancient hamlet, but although there were houses there were no schools for the children and only one pew reserved in St Peter's Church, Derby, for the people from the township. Litchurch itself had had no church since the disappearance of the ancient church from which the township took its name some centuries before.

It is to John Erskine Clarke, who became Vicar of St Michael's, Derby in 1856, that we owe the existence of what became known as the railwaymen's church, St Andrew's*. His own church, which held services most suited to the lowly railwaymen, became crowded out, and he was given permission by the Vicar of St Peter's Church, to whose parish Litchurch was attached, to put up an iron church near the station, with the object of erecting a more permanent church later. The most suitable site was land adjacent to Hulland Street, for between there and the railway bridge there lay a "swampy waste". This area of land belonged to J. C. B. Burrough of Chetwynd Park, Salop, from whom most of the site for the works and station had also been purchased. He promised £1,000 towards the purchase of the site if a church, parsonage and schools were built. The matter of financing the building was brought up at the Midland Railway Company's half-yearly general meeting in February, 1862, by Mr Michael Bass MP who asked for support from the Company's shareholders. In three weeks some £1,100 had been raised, and the building committee decided to erect brick Sunday Schools for temporary use while the church itself was built. The two-storey schools were built and opened in September, 1863 and on March 29, 1864, the foundation stone of the church itself, to be built to the designs of Sir Gilbert Scott RA (Architect of St Pancras station and

*St Andrew's Church, Derby – The Story of its Early Years by Rev M. R. Austin

the Law Courts in London), was laid by the Duke of Devonshire. The church, complete except for the spire which was not finished until some 25 years later, was consecrated on Ascension Day, 1866, by the Bishop of Lichfield.

Clarke did not relax his efforts here, however, but founded clubs, in opposition to the many public houses in the area, in which the workers could relax in the evening, and in 1858 opened a nursery where wives, who were forced to go out to work to help support the family, could leave their children. This nursery was open from 7.30am to 7.30pm in the winter and 5.30am to 6.30pm in the summer, Saturday hours being 5.30am to 3.00pm. These times of opening and closing give some idea of the working hours of those days. Clarke was a true social worker and a most exceptional man in every way, and after the consecration of the new St Andrew's Church he resigned his living at St Michael's to become the new church's first vicar.

The Sunday School thrived and by April, 1864, its doors were open as a day school to all children under 10 years of age for the sum of 3d per week. These contributions together with a government grant and regular contributions from the congregation paid for the expense of running it, although Clarke frequently met deficits in the yearly accounts out of his own pocket. By August, 1864, 140 pupils under 10 were being taught by one teacher, the following July a school for older girls was opened and in January, 1866, a boys school was also begun, all in the same building. Further schools were begun under the auspices of the church until by January, 1879, over 800 pupils were being taught in seven separate schools.

Adult education was not forgotten either, for in November, 1864 a free evening class was started meeting on two evenings a week to teach Reading, Writing and Arithmetic to men over the age of 18, and there already existed a library of over 300 books for the use of parents or their children at a charge of 3d per month for adults and $\frac{1}{2}$d a month for the children. In the adults school new subjects were added year by year and the frequency of classes increased.

It is not to be thought that the St Andrew's Church was working alone in this task of educating and caring for the new inhabitants of the town. Similar stories could be told of other churches, both established and non-conformist situated throughout the town.

Thus the social welfare of the new railway community was gradually catered for, largely by the church playing a role which these days is regarded as an obligation of the state and the local authorities to fill.

CHAPTER EIGHT

Trials and Triumphs
(1887-1890)

TURNING ONCE MORE to the locomotives built, Johnson, as we have seen, already provided several new classes and developments of old ones, but for the Settle–Carlisle line traffic, with its heavier Pullman-car trains, he decided to rebuild the famed Kirtley 800 class of 2-4-0s with larger cylinders and his own style of boiler having in all three different variations of heating surfaces.

The most powerful were those with an unclassified special boiler pitched 7ft 2in above rail having 1,333sq ft of heating surface of which the 264 tubes of 1⅝in diameter provided 1,215sq ft, and the firebox 118sq ft, the shell being 6ft 2in long and 4ft ½in wide outside. Larger 18in diameter × 26in stroke cylinders were provided and new motion and crank axle, but the original full-length double frames and 6ft 8in driving wheels were retained.

A new leading axle with new axleboxes was provided, the springing being provided rather unusually by two pairs of spiral form springs mounted below the axle.

There were 10 locomotives of the 800 class rebuilt in this form to order 155 and these were 800, 804, 805, 807, 811, 813, 814, 816, 818 and 819 all in 1877, following the trial rebuilding of 169 in September, 1876. This had a B boiler carrying only 1,142sq ft of heating surface with 221 tubes of 1¾in diameter, and working at 140psi pressure. All of these had new 2,950gal tenders having outside axlebox springs below the platform level.

The remainder were rebuilt with 18in × 24in cylinders, retaining original frames and motion, but with B class boilers carrying 1,233 or 1,223sq ft of heating surface pressed to 140psi, being rebuilt between 1876 and 1882. These were the rest of the range 800–29 and Nos 165–9 and 60–66, and were fitted with 2,950 or 2,750gal tenders except for Nos 820, 823 and 827 which were temporarily supplied with the old pattern 2,000gal type.

The loaded weights of the rebuilt locos were as follows:
Large class: leading 12 tons 10cwt 3qtr, driving 13 tons 17cwt 2qtr, trailing 11 tons 5cwt 3qtr, totalling 37 tons 14cwt, tender 34 tons 12cwt 2qtr (all water and 4 tons of coal).
Smaller class: leading 11 tons 13cwt, driving 14 tons 1cwt 3qtr,

trailing 10 tons 19cwt, totalling 36 tons 13cwt 3qtr, tender (2,950 gal) as above.

From 1880 onwards some of these engines were fitted up with new type Westinghouse air-brake equipment, these being Nos 800–819, 22, 60, 62–5 and 165 except 803 and 812 which, together with 829, were fitted up with the old type. Charles Rous-Marten gives details of several runs behind these locomotives in the *Railway Magazine* for 1901, page 366, for those interested in locomotive performance.

The same year some of the 890 class of 2-4-0s were also fitted up with this equipment, Nos 900–903, 906 and 907 being the engines in question. Johnson later rebuilt this class, Nos 890–909, built originally by Neilson & Co in 1871, with his standard P class boiler beginning with 902 in September, 1885. This was pitched 7ft 2in from rail and carried 1,244sq ft of heating surface, except Nos 890 and 891 with 1,242sq ft. The last to be rebuilt was 904 in December, 1889. They had new frames, with strengthening plates of the same 1in thickness attached to the inside of the main frame around the driving axleboxes, and had 6ft 8in driving and 4ft 2in leading wheels, on standard wheelbase, 18in × 24in cylinders, and screw reversing gear.

On the subject of boilers Johnson was to introduce a group of basically standard types, although there were many slight variations in heating surfaces in each class, within each boiler class every boiler having the same main physical dimensions. Generally speaking they were the following:

A   Johnson 17in 0-6-0T as built 1874–92
A1   Variant of A with 4in deeper firebox, fitted to Johnson 17in 0-6-0T built 1895–1900. (A1 boiler discontinued after construction of above engines and A boilers built for all subsequent replacements.)
B   Johnson 4-4-0s as built 1876–91, and a few later engines Johnson 0-6-0s as built 1875–1902, and rebuilds of Kirtley 0-6-0s
        Some 2-4-0s as rebuilt
        Some Kirtley 0-6-0WTs as rebuilt
        Some Kirtley 2-2-2s as rebuilt
C   Johnson 0-4-4Ts as built 1875–93, and rebuilds of Kirtley 0-4-4WTs
        Rebuilds of some Kirtley 2-2-2s and 2-4-0s
C1   Variant of C with 4in deeper firebox, fitted to:
        Johnson 0-4-4Ts as built 1895–1900
        Johnson 18in 0-6-0Ts as built
        C1 boiler discontinued after construction of above engines,

and C boilers built for all subsequent replacements.

D Some Johnson 4-4-os as built
4-2-2s as built 1887–96
Some Kirtley o-6-os rebuilt with second-hand D boilers

E Some Johnson 4-4-os as built
4-2-2s as built 1896–9
Some Kirtley o-6-os rebuilt with second-hand E boilers

F 4-2-2s as built 1899–1900 (10 engines only)

GX "Belpaire" 4-4-os as built 1900 (10 engines only)

G8 "Belpaire" 4-4-os as built 1902–5

G8½ Johnson Compound 4-4-os

H,H1, & o-6-os as built 1903–8, rebuilds of earlier o-6-os

HX 4-4-os as rebuilt 1904–8
o-6-4Ts as built
(The H, H1 and HX boilers had the same external dimensions, but the H1 had the tubes arranged in vertical rows.)

J Small Johnson o-4-oST

J1 Large Johnson o-4-oST

J2 As J1, but with minor variations, used on Deeley o-4-oT

P As B but with 2in shorter barrel, fitted to:
Johnson 2-4-os as built
Rebuilds of some Kirtley 2-2-2s and 2-4-os

The main dimensions of these types of boilers are given in Appendix III.

This list covers all locomotive boilers supplied by the works under Johnson, except for the occasional special boilers. Some have already been mentioned, but the remainder will be referred to later in our story.

In the years 1874–6 Messrs Neilson & Co and the Vulcan Foundry Co supplied 40 o-6-o tanks of a new type that were to become a basic standard for almost 30 years. These were Nos 1102–26 (Neilson) and 1127–41 (Vulcan) all with A class boilers, and having inside frames only, 17in × 24in cylinders and six driving wheels of 4ft 6in diameter on a wheelbase of 7ft 4in + 7ft 8in. The round-topped boiler, pressed to 140psi carried a total heating surface of 1,120sq ft comprising tubes 1,030 and firebox 90sq ft respectively. The tubes were 220 in number and 1¾in in diameter, and the sidetanks carried 900gal of water and the bunkers 24cwt of coal, the working weights being as follows: leading 12 tons 11cwt 3qtr, driving 12 tons 19cwt 3qtr, trailing 13 tons 14cwt 2qtr making a total of 39 tons 6cwt (with full tanks and 1 ton of coal). The Neilson's cost £2,550 each and the Vulcan's £2,135 for the first five and £2,185 for the remainder

They had enclosed cabs as built and proved to be very useful little locomotives. Two hundred and eighty of this general type were to be built up to 1902. The first to emerge from Derby was No 1377, of the range 1377–86, in May, 1878 followed by the rest of the order, 204, the same year. There was a difference in the boilers of these however for they had only 213 tubes of 1¾in diameter (1,024sq ft) plus 91sq ft firebox heating surface, giving a slightly smaller heating surface of 1,115sq ft which was used on the subsequent orders. They cost £1,691. 14s 0d each. Another order, 218, for a further 20 locomotives, Nos 1387–96 and 1347–56 was begun the same year and completed by 1879 followed by O/239 for a further ten, Nos 220, 221 and 1420–27, also built in 1879. More orders followed as listed below (see Plate 44).

Order	Locomotive Nos	Year built	Cost
O/262	1410–19	1880	£1,531. 11s 6d
O/340	1552–61	1882	£1,514. 17s 3d
O/414	210–12, 215, 216, 218, 219, 1397–9	1883	
O/496	1677–86, 1090–92, 1094, 1095	1884	
O/499	1687–96, 1096–1100	1884–5	

There was gap of four years here between O/499 and the next order for this type, and the remainder will be referred to later. Some variations in the above orders ought to be mentioned, as follows: the last five locomotives of O/414, viz Nos 218, 219 and 1397–9, were built with all-over cabs and vacuum-brake gear for use on the Keighley and Worth Valley line. All the others had only half cabs, and Nos 1552–61 had cut-down half-cabs and shortened chimneys (11ft 5½in top to rail) and domes, and were used on the Midland's London branches (see Plate 46).

There were other variations of a minor nature and these, along with a large amount of other interesting information appear in an article by G. H. Daventry in the SLS Journal for October 1965, with supplementary notes in the May and July 1966 issues.

These locomotives were used not only on goods workings, but also on passenger trains on some secondary routes, especially in the Swansea area, and the class were allocated over the whole Midland system.

As to goods engines of the 0-6-0 tender variety, Johnson was to follow Kirtley's example, and build vast numbers of these, although all were of the inside single-framed variety, rather than in the later double-framed style of Kirtley.

One hundred and twenty were ordered from four makers, in 1875, and delivered during that and the following year. The list is given opposite.

Makers	Locomotive Nos	Year built	Cost each
Kitson & Co	1142–61, 381–5, 400–404	1875–6	£2,920
Dübs	1162–91	1875	£2,735
Beyer Peacock & Co	1192–1221	1876	£2,650
Neilson	1222–51	1876	£2,635

These had 17½in diameter × 26in stroke cylinders, and six 4ft 10in diameter driving wheels on a standard wheelbase of 8ft + 8ft 6in. The boiler carried a heating surface of 1,233sq ft (tubes 1,123sq ft, fire box 110sq ft) and was pressed to 140psi except for Nos 1192–1221 with a total heating surface of 1,223sq ft (tubes 1,112sq ft, firebox 110sq ft) and the tender was the Johnson pattern 2,350gal type holding 4 tons of coal. Working weights totalled 34 tons 3cwt for the engine and 28 tons 19cwt 1qtr for the tender (full).

A further 20 locomotives were delivered by Messrs Dübs in 1878, class H, Nos 1357–76, generally similar to the previous lots, but with larger 5ft 2½in diameter driving wheels, and in 1880 Derby Works turned out their first Johnson goods tender locomotive of this type to O/240, this being No 1452 in March, followed by Nos. 1453–61 the same year. These had the same size driving wheels and cylinders as the Dübs engines, and the B boiler carried 1,223sq ft of heating surface (tubes 1,113 sq ft, firebox 110sq ft). A 2,250gal tender was fitted and weights of a Dübs locomotive in working order were: engine 37 tons 14cwt 2qtr, tender 29 tons 12cwt 1qtr, totalling 67 tons 6cwt 3qtr. The Dübs locomotives cost £2,274 each and the Derby product £1,990. 9s 6d, a considerable saving.

Although contractor-built locomotives are not strictly within the scope of this work, brief mention of these is necessary to obtain a balanced picture of the locomotive scene since all orders placed outside reflected on the capacity of the Derby Works. From Stephensons in 1880–81 a further batch of these class H goods locomotives, Nos 1432–51, 1462–71, appeared followed in 1882–4 by a further 50, Nos 1582–1631, from Beyer Peacock & Co at unit costs of £2,234 and £2,460 respectively.

Many of the above were provided specially for the large increase in traffic expected with the opening of the through route to Scotland via the Settle-Carlisle line.

In 1881 a further large series of 0-4-4 tank engines began to emerge from Derby (see Plate 57) following the building of a further 30, Nos 1252–81, by Messrs Neilson & Co in 1875–6, being Class D. These incidentally had the largest driving wheels on this type produced by the Midland, these being 5ft 6in driven by 17in × 24in cylinders, and having a working weight of 43 tons 17cwt 1qtr with the 1,000gal tanks ¾ full and ½ ton coal on board. The boilers carried 1,227sq ft heating surface. The 223 tubes of 1¾in diameter provided a heating surface of 1,123sq ft and the firebox 104sq ft.

The Derby series began with No 1532 which emerged from the works in August, 1881, and a summary list is given below:

Order	Locomotive Nos	Year built	Notes
O/289	1532–51	1881–2	1547–51 Metropolitan cond.
O/415	1632–6	1883	
O/460	1637–56	1883–4	
O/538	1718–27	1885	1718–27 Metropolitan cond. O/757
O/589	1728–37	1886	1728 Metropolitan cond.
O/763	1823–32	1889	
O/981	1322–6, 202, 1428–30, 1697	1892	

These all had 5ft 3½in diameter driving wheels and the trailing bogie wheels were 3ft ½in diameter. All the earlier ones of the group have 17in × 24in cylinders, but the engines of the last two orders had 18in × 24in cylinders, as later fitted to the whole range of locomotives. Some of the first 15 built were used to work the service between Manchester London Road and Central stations via Stockport, while Nos 1547–51 and 1718–28 were fitted with condensing apparatus for working the Metropolitan lines traffic, the first 10 as built, and the remainder converted to O/757, (see Plate 45). All had 1,150gal capacity tanks and coal space for 42cwt of coal. The standard wheelbase was 8ft for the leading and driving wheels and 11ft 3in from driving wheel to the bogie centre, the wheels of which were at 5ft 6in centres equally spaced. All over cabs were provided having two round windows in front and back plates, except on the Metropolitan condensing locomotives which had only a front weatherboard.

Working weights were as follows: leading 14 tons 17cwt 3qtr, driving 15 tons 17cwt 3qtr, bogie 19 tons 14cwt, totalling 50 tons 9cwt 2qtr (empty 40 tons 11cwt 3qtr).

The distance from rail to centre-line of boiler was 6ft 11¼in and to top of chimney 12ft 11¹³⁄₁₆in. Length over buffers was 33ft ⁵⁄₁₆in. These dimensions applied also to the condensing engines which were slightly heavier of course, carrying the following weights when in working condition: leading 14 tons 15cwt 3qtr, driving 15 tons 12cwt, bogie 20 tons

9cwt 3qtr, totalling: 50 tons 17cwt 2qtr (empty 41 tons 14cwt 1qtr).

Concurrent with the building of these, the works were turning out 4-4-0s, 0-6-0Ts, 0-6-0 goods tender engines, and latterly (1887) the famed 4-2-2s of which more later. However, in 1883 there emerged from the Works the first 0-4-0ST engine to be built at Derby, indeed the first locomotive of that wheel arrangement ever turned out for the company (see Plate 56). The new machines were only designed for shunting work in the locomotive works yard as replacements for four old Manning Wardle locomotives, but even so were vastly superior to their forebears of years gone by. Five were built, Nos 1322–6, to order 341 in August and September, 1883, having 3ft 9½in diameter driving wheels at 7ft centres, single frames and inside cylinders 13in diameter × 20in stroke. They had no cab, merely a "protection plate at the front" and guard-rails at the rear. The round-topped J class boiler with raised round topped firebox and pressed to 140psi, carried a total heating surface of 535.02sq ft of which the 113 tubes of 1¾in outside diameter provided 490.673sq ft and the firebox 44.347sq ft. The grate area was 8sq ft the firebox being 3ft long (outside) × 4ft ½in wide (outside).

The distance from rail to the top of the "stovepipe" or plain chimney was 11ft and from rail to centre-line of boiler 5ft 4½in. Both chimney and dome, which was on the first ring of the boiler and fitted with twin Salter safety valves, passed through the saddle tank which was 9ft 7½in long (outside). The class was renumbered 1322A–6A in February March 1892, and later became Nos 1500–1504 in 1907, being withdrawn between 1921 and 1934 although No 1323, the first to be withdrawn, was considerably rebuilt, with new frames and emerged as No 1533 in July, 1921 (see later).

The saddle-tank capacity was 400gal and there was bunker space for 8cwt of coal, and the working weights were: leading 8 tons 9cwt, driving 13 tons 5cwt, totalling 21 tons 14cwt (18 tons 18cwt 2qtr light). The length over buffers was 22ft 1⅝in as built.

A further five locomotives of the same type, Nos 202, 1428–30 and 1697 were built at Derby to O/816 during 1889 and 1890, also going into the Duplicate list as A's in February and March 1892, and being renumbered 1505–7 in 1907, Nos 202A and 1429A having been withdrawn in January, 1907 and January, 1905 respectively, before the general renumbering took place. These small shunting engines were nicknamed "Jinties" on account of their J class boiler, a name later wrongly applied to the Class 3 0-6-0 tank engines.

Before returning to the subject of passenger engines a quick note about the ever increasing numbers of Johnson 0-6-0 goods tender engines is in order, and a new range of 4ft 10½in diameter driving wheel locomotives, with slightly larger 18in diameter cylinders, began to emerge from the works commencing with No 1698 in February, 1885, the range of which is tabulated below for ease of reference:

Order	Locomotive Nos	Year built
O/530	1698–1707	1885
O/544	1708–17	1885
O/617	1758–67	1886
O/633	1768–77	1887
O/663	1778–97	1887–8

These were fitted with B class boilers having one slight variation in heating surface, but all set at 140psi. The first 10 had boilers carrying 1,142sq ft of heating surface and the remainder had 1,260 sq ft. Many of these were fitted from 1903 onwards with H class boilers carrying 1,404sq ft of heating surface and set at 175psi, and a few with H1 class boilers carrying fewer tubes, 242 of $1\frac{3}{4}$in diameter instead of 258 on the ordinary H class. Firebox heating surface was 118.75sq ft against 118.5 sq ft and there was a common grate area of 21.1sq ft and later still many of this (and later classes too) were also rebuilt, from 1926, with the Belpaire G6 type boiler set at 140psi or 160psi. These carried 196 $1\frac{3}{4}$in diameter tubes giving 977.5sq ft of heating surface which, with the firebox (103sq ft), gave a total of 1,080.5sq ft with a grate area of 17.5sq ft. These figures are computed as agreed by the Association of Railway Locomotive Engineers in November, 1914.

Eleven of these were also rebuilt, commencing in 1920, with G7 Belpaire type boilers as were large numbers of the later builds of goods engines. This boiler was larger altogether, carrying 254 tubes of $1\frac{3}{4}$in diameter giving 1,265.5sq ft heating surface + firebox 122.75sq ft totalling 1,388.25sq ft heating surface. Grate area was 21.1sq ft. The principal difference between the G7 and G6 was the larger barrel diameter, 4ft 8in against 4ft 1in, length and depth of firebox and the position of the dome in relation to the tubeplate at the smokebox end together with an increase in the length of firebox from 6ft to 7ft.

Johnson's passenger engines were of course being turned out of the works in larger numbers, along with the other types, and following the first two batches of 4-4-0 passenger tender engines built by Messrs Kitson & Dübs and mentioned earlier, the Derby shops commenced building this type in 1882, No 1562, turned out in September of that year being the first of order 370 for 10 locomotives, to be followed over the years by many more, the whole series numbering 265, although there were many variations which created sub-divisions within the class (*see Plate 47*).

The first eight orders for the 4-4-0s are listed opposite.

Order	Locomotive Nos	Year built
O/370	1562–71	1882
O/400	1572–81	1882–3
O/430	1657–66	1883
O/554	1738–47	1885–6
O/615	1748–57	1886
O/678	1808–17	1888
O/734	1818–22	1888
O/920	80–87, 11 & 14	1891

All the above had inside 18in × 26in cylinders, Stephenson's valve gear, and B type boilers of two types, the first three orders having boilers with total heating surface 1,142sq ft comprising 205 tubes of 1⅞in diameter (1,032sq ft) and firebox (110sq ft) with a grate area of 17.5sq ft set at 140psi working pressure; and the remainder had steel boilers with a larger heating surface of 1,261sq ft comprising 246 tubes of 1⅝in diameter (1,151sq ft) and firebox (110sq ft) with the same grate area but set at a higher working pressure of 160psi. The tenders were of the six-wheeled 2,950gal variety carrying 2½tons of coal for the first three orders and O/678 and O/734, and 3,250gal for the remainder, carrying 3 tons of coal.

For the first three orders, the 6ft 8½in diameter driving wheels were on 8ft 6in centres and the bogie centre was 10ft in front of the leading driving wheel, the bogie wheels being 3ft 6in diameter at 6ft centres. The boiler was provided with Salter safety valves on the dome as was the usual practice and a lock up safety valve over the firebox. Height to centre-line of boiler from rail was 7ft 2in and to top of chimney 12ft 11 9/16in.

For O/554 and O/615 the dimensions were generally similar but the driving wheels were 7ft ½in and distance from leading driver to centre of bogie was 10ft ½in, height to centre line of boiler from rail 7ft 3¾in and to top of chimney 13ft 1 5/16in. The ten locomotives built to O/400 were fitted with Westinghouse air brakes, the cylinders being mounted vertically between the splashers.

The remaining three orders, with 6ft 6in diameter driving wheels, were on the same wheelbase, but the bogie wheels were only 3ft 3in diameter. Height to centre line of boiler from rail was 7ft 3in and to chimney top 13ft 9/16in. These orders were O/678, O/734 and O/920.

Working weights of these engines varied from 41 tons 19cwt 1qtr to 42 tons 19cwt 1qtr divided thus: bogie 14 tons 4cwt 2qtr, driving 14 tons 19cwt 3qtr and trailing 12 tons 15cwt for those with 6ft 8½in driving wheels. Those with the smaller 6ft 6in wheels were bogie 13 tons 15cwt 3qtr, driving 15 tons 14cwt, trailing 12 tons 9cwt 2qtr, and the largest size with 7ft wheels, were bogie 13 tons 3cwt 3qtr, driving 17 tons 4cwt 1qtr and trailing 12 tons 11cwt 1qtr. The 2,950gal tenders weighed 35 tons 3cwt 1qtr in working order and the 3,250gal type 37 tons dead.

Of the first order Nos 1562–5 were allocated to Leicester and the remainder to Nottingham, and later Derby.* Nos 1572–81, having the Westinghouse air brakes, were allocated to Carlisle and later to Skipton while Nos 1657–66 went to Manchester. The next order all went to London, as did No 1757; Nos 1748–9 went to Carlisle, and the remainder (1750–6) were divided between Nottingham and Leeds. Nos 1808–13 went to Newton Heath (Manchester) and Nos 1814–18 to Sandhills (Liverpool) the remainder, 1819–22, going to Hellifield, as did most of O/920.

All of these engines were later rebuilt from 1904 onwards with H or H^x class boilers to orders 2675, 2676A and 2676B, working at 175psi and many had Belpaire type G7 boilers fitted in later years, some saturated and some superheated together with bogie brakes (although these were removed by Stanier). Issued in 1903, O/2675 was for rebuilding those with 6ft 6in driving wheels; in 1906, O/2676A was for rebuilding those with 6ft 8½in driving wheels, and in 1906, O/2676B was for rebuilding those with 7ft driving wheels.

One of these 4-4-0s, No 1757, carried the nameplate *Beatrice* and was exhibited at the Royal Jubilee Saltaire Exhibition of 1887 where it won a gold medal. It was named after Princess Beatrice who opened the exhibition, and afterwards, among other duties, worked holiday traffic from St Pancras to Southend for many years, being allocated by agreement with the LT & SR to Shoeburyness. She was also used to draw the royal train carrying Queen Victoria from Derby on her way to Scotland in May, 1891.

A further batch of ten 4-4-0s Nos 1667–76, built to O/444, were turned out of the Derby Works in 1884–5 beginning with 1667 in May, 1884. These were a considerable departure from any engines built before in that they had Joy's valve gear and were the result of David Joy's personal approaches to Billinton, the Chief Locomotive Draughtsman. Apparently, according to Joy's diaries, they discussed the building of a new lot of passenger engines, and talk ranged from four coupled 7ft 3in driving wheel bogie engines to singles with 7ft 6in diameter wheels, and eventually Joy worked out his own scheme for a large, single engine with bogie in front and radially controlled axle behind, inside compound cylinders, one 20in × 26in and one 30in × 26in, with a boiler working at 200psi carrying 1,600sq ft of heating surface. This was to have Joy's gear operating slide valves, placed over the cylinders, having early cut off, and Joy expected an economic coal consumption of

*Locomotive and Trains Working in the latter part of the Nineteenth Century.*Vol II by E. L. Ahrons.

say 24lb per mile. However this was not to be and Johnson, perhaps against his better judgement, was persuaded to allow 10 four-wheel coupled-bogie engines to be built, having inside 19in diameter × 26in stroke cylinders with overhead slide valves, and 7ft diameter driving wheels at 8ft 6in centres. The bogie centre was placed 10ft in front of the leading driving wheel and the bogie wheels were 3ft 6in diameter at 6ft centres. Height from rail to centre line of boiler was 7ft 4in and to top of chimney 13ft 1$\frac{9}{16}$in. The B class boiler set at 140psi carried 175 copper tubes of 1$\frac{3}{4}$in outside diameter and 30 copper tubes of 1$\frac{1}{2}$in outside diameter, giving a heating surface of 1,032sq ft with firebox heating surface 110sq ft and total heating surface 1,142sq ft. Working-weight of engine was 42 tons 16cwt and they were provided with 2,950gal tenders. As built they were allocated as follows: London Nos 1667–9 and 1675–6, these last two having Westinghouse brakes for working Scottish expresses, the rest having Smiths vacuum brakes; Nos 1671 and 1673 were at Nottingham and 1670 and 1672 at Derby.

However these engines were not a success, and the boilers were soon found to be inadequate for the size of cylinders provided. In August, 1886, No 1669 was fitted with a B boiler set at 160psi, the first at this pressure incidentally, and having a larger heating surface of 1,261sq ft, the same as that provided for O/554 onwards, and all 10 were so rebuilt over the next two years. Two, Nos 1670 and 1672, were fitted in 1890 with cylinders having piston valves over the top to O/930, but some seven years later No 1670 was altered back to the ordinary type, when it was again rebuilt in November, 1897.

Even this reboilering did not improve the design over-much and Johnson decided to rebuild the whole class with new cylinders having piston valves, Stephenson link motion, new boilers and new frames. These retained some parts of the old class including the bogies, but were officially considered as new engines. Five were rebuilt to O/1460, beginning with Nos 1672 and 1675 in October, 1896, followed by 1668 in December of that year and 1667 and 1676 in March, 1897. Two more were similarly rebuilt to O/1707 (Nos 1669 and 1671) in 1898 and the remainder to O/2072 in 1901. These were much better engines although they were to be rebuilt yet again between 1912 & 1914 to O/3942 with new frames and G7s boilers, all being, taken over by British Railways.

From 1887 to about 1903 Johnson built almost all his express engines with flush smokeboxes, retaining the raised type on other types of locomotives. Kirtley had for a very long time used the double, rectangular, side-opening, smokebox doors, but they were liable to draw air and were gradually replaced by the dished type. An intermediate design with strap hinges and central locking wheel appeared late in 1901 and was used on the 2781 series of 4-4-0s and the compounds. In the future, commencing in 1905, the Midland were to go to the flat type of door secured round the edges by six "dog" bolts, these later still giving way to the dished type secured in the same manner.

Before closing this chapter mention should be made of the building of No 4 shed. Johnson reported to the Locomotive Committee on February 28, 1888, that when the plan of the new workshops was prepared in 1873–4, provision was shown for increasing the number of running sheds, but the subject was not considered further in the face of the more pressing need at that time for additional workshops. However the engine stock had risen in number from 1,052 to 1,867, an increase of 815 engines without any increase in running shed room at Derby. Ninety-nine engines were regularly in steam at Derby and all the engines ex-shops had to be accommodated also during several days of trails. Eight hundred and eighty engines had passed through the Derby shops during 1887. Shed room was now available for only 40 engines, ie 16 in No 2 shed and 24 in No 3 shed. No 2 shed was now required for spare engines in stock and others coming from the paint shop after trials, leaving space for only 24. It was therefore ordered that plans and estimates be got out for a 48-engine shed with necessary sidings, etc.*

The original plan provided for two twin-turntable sheds of rectangular shape positioned adjacent to each other, but off-set end to end. The contract for the first engine shed, with twin 50ft 22 road turntables, with central through line, housed in a rectangular shed 340ft long × 180ft wide was let to Messrs William Walkerdine of Derby, and the tender signed on November 1, 1888 the shed being brought into use early in 1890 at a cost of £29,800. The two turntables were supplied by Messrs Cowans Sheldon at a cost of £640 each.

The second shed was never constructed but one 60ft turntable supplied by Messrs Eastwood Swingler & Co, costing £1,065, was installed on the site and 16 radiating lines provided mainly for stabling engines in steam, being brought into use in 1900–1901.

Early in 1895 a new 50ft turntable was installed by the North Stafford shed to replace the old 46ft one, being supplied by Messrs Eastwood, Swingler & Co at a cost of £299. 15s od. Alterations to the foundations cost a further £195 plus alterations to the sidings.

Also approved about this time was the erection of an extensive system of carriage sidings, with carriage sheds, at a cost of £33,770, this getting its second reading on June 2, 1899. This was for the Chaddesden Sidings site, the Etches Park carriage sheds having been completed shortly after No 4 shed was brought into use.

*BTHR Mid 1/178.

32 No 4 shed, a view taken in 1890 with an assortment of Kirtley and Johnson 0–6–0s and S&DJR No 60, just built by Neilsons and running trials before delivery to Highbridge.

33 John Lane, first to be styled "Works Manager" 1893–1901.
[*W. W. Winter, Derby*

34 Francis Holt, Works Superintendent 1874–93.

35 Cecil Walter Paget, Works Manager 1903–7 and General Superintendent 1907–19.
[*W. W. Winter, Derby*

36 Richard Mountford Deeley, Works Manager 1902–3 and Locomotive Superintendent 1904–9.
[*W. W. Winter, Derby*

37 James Edward Anderson, Chief Locomotive Draughtsman 1906–13 and Works Manager 1910–13.

38 Sandham John Symes, Chief Locomotive Draughtsman 1913–22 and Works Manager 1923–28.

39 Sir Henry Fowler, Works Manager 1907–09, Chief Mechanical Engineer MR 1910–22 and CME of the LM&SR 1925–31.

40 T. F. B. "Freddie" Simpson, Works Manager from November, 1947 to February, 1965.

41 Johnson single No 1865 as originally built in December, 1889.

[Author's Collection

42 The first batch of Baldwin American 2-6-0s being erected in the open at Derby in the summer of 1899 during the great locomotive shortage.

43 A Schenectady 2-6-0 being assembled in No 8 erecting shop in September, 1899 during the great locomotive shortage.

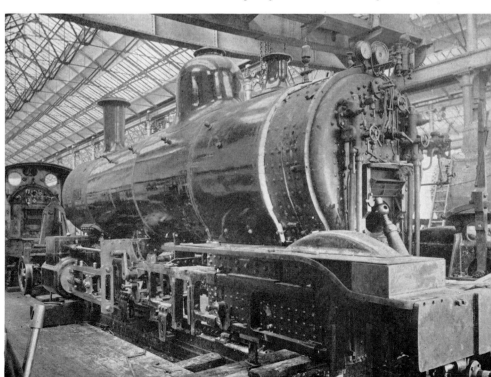

44 Johnson 0-6-0T No 1413 in original
form as built at Derby in June, 1880.

45 No 1549, one of Johnson's 0-4-4 condensing tank engines built at Derby for the
Metropolitan Lines in March, 1882.

46 No 1557, one of Johnson's 0-6-0STs
built in 1882 with shortened chimney,
dome with side mounted salter safety
valves and cut down cab for London area
trip working.

47 "Beauty at Rest". One of Johnson's
elegant 4-4-0s No 1756 built at Derby in
September, 1886.   [*Author's Collection*

48 Johnson Class 3 4-4-0 No 819 as
built in December, 1902. This was one of
Johnson's last designs incorporating a
bogie tender designed to reduce the number of double headed trains on the Settle-
Carlisle route.   [*Author's Collection*

49 The second of Johnson's three-
cylinder compound 4-4-0s No 2632
shown as originally built with two sets of
reversing gear for high and low pressure
systems in January, 1902.
[*Author's Collection*

50 A *c.* 1890 view of the works from the North Stafford depot before the erection of No 4 shed. In the foreground are the Pullman car sheds and two North Stafford "break vans" in the North Stafford siding.

51 Deeley compound No 1019 heading south past High Peak Junction with a train of clerestory coaches from Manchester in the summer of 1911.

52 Johnson 4-4-0 No 451 slips down the Ambergate avoiding line with an express from Sheffield in the summer of 1911.

53 Johnson class 3P 4-4-0 No 705 heads a southbound express through Cromford in the summer of 1911.

54 An express from Bristol headed by Johnson locomotives No 197 and single No 630 being banked up the Lickey Incline in mid-1911.

55 One of the small well tanks No 214, built as a 2–2–2 at Derby in July, 1855 and rebuilt as an 0–6–0 tank engine in January, 1872. Shown as reboilered by Johnson in February, 1876.

56 Johnson 0-4-0ST No 1322 as built in August, 1883 for shunting in works sidings, etc.

57 Johnson 0-4-4T No 1832 as built at Derby in May, 1889.

58 A 1905 view inside the historic old No 1 shed, the oldest engine roundhouse in the world, now converted into a crane repair shop.

59 A view in old No 2 erecting shop probably taken in 1888. This later became No 4 electric shop.

60 Shunting by horsepower on the bottom yard *c*. 1890. The shop is the forge with its louvred windows for cooling the inmates!

61 No 8 erecting shop filled to capacity in the palmy days of steam. The photograph was taken in November, 1895.

62 Thread chasing the old fashioned way in a "Cooper" centre lathe using a two start hob. A view in the machine shop brass corner in December, 1908.

63 A Craven tyre turning lathe at work in the wheel shop about 1907. The turner operated the feed on both tool posts by means of the ratchets and chains shown. Beyond the machine (top left) can be seen the steam driven beam engine driving the counter shafting for the shop machines.

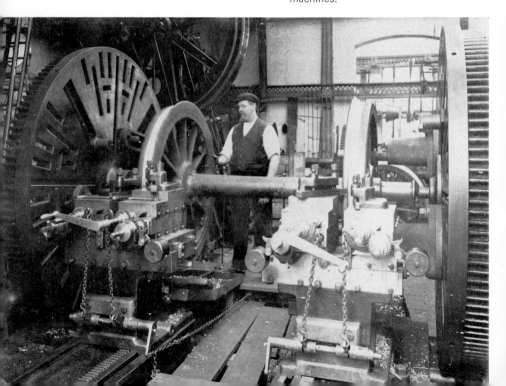

64 One bay of the wheel shop as it appeared in November, 1895, showing tyre turning and crank-axle machining lathes.

65 No 9 machine shop, a later view taken in September, 1938 showing the replacement of belt driven machines by up to date capstan lathes.

66 Derby Locomotive Works fire brigade seen in 1919 with their Merryweather fire engine mounted on a flat truck for use anywhere on the system.

67 The No 3 mess room, set aside for those who enjoyed hymn singing and a word from the Bible with their meal. The "pulpit" and organ can be seen on the right and the men's lunch baskets are in their places containing their midday meal ready for the cooks to prepare.

CHAPTER NINE

The Johnson Singles
(1887-1900)

SINCE THE YEAR 1866 no single driver locomotives had been built for the Midland, although a practically new engine, No 4 had been turned out in April, 1869, being the rebuild of an earlier engine of 1861. Even some of those singles still on the books had, by 1884, been taken off the road as a result of a circular instruction forbidding their use owing to the many delays to trains being caused by the single driving wheels slipping. One of these engines was stationed at Leicester, and was used solely for supplying steam to stationary engines at pumping stations whilst their boilers were under repair, the engines being sheeted over when not in use to hide their shame.

At this time Robert Weatherburn, a valued servant of the company, was the District Locomotive Superintendent at Leicester, and he records that he never passed the laid-up engine without the strong desire to make use of it. Eventually the temptation was too great. He had the tarpaulin cover removed and, after examination of springs and tyres, gave instruction for the driving springs, both inside and out, to be strengthened by the addition of an extra plate. The sand-boxes were brought nearer to the wheels and two pipes trained as closely as possible to the tyres to ensure that the sand was delivered onto the rail and not blown away. These alterations were completed the day before Leicester Fair and Weatherburn changed the engines of one train at Leicester, putting the single on to work south to London. He records that it did well, and he kept it at work for some months, almost forgetting Johnson's instruction concerning these singles, until one day he was summoned to Derby and there met by Billinton who told him his violation of the instruction had been known for some time, but that his alterations were considered successful, particularly the running up Barden Hill and stopping and starting at difficult places. Billinton concluded by saying that Johnson had almost decided on the use of new single wheelers for the southern section.

Upon being ushered into Johnson's presence Weatherburn was admonished on the value of circular instructions, then made to recount exactly the details of his alterations, loads, etc. Johnson estimated the driving axle-load to be 17 tons, and when weighed it proved to be 17 tons 3cwt. It was decided to continue using the locomotive in question,

G

and a somewhat emboldened Weatherburn strongly advised the use of a leading bogie as part of the new design.

It ought to be mentioned in passing that Robert Weatherburn's father, of the same name, assisted George Stephenson and his son Robert on the footplate of the Leicester and Swannington Railway Company's locomotive *Comet* when that particular line was opened on July 17, 1832, being the regular driver of that engine from its reception and for some years afterwards. He was appointed locomotive running-shed foreman at Derby in June, 1848, but removed to a similar position at Leeds the following August.

Shortly after this event with the Leicester single-wheeler another development was to take place which further strengthened the argument for single-wheelers, this being the introduction of compressed air sanding gear which delivered a jet of air and sand directly at the space between tyre and rail instead of by means of the former gravity fed system, the value of which was extremely suspect and varied considerably with the prevailing conditions. This new air-sanding owed its origin to Francis Holt, at that time the Works Manager at Derby, and he had the system fitted to several engines, working on the heavily graded Settle–Carlisle line in 1886, the air being supplied from the Westinghouse braking system fitted to these locomotives.

However the Westinghouse Company raised objections to this use of air from their system, claiming rightly that it could upset the brake, so Holt modified his device and used steam from the boiler instead of air. This system had a marked effect on the whole of British locomotive policy, and was ultimately commercially marketed by Messrs Gresham & Craven.

Johnson had several of the four-wheel coupled engines, Nos 1306–11, fitted with this gear, and removed the coupling rods, running them as singles. The engines did quite as well on the level with the same trains, as the rest of the class, yet strangely showed up better on the gradients, there being also a considerable economy in fuel.

Johnson had also been impressed by the performance of Stroudley's single wheeler *Grosvenor* which had competed at the Newark Brake Trials, some few years previously and had, by its design and performance on that occasion, left a considerable reputation behind it. It must also be remembered that the Chief Locomotive Draughtsman at this time was Billinton, who had formerly held the same position under Stroudley on the LB&SCR.

The foregoing circumstances all prompted Johnson into producing the first of his 4-2-2 type tender engines which were to many the essence of beauty in a locomotive, and certainly among the best looking engines of the day. First to be built was No 25 in June, 1887 and over the next

14 years a total of 95 locomotives of this type were produced, all by the Derby Works.

It should be mentioned here that Johnson was not a man easily converted to revolutionary ideas but rather waited patiently for the stage of co-operation and development to arrive when he could be ensured of success. This was particularly the case with steam brakes, steam and automatic vacuum brake combined and later the train-heating apparatus, all successfully introduced during his term of office, as were the famous compounds to be described later.

To return to the singles, the first five built to O/655 were Nos 25–9, turned out between June and August, 1887. The single pair of driving wheels were 7ft 4in diameter, the largest yet used on main line locomotives on the Midland. The leading bogie was centred 10ft ½in in front of the driving wheel and the 3ft 6in diameter wheels were at 6ft centres. The trailing wheel of 4ft 2½in diameter was placed 8ft 9in behind the driver. Length over buffers (engine and tender) was 52ft 3in.

The boiler barrel was 10ft 4in long and 4ft 1in outside diameter, and the distance between tubeplates was 10ft 8⅝in. This was incidentally the first use of an all-steel boiler on passenger engines, but five B class steel boilers had been built to O/658 and fitted to 0-6-0 goods engines 431, 942, 1020, 252 and 947 in December, 1886, the first ever use of the all steel boiler on the Midland.

The D class steel boiler, set at 160psi, carried a total heating surface of 1,240.6sq ft of which the tubes, 242 of 1⅝in outside diameter and 2 of 1½in outside diameter, provided 1,123.6sq ft and the firebox 117sq ft. The grate area was 19.678sq ft and the firebox measured 6ft 6in long × 4ft ½in wide outside. Boiler centre line from rail was 7ft 5in and to top of chimney 13ft ½in. Twin Salter safety valves were provided on the dome with a lock-up safety valve over the firebox. Screw reverse was provided on the right-hand (driving) side. The new steam sanding device was applied in front of the driving wheels. The inside cylinders were 18in × 26in and the slide valves were actuated by Stephensons motion. They had deep double-frames.

The driving axle had both inside and outside bearings, the outside springs being underhung and the inside springs overhung whilst the bogie axles had only inside bearings and the trailing wheel outside bearings only with overhung leaf springs. Working weights were: bogie 14 tons 7cwt 3qtr, driving 18 tons 10cwt, trailing 10 tons 12cwt, totalling 43 tons 9cwt 3qtr, tender 37 tons dead. They were the first Midland engines to have a drumhead smokebox flush with the boiler barrel.

Six-wheeled tenders of 3,250gal capacity and carrying 3 tons of coal were provided to O/656.

Nos 25–7 were allocated to Kentish Town and 28 and 29 to Nottingham initially, although they too went to London the following year. These locomotives were, to the surprise of some, a huge success and Johnson embarked on a long building programme which extended right up to 1900. Three of the class, Nos 25, 28 and 29 later had their cylinders bored out to 18½in diameter. They were broken up between 1919 and 1928, No 25 being the last to go in July of that year.

The next batch to O/745 were split up into Nos 30–32 having 7ft 4in diameter driving wheels and being identical to Nos 25–9 as built, and Nos 1853 and 34 with 7ft 6in diameter driving wheels and 4ft 4in diameter trailing wheels, and having larger 18½in × 26in cylinders giving somewhat greater power. These adjustments in size were made as a result of experience gained with the first batch in service, and Nos 30–32 went to Nottingham, whilst the other two were sent to London.*

No 1853 was sent to the Paris International Exhibition of 1889 along with one of Mr Clayton's carriages a "soft third-class", twelve-wheeled, pressed-steel bogie composite coach with toilet facilities as provided for the first class passengers. The French judges were somewhat staggered by this grandeur and awarded the coach the Grand Prix and Mr Johnson's locomotive a gold medal.

Incidentally Nos 1853 and 34 were among the first Midland engines to have all wheels made of Siemens Martin cast steel, a change which was continued on some other engines of the type and later became standard practice. Hitherto wheels had been of wrought iron, forged throughout, the spokes being forged in a solid "T" head and welded at the centre of each spoke. Balance weights were also forged solid in the rim of all driving wheels.

The same year, 1889, saw the next batch of five engines, Nos 1854–7 and 37, built to O/796, emerge from the works between June and August They were of the same dimensions as Nos 25–9 when built, as were Nos 1858–62, part of O/809 built between September, 1889 and January, 1890. The remainder of the order, Nos 1863–7, were of the larger size, with 7ft 6in driving wheels, identical to 1853. These too had cast steel wheels (see Plate 41). The series are tabulated opposite for ease of reference.

As will be noticed there were further variations in size of driving wheels and cylinders. Engines built to O/1124 were first to have the larger 19in × 26in size and were also the first to have 8½in diameter piston valves in place of the slide valves used formerly.

From O/1474 onwards, the first engine of which, No 115, ran out on December 8, 1896, the distance between the driving wheel and bogie centre line was increased to 10ft 2½in to accommodate the E class boiler

*Locomotive and Train Working in the latter part of the Nineteenth Century. Vol II by E. L. Ahrons.

TABLE I.
THE JOHNSON SINGLES.

Order Nos	Locomotive Nos	Year Built	Engine only Wts			Driving Wheel	Cylinders dia × stroke	Valves	Firebox Length	Grate Area
			T	C	Q					
O/655 Part	25–9	1887	43	9	3	7ft 4in	18in × 26in	Slide	6ft 6in	19.6sq ft
O/745 Part	30–2	1888	43	9	3	7ft 4in	18in × 26in	Slide	6ft 6in	19.6sq ft
O/745	1853, 34	1889	43	9	3	7ft 6in	18½in × 26in	Slide	6ft 6in	19.6sq ft
O/796 Part	1854–7, 37	1889	43	9	3	7ft 4in	18in × 26in	Slide	6ft 6in	19.6sq ft
O/809 Part	1858–62	1889–90	43	9	3	7ft 4in	18in × 26in	Slide	6ft 6in	19.6sq ft
O/809	1863–7	1889–90	43	9	3	7ft 6in	18½in × 26in	Slide	6ft 6in	19.6sq ft
O/935	1868–72	1891	44	3	0	7ft 6in	18½in × 26in	Slide	6ft 6in	19.6sq ft
O/998	8, 122, 145, 20, 24, 33, 35, 36, 38, 39	1892	44	3	0	7ft 6in	18½in × 26in	Slide	6ft 6in	19.6sq ft
O/1080	4, 16, 17, 94, 97, 100, 129 & 133	1892	44	3	0	7ft 6in	18½in × 26in	Slide	6ft 6in	19.6sq ft
O/1094	149, 170–78	1893	44	3	0	7ft 6in	18½in × 26in	Slide	6ft 6in	19.6sq ft
O/1124	179–83	1893	44	4	0	7ft 6in	19in × 26in	Piston	6ft 6in	19.5sq ft
O/1454	75–7, 79, 88	1896	44	4	0	7ft 6in	19in × 26in	Piston	6ft 6in	19.5sq ft
O/1474	115–19	1896–7	47	2	1	7ft 9in	19½in × 26in	Piston	7ft 0in	21.3sq ft
O/1659	120, 121, 123–8, 130, 131	1899	47	2	1	7ft 9in	19½in × 26in	Piston	7ft 0in	21.3sq ft
O/1926	2601–5 & 19–23	1899–1900	50	3	0	7ft 9½in	19½in × 26in	Piston	8ft 0in	24.5sq ft

with longer barrel, and the boiler pressure was raised to 170psi for O/1474 and O/1659, and further increased to 180psi for O/1926, the engines for which were fitted with double bogie 4,000gal tenders having coal capacity of 5 tons and weighing 50 tons 13cwt 3qtr in working order. These were for the longer non-stop runs, for there were as yet no water troughs on the Midland. A further boiler change to F class was made for O/1926 which also necessitated increasing the distance between driving and trailing wheels to 9ft 9in to allow for the 8ft long firebox.

Another modification was in the outside driving-wheel springs which were changed from plate to twin-spiral springs for engines built to O/935 and onwards.

There were also some variations in the boilers provided, a change being made for the last four engines of O/998 which had D class boilers having 1,223sq ft of heating surface, and this type was used until O/1454 which had the same type boiler with 1,205sq ft heating surface. No further D class boilers were fitted to the singles beyond this, E class boilers set at 170psi and having 1,233sq ft heating surface being fitted to orders 1474 and 1659, and F class boilers having 1,217sq ft of heating surface were used for O/1926, set at 180psi.

On the last order of locomotives the dome was placed farther back from the chimney, directly above the driving splasher, which somewhat destroyed the symmetry of the design in many eyes, although one of the class won a valuable prize as mentioned below.

There was of course some variation in weights. The engine with the largest 7ft 9½in diameter driving wheels weighed 50 tons 3cwt giving a total working weight of 100 tons 16cwt 3qtr, whilst those with the 7ft 9in diameter driving wheels weighed 47 tons 2cwt 1qtr, which with a tender weighing 38 tons dead gave a total weight of 85 tons 2cwt 1qtr in working order. There was only 1cwt difference in weight (working) between all the locomotives with the 7ft 6in diameter ones, the last two orders carrying 14 tons 17cwt 3qtr on bogie wheels, 18 tons 10cwt on drivers and 10 tons 16cwt 1qtr on trailers, whilst the earlier locos had 14 tons 13cwt 2qtr on the bogie, the same on the driving wheels but 10 tons 19cwt 2qtr on the trailing wheels.

The locomotives with the 7ft 9in wheels varied only in the bogie (15 tons 16cwt 2qtr) and trailing wheels (12 tons 15cwt 3qtr) and these were 53ft 2in over buffers being 3in longer in front of the bogie and 2in longer between bogie centre and driving wheel and 6in longer behind the trailing wheel. Those with the largest wheels, but to O/1926 also had the 7ft 1in overhang in front of the bogie centre, but were 9ft 9in from driver to trailing wheel and 9ft 10¾in from there to the leading tender wheel, giving an overall length over buffers of 58ft 11in. There were also variations in the height to centre-line of boiler and chimney-top ranging from 7ft 5½in and 13ft 1in respectively on the first order to 8ft 1in and 13ft 3½in on the last order.

One locomotive of the last order No 2601 was named *Princess of Wales* and represented the Midland Railway Company at the Paris Exhibition of 1900 where it stood alongside Webb's compound *La France* and *Claud Hamilton* representing the Great Eastern Company, but nevertheless it was the Midland engine which was awarded the Grand Prix. The name was taken off for a short period but restored in 1914 again, and was painted around the rim of the driving wheel splasher. When the engine was scrapped in November, 1921, the driving wheels were mounted on a pedestal near the offices in Derby Works yard where they remained until the 1930s.

The allocation of Nos 25–9 has already been mentioned, and the remainder were allocated between Nottingham, London, Leeds, Leicester and Liverpool, with only a few odd ones at Derby. In 1892 it was decided to try the class on the difficult Derby-Bristol road and the great number of engines built in that year went either to Bristol or Birmingham.

As a whole the class gave excellent results, being among the most economical ever turned out from the Derby Works, consuming between 20 and 21lb of the local coal per mile with their usual average load of 115 tons. The drivers were thrilled with them and they were great favourites, becoming nicknamed "spinners" on account of the odd spasm of slipping which they suffered from when starting with heavy trains; yet once in motion they swept along with seemingly effortless ease, there being of course no visible moving parts of the motion, just the large whirling wheels. They were subsequently replaced on the best trains by heavier, more powerful coupled engines of later design, but came into their own again during the 1912 coal strike when, on account of their economy, they were once again put to work on some of the fastest trains for a brief period. They were re-numbered in 1907 as Nos 600–94 in order of building, and were one of the few classes not to undergo a metamorphosis under Deeley, although they escaped by only a narrow margin, as will be recounted later in our story.

One of the singles was however somewhat modified under Deeley by having one of his design of cab fitted. This was No 600 which was so fitted in 1917 under O/5001 which also provided for the addition of vacuum controller gear for working the General Superintendent's service saloon. The saloon itself was most interesting, having been converted from the second of two steam rail motors mentioned later in the book as having been constructed to O/2741 for working the Heysham branch. This was numbered 2234 in the coaching stock, and retained this number after conversion. It was later to be renumbered DM45010 and is fortunately still in existence in private ownership which has secured its preservation at least for the time being.

The singles were withdrawn between 1919 and 1928, beginning with Nos 601 (ex-26) and 696 (2602) which was probably the first to actually be withdrawn since the boiler is shown as being broken up in December, 1916, and no replacement shown. Last to go was 600, mentioned above, which was taken out of service in July, 1928, but fortunately one, 673 built as No 118, was put to one side for possible preservation when withdrawn in July, 1928, and was later restored to Midland crimson lake livery as 118, being placed in the Work's Museum in January, 1931. After being preserved for over 35 years in the works, she was regrettably moved to Leicester for exhibition in the Museum of Transport.

It is most unfortunate that only after the departure of all the preserved locomotives from Derby did the civic authorities wake up to the fact that the town should have some kind of permanent exhibition to mark the great part that it had played in the industrial history of this country. Belated attempts are now being made to rectify this, but it is tragic that a town which owes its present prosperity to the railways should have done so little to mark the fact.

CHAPTER TEN

The Closing Years of Johnson's Era
(1891-1903)

WE MUST NOW catch up on the other locomotives being turned out of the works. In 1889 the first of a new order of 10 six-wheel coupled tank engines, Nos 200, 201, 213 and 214 built to O/824, were turned out, followed by the remainder, Nos 217, 222, 223, 1093, 1101 and 1431, the following year, during which no less than four further orders for a total of 35 locomotives of this type were completed, followed by three more orders as follows:

Order No	Locomotive Nos	Year built
O/854	1843–7, 85–7, 11 & 14	1890
O/869	203, 1848–52, 1973–6	1890
O/924	1977–81	1890
O/883	880–89	1890
O/968	1982–91	1891
O/991	1992, 1107–15	1891
O/1395	1121–30	1895

These all had 4ft 6½in diameter coupled wheels on a wheelbase of 7ft 4in + 7ft 8in (except the last order) and carried an A class boiler set at 140psi with three different heating surfaces but standard grate area and firebox heating surface except for the last mentioned order which carried A1 class boilers with a 4in deeper firebox. All had half cabs as built apart from O/1395, and Nos 1982–91 were built with a cut down cab, shortened chimney (11ft 5½in from chimney top to rail) and dome with Salter spring balance safety valves mounted on the side, these alterations enabling them to work the Victoria Docks–Mint Street traffic. Nos 1111–15 were later fitted with gangway doors (1910) to work the Worth Valley branch.

The engines of the last order, Nos 1121–30, were somewhat different in that the coupled wheelbase was 6in longer being 7ft 4in + 8ft 2in, and the cabs for these were totally enclosed. They had larger 800gal tanks, like the Vulcan and Neilson Class A engines, compared with the 740gal tanks of the remainder. All of these had bunker space for 42cwt of coal. Further orders built by Vulcan, Sharp Stewart & Co and Robert

Stephenson & Co brought the class total to 280. They were renumbered 1620–1899 consecutively in the 1907 renumbering undertaken by Deeley to be mentioned later.

In 1888 Johnson brought out the first of a new range of six-coupled goods engines having 5ft 2½in diameter driving wheels and 18in × 26in cylinders. This was No 1798 which emerged in September of that year built to O/713, and she was followed by the remainder of the order, Nos 1799–1807, the last being completed in November. These engines had second-hand 2,750gal tenders off earlier passenger engines, which received the new tenders built to O/714 intended for these goods engines.

This class were fitted with the standard B class boiler, having a total heating surface of 1,260sq ft, five being later rebuilt with H class boilers, four later had G7 class boilers and new frames and five, Nos 1798, 1803–5 and 1807, had a G6 class boiler put on the old frames.

Only one other order for this type was built at Derby up to the turn of the century, and this was O/1353 fulfilled in 1894–5, for locomotives Nos 361–70. These had the same basic dimensions, with B boilers of 1,252sq ft heating surface and 150psi. Four were later rebuilt with H or H^x boilers and six with G7 boilers. One No 367, was rebuilt with a G6 boiler. In addition 555 of this class were built by outside contractors between 1890 & 1902.

As mentioned earlier the main locomotive offices were structurally altered towards the end of 1893 by the addition of an extra storey, making three floors in all. This was to relieve the serious overcrowding of the clerical staff which had come about as their numbers were increased to match the expansion of the workshop area and staff. In April, 1893, the cost was reported to be £2,500 and the Locomotive Committee referred the project to the Way and Works Committee, and later brought it before the General Purposes Committee who gave it their usual two readings before work was commenced.

As regards the workshop area itself Johnson began, in the summer of 1891, to press for more improvements, making the following suggestions:

(1) The space between the wheel and turning shops to be covered in and machinery from the press shop installed.
(2) The then press shop to be fitted with hydraulic flanging press and annealing furnaces.
(3) Two additional bays should be added to the boiler shop.
(4) The space between the machine and paint shops to be covered in and additional machinery installed, a place at the end being set aside for the repair of weighing machines in lieu of the millwrights doing this work in their shop.
(5) Extension of the mess rooms recommended.

The total estimated cost of this work was given as £44,010 the cost of new machinery being £16,010, and the buildings £28,000. The proposal was referred to the General Purposes Committee who approved the scheme at the second reading on October 2, 1891. Total workshop area had already increased from 2½acres in 1844 to 12½acres, the total area now being 80 acres from the original 8½.

An interesting minute of January 17, 1899, records approaches by the workmen in the Derby shops to Mr Johnson by deputation asking that they be granted reduced-rate privilege tickets for travel on the companies system "like the Great Northern and other railway Companies". After consideration this was granted in August, 1899, and a memorial, recording their grateful thanks for the award of 12 privilege tickets per year, was signed by 1,687 men. They asked that the principle be extended to one per week for the workmen living away from home. This was later granted, and in September, 1895, the interchange of privilege tickets over other companies was introduced, a large meeting in the bottom yard sending their thanks to the Locomotive Committee for their efforts in this direction.

Francis Holt, the Derby Works Manager, died on January 7, 1893, and John Lane, still Inspector of Boilers, was promoted to fill the vacancy at a salary of £600 per annum from February 16. He was to keep this post until he retired under the age limit on December 31, 1901. He died on January 16, 1923.

In 1893 a further group of five small 0-4-0STs for shunting purposes was built in the Derby shops to O/1162. These were Nos 1116A–1120A, being numbered straight into the duplicate list, and all were turned out during June and July. They were almost identical to those built to O/341 and O/816 mentioned previously except that the working weight was 22 tons 19cwt 3qtr as against 21 tons 14cwt.

The following year more of Johnsons four-wheel coupled-bogie passenger engines were constructed at Derby, followed by these others:

Order No	Locomotive Nos	Year Built	Driving Wheel	Valves	Firebox Length	Grate Area
O/1235	184–93	1894	6ft 6in	Slide	6ft 6in	19.5sq ft
O/1276	194–9, 161–4	1894	6ft 6in	Slide	6ft 6in	19.5sq ft
O/1410	230–9	1895	6ft 6in	Slide	6ft 6in	19.5sq ft
O/1458	156–60	1896	7ft 0in	Piston	6ft 6in	19.5sq ft
O/1460	*1667, 1668, 1672, 1675, 1676	1896–7	7ft 0in	Piston	6ft 6in	19.5sq ft
O/1597	150, 153–5, 204–9	1897	7ft 0in	Piston	6ft 6in	19.5sq ft
O/1635	60–66, 93, 138–9	1898	7ft 0½in	Piston	7ft 0in	21.3sq ft
O/1707	*1669, 1671	1898	7ft 0in	Piston	6ft 6in	19.5sq ft
O/1834	67–9, 151–2, 165–9	1899	7ft 0½in	Piston	7ft 0in	21.3sq ft
O/2041	805–9, 2636–40	1901	7ft 0½in	Piston	7ft 0in	21.3sq ft
O/2072	*1670, 1673, 1674	1901	7ft 0in	Piston	6ft 6in	19.5sq ft

*Rebuilds of original Joy's valve gear engines built to O/444 but considered to be new engines.

All the engines to the first three orders together with Sharp Stewart's Nos 2203–17 built for the new Dore & Chinley line, were later rebuilt with H class boilers and 30 were rebuilt to O/4476 and O/5664 with G7 class superheated boiler and new 7ft ½in diameter driving wheels between 1914 and 1923. Two, Nos 162 and 232 were fitted with G7 saturated boilers in 1910.

These engines as built were very similar to the earlier orders, having a bigger distance between driving centres of either 9ft or 9ft 6in, (to enable a longer firebox to be used), the bogie with wheels at 6ft centres being placed either 10ft ½in or 10ft 2½in at its centre from the leading driver. The bogie wheels on the first three orders were 3ft 3in diameter, but this was raised to 3ft 6in on the engines having 7ft and 7ft ½in driving wheels.

Those with the longer driving centres and bigger distances to bogie centre were O/1635 onwards, except for the rebuilt Joy's valve-gear engines, reconstructed to O/2072. All these engines had the short Johnson smokebox and the combined splasher with the access hole at footplate level.

So far as the original boilers were concerned, those built to O/1458 for example had a boiler carrying 242 tubes of 1⅝in external diameter and 2 tubes of 1½in od providing a heating surface of 1,123.6sq ft and with the firebox of 117sq ft this made a total of 1,240.6sq ft. The grate area was 19.678sq ft. As a comparison the smallest 4-4-0s with 6ft 6in driving wheels carried somewhat less heating surface, of which the 240 tapered tubes (1 11/16in od at smokebox end and 1⅝in od at the firebox end) gave 1,106.1sq ft and with the same ample size of firebox, the total was 1,223.1sq ft. Grate area was the same. The boilers on both types were pitched 7ft 4in from rail and the height to the top of the chimney was 12ft 11½in.

These engines were allocated as follows: Nos 184–99 to Carlisle, 161–4 Leicester, 230–35 Leeds, 236–9 Hellifield, 156–60 and certain of O/1460 went to Nottingham as did 151 and 152, the rest going to Derby and Kentish Town. Nos 60–69, 150 and 153–5 went to Leicester, 204 to Birmingham and the remainder of that order to Manchester. Derby had Nos 93, 138, and 139, and apart from the rebuilds the remainder, to O/2041, went to Carlisle (805–9) and Leeds (2636–40).

Also built in the Derby Works about this time were the first engines supplied by the Midland Railway to the Somerset and Dorset Joint Committee, the Locomotive Department of which became the responsibility of the Midland Company when the old Somerset and Dorset Company was leased jointly to the Midland and London and South Western companies for 999 years from November 1, 1875.

After the first Midland nominated Locomotive Superintendent, Mr

W. H. French, who was appointed May 17, 1883, had lost his life at Highbridge after being crushed between two wagons, on November 1, 1889, Mr Alfred W. Whitaker took over, and it was he who instigated the supply of a number of Derby built "quality" locomotives to the line rather than those of outside contractors as supplied heretofore. He also undertook the rebuilding and re-equipping of the company's own shops at Highbridge. Whitaker was a former pupil of Matthew Kirtley, and had been in charge of the Midland locomotive depots at Carlisle and Leeds before moving to Highbridge in the November of 1889.

The first Derby order for the S&DJR, O/872, was for 4 four-wheel coupled passenger engines Nos 15–18 which were built in May, 1891, the boilers being supplied by Messrs Kitson and Co and the 2,200gal tenders with outside springs above the platform plate, being constructed in the S&DJR Committee's own workshops to O/873. They had 5ft 9in diameter driving wheels at 8ft 3in centres and 3ft bogie wheels and the two inside cylinders were 18in diameter × 24in stroke. Boiler pressure was 160psi and weight in working order was 66 tons 12cwt 2qtr.

Further engines of this type were to follow, two Nos 67 and 68 to O/1431 in January, 1896, and two more Nos 14 and 45 to O/1482 in January and February, 1897. They were rather diminutive locomotives with Salter valves on the dome, inside cylinders and half cabs, but they were put to work on the main line trains now running faster with heavier loads and being too much for the 0-4-4 types used up to that date. The last two had steel boilers set at 150psi. Only three more of this wheel arrangement were built for this Committee in Johnson's time, these being Nos 69–71 built to O/2588 in 1903. These had 6ft driving wheels at 8ft 6in centres and 18in × 26in cylinders and were much larger engines altogether.

In addition to these Derby supplied the Joint Committee with five of their standard 0-6-0 goods engines to O/1449 between January and March, 1896, these being Nos 62–6. They had 5ft 2½in driving wheels at the standard 8ft + 8ft 6in centres and 18in × 26in cylinders and were fitted with 2,950gal tenders and had automatic vacuum train brakes. The boilers were set at 150psi.

A few more locomotives turned out before the turn of the century must be recorded, the first being two further orders for 0-4-0 saddle tank engines. O/1534 was for five locomotives Nos 2359, 2360 and 1131A–3A and O/1552 was for five more, Nos 1134A–8A. These were generally similar to those described above, O/1534 being the same as O/1162, but those to the second order mentioned were somewhat larger having a 7ft 6in wheelbase, and a length over buffers of 25ft $\frac{7}{16}$in after thicker beams had been added at the front end. 15in × 20in inside cylinders were fitted instead of the former 13in × 20in, and a larger 650gal saddle tank 11ft long. The working weight was 30 tons 19cwt 2qtr. Height from rails to top of chimney was 12ft. These last mentioned locomotives were built specially for working the Staveley Works sidings under the standing agreement with the Midland. They carried the J1 class boiler having 147 tubes of 1¾in diameter giving a total heating surface of 759.4sq ft including firebox heating surface of 62.4sq ft. The grate area was 10.5sq ft and the distance between tube plates was 10ft 8⅝in. Working pressure was 150psi. The engines to O/1552 originally carried a tool box beneath the footplate, but in August, 1897, these were replaced by new cast iron tool boxes on the running plate at the front end.

Only one more class (with two peculiar exceptions) needs to be described to bring us to the end of the 19th century, and this was the 690 class 0-4-4 passenger tanks, built to O/1602 and turned out between February and May, 1898. They were Nos 690–95 and 780–83 and were the same as Nos. 2233–47 turned out by Messrs Dübs & Co of Glasgow in 1895. They had 5ft 3½in diameter driving wheels at 8ft centres and a bogie having 3ft ½in diameter wheels at 5ft 6in centres placed 11ft 3in behind the driving wheel. The inside cylinders were 18in ×24in and the C1 class boiler carred 1,252sq ft of heating surface, being pressed to 150psi. The side tanks carried 1,270gal of water and the bunker (with coal rails) 42cwt of coal. There was an all-over full cab provided, and the working weight was 5 tons 18cwt 3qtr of which the driving wheels carried 14 tons 1qtr and 16 tons 16cwt 1qtr respectively.

The exceptions mentioned above were the American 2-6-0 tender engines erected at Derby in 1899. These were supplied by two companies Messrs Burnham Williams and Co of the Baldwin Locomotive Works, Philadelphia and the Schenectady Locomotive Works, New York, and recourse was had to America since the Derby shops were full to capacity with work and the private locomotive builders, in the middle of a tremendous boom and yet suffering under a strike, could not provide a single locomotive in under 15 months. Since more locomotive power of the six coupled main line goods type had to be obtained Johnson, in company with his opposite numbers on the Great Central and Great Northern Railway Companies, obtained sanction to purchase from across the Atlantic and orders for 30 locomotives and 10 locomotives were placed with the two companies respectively.

Within a few weeks the first crates arrived at the Derby Works on May 24, 1899, the engines having been previously assembled and then dismantled again at the parent companies works. Space was found at the bottom end of No 3 bay in No 8 shop at Derby for the re-erection of the 10 Schenectady locomotives (*see Plate 43*), but the 30 Baldwin's were just too much for the capacity of the shops and space was cleared in front of the Locomotive Works offices and they were erected out in the open, this fortunately being summer time! (*see Plate 42*).

The first Baldwin was ready to go into service by the end of May, the range of running numbers allocated to this type being 2501–10 and 2521–40, and the first 10 locomotives were completed by the end of the following month. These engines were almost entirely American save the Johnson coal-rails and MR buffing and drawgear. They had bar frames, common American practice, and outside cylinders 18in × 24in with inside valve gear. The driving wheels were 5ft diameter on a wheelbase of 6ft 3in + 8ft 6in and the pony truck wheels were 2ft 9in diameter, being 7ft 5in in front of the leading driving wheel. The boiler was pressed to 160psi and pitched 7ft 2⅛in from rail, having three "domes" of varying sizes, one being a sand box on the first ring of the boiler, the next the steam dome housing the regulator and twin "Coale" pop safety valves and the last and smallest one housing chime whistle and spring safety valve. The cabs were very large by Midland standards with two side windows. One unusual feature was the bar steel support struts from the smokebox to the footplating over the pony truck. The tenders were of 3,250gal capacity on two four-wheeled bogies of total wheel base 14ft 4in, the bogie wheels being 3ft diameter and 4ft 8in apart on each bogie. The length over buffers was 51ft 1in and total wheelbase 43ft. Working weight of engine was 45 tons 16cwt 1qtr and tender 34 tons 12cwt 2qtr The last 20 Baldwins were built between September and November, 1899 and the class was divided between the Toton, Sheffield and Leeds running depots. A driver of that day, James Gibbs Hardy, observed "very rough workmanship" when the crates of material arrived, but modified his criticism when the first commenced running on June 21, commenting in his diary "splendid weather cab, upholstered seats and the engine looks considerably better now it is in working order". He had one of these engines No 2503, booked to him to do 1,000 miles on and found them hard to reverse and rather poor steamers. He took the first one to Normanton where everyone stared at it, and on July 24 took the first one up the Peak to Manchester, recording that she went up the bank with 80–90lb of steam. By August 8, he had completed his 1,000 miles and was "very glad to get rid of her".

The Schenectadys were rather nearer to looking like Midland engines, although they too had the unusual type of bar frame (to British practice that is). The outside cylinders were 18in diameter × 24 in stroke and the tapered boiler was pitched 7ft 1in from rail, the working pressure being 160psi. Driving wheels were 5ft diameter on a 7ft + 8ft 6in wheelbase and the pony truck, having 3ft diameter wheels was placed 7ft 6in in front of the leading driving wheel. Total wheelbase was 43ft and length over buffers 51ft 11¼in with basically Midland 3,250gal tender on a shorter 12ft 3in wheelbase. Working weights were engine 49 tons 15cwt 2qtr and tender 37 tons. These were all stationed at Wellingborough.

As can be gathered from Hardy's comments these engines were not popular and some criticisms reached America causing bad feeling. Johnson gave some comparable figures quoting that, work for work, they consumed 20–25 per cent more coal, and 50 per cent more oil than his standard goods engines, while repairs cost 60 per cent more. To their credit he observed that the engines cost £400 less than their British counterparts, and were at least supplied within a few months of the contract being placed, while he had to wait about three years for locos ordered from British firms, due in the main to the engineering strike which had forced the Midland Company to buy "Yankee" in the first place.

Supervising the contract for the Baldwin engines being built in America for the Midland was J. W. Smith, who was on January 1, 1901 to become the Chief Locomotive Draughtsman in place of T. G. Iveson. We can at this point examine the changes in this position since the appointment of Billinton in 1874.

As we have mentioned, Billinton came to Derby to be Johnson's Chief Draughtsman, from a similar position under William Stroudley on the LB&SCR. In 1889 Stroudley went to the Paris Exhibition of that year with his Gladstone class locomotive *Edward Blount*, but in putting it through its paces on the line from Paris to Laroche he caught a cold. Complications set in, and he died in Paris at the age of 56. So the LB&SCR found itself in need of a new Locomotive, Carriage and Marine Superintendent and who better to offer the post to than Billinton, Stroudley's former chief assistant. He gladly accepted the position, and resigned from the Midland on January 31, 1890. He was still in office on the Brighton line when he died on November 7, 1904.

Johnson was thus stuck for a Chief Draughtsman and in Billinton's place he appointed Thomas G. Iveson, a fairly old, amiable gentleman who stuttered rather badly, and worse than usual when trying to answer a question to which he did not know the answer. A story is told of his earlier life in London when he daily passed the Railway Clearing House. There being no outward sign of this building's use, he one day plucked up courage and entered, saying to the attendant "If you p-p-please, wh-what is this p-p-place". This seemed to annoy the servant of the RCH who promptly ejected him with the words "Now out you go", and Iveson was so confused he could not stutter out any reply to smooth over the situation. He had served in his earlier years as a draughtsman at Messrs E. B. Wilsons, and had produced a fine line drawing of *Jenny Lind* in December, 1851.

Iveson lasted in the position of Chief Draughtsman for 10 years, being replaced, on his retirement, by the J. W. Smith mentioned above. He had been trained on the North Eastern Railway at Gateshead on Tyne and had come to the Midland in October, 1891, filling many widely differing positions which had enriched his extensive and comprehensive mechanical experience. Smith was to continue in office until August, 1906, and was to be responsible for the development of the compounds first under Johnson and later under Deeley.

Before taking the locomotive side of the story further some facts and figures, regarding the Locomotive Department about this time are available. By the end of 1894 the covered workshop area was 20 acres, including the general stores, the whole ground area amounting to 80 acres, 4,089 workmen were employed in the shops and the numbers of foremen, clerks, draughtsmen, etc, was 257, the average weekly wage bill being £5,272. The machine shop housed 500 machines, and the erecting shop capacity was 108 engines. The Iron Foundry's four cupolas each had a capacity of about 5 tons of molten iron, the weekly output of castings of all kinds being of the order of 350 tons. Gas lighting and heating was of course general at this time, especially in the form of portable jets on the end of rubber piping for use in illuminating the various shops, including inside the engine erecting pits, and boilers and tender tanks under repairs. For this demand the company's gas works in the Locomotive Works, formerly belonging to the Derby Gas Company, produced a total of over 122m cu ft of gas in 1894. Locomotive stock at this time was 2,400 plus 23 stationary engines, the former running up a total yearly mileage of 40,628,405.

The works was responsible for producing an average of between 20 and 30 new locomotives per year, rebuilding about 120 engines with new boilers and giving heavy repairs to between 750 and 800 locomotives. The paint shop could hold between 30 and 40 locomotives, depending on the size, and was responsible for turning out an annual quota of between 600 and 700, repainting being necessary every three or four years. One interesting fact was that if all the companies stock was marshalled into one long train it would have reached from London to Edinburgh and would include over 20 miles of locomotives! There were of course out-station repair shops at various main locomotive depots which assisted by doing fairly heavy repairs to locomotives.

The new footbridge into the works leading from Hulland Street was opened on January 9, 1899, and in building this, the demolition of the North Stafford "Cosy Corner" had to take place. Here, for many many years Old John Faulkner had held court in his harbour of refuge for the privileged few. The room was "like a bar with no drinks and a barber's shop with no barber". John was a temperance figure and offered homely advice as seasoning to the every day chat of local gossip and government policies. One of the "regulars" was William Burdett, the last of the Derby stage-coach drivers, who finished his days on the station omnibus from the Market Place. Sad to relate, during the demolition of the Corner, Old John took a chill and died, and thus another small link with the past was broken. Approaches had been made for this new entrance as early as December, 1883, this first request being for a subway passing underneath the tracks at the south end of the station.* Nothing further was done until a memorandum from 1,003 workmen was received in July, 1891 requesting a "new additional road entrance to the Locomotive Works across the line to Nelson Street either by Iron bridge or underground passage". It was ordered that an estimated cost be obtained for a suitable iron bridge, and the estimate for the subway, made in 1883, was again brought before the committee on December 4, 1891.

At this meeting the cost of a 15ft wide footbridge was stated to be £9,095 and that for the subway £9,040. The scheme for a subway was approved and passed its first reading but the matter was then referred back for reconsideration and a new estimate of £7,862 was made, when it was stated that £3,210 per annum would be saved by the men getting quicker to work, a bridge would mean less time conveying stores and parcels into the Works, and would avoid the necessity of providing a new messroom.

The scheme for the footbridge was finally approved by the General Purposes Committee on September 17, 1896, and the tender of Sir W. G. Armstrong Whitworth to supply two hydraulic lifts, for the bridge, at a cost of £300 each, was accepted.

Also about this time, in July 1887, it was agreed that a road be made into the Locomotive Works for workmen residing at Osmaston, Alvaston and Newtown. As a result of a petition signed by 138 workmen affected, the road and a gate-house were constructed, a fenced cinder path 6ft wide being provided lighted by 10 gas lamps, in 1888.

We can now study the few remaining years of Johnson's superintendence. There are but three further classes to be described.

In September, 1900, the first of Johnson's large two-cylinder 4-4-0 passenger locomotives emerged from the Derby Works (*see Plate 48*). These were the 700 class as they later became known although they were colloquially referred to as the "Belpaires", and the first order O/1869, was to 10 locomotives, Nos 2606–10 and 800–804 turned out between September, 1900 and June, 1901. They were produced for the Settle–Carlisle line to reduce the number of double-headed trains then being run over this difficult section.

*BTHR Mid 1/177.

The driving wheels of these engines were 6ft 9in diameter at 9ft 6in centres and the 3ft 6½in diameter bogie wheels at 6ft centres, were placed 10ft 2½in in front of the leading driver. The inside cylinders were 19½in diameter and 26in stroke and had piston valves. For the first time Johnson used a Belpaire GX type boiler set at 175psi, and pitched 8ft 3in from rail. This carried a total heating surface of 1,519sq ft of which the 272 tubes of 1¾in diameter provided 1,374sq ft and the firebox 145sq ft. The grate area was 25sq ft. They were provided with "water-cart" tenders of the twin four-wheeled bogie type of 4,000gal water capacity and 3½tons of coal, the working weights being as follows: leading bogie 17 tons 5cwt 2qtr, driving 18 tons 5cwt 2qtr, trailing 16 tons 6cwt 2qtr, totalling 51 tons 17cwt 2qtr. The tender weighed 52 tons 7cwt 1qtr.

The appearance of these engines was further altered by the use of a closed round-topped dome and twin Ramsbottom safety valves enclosed in an oval canister-shaped housing over the firebox. A lock-up safety valve was added on later engines. The bogies of these engines had a somewhat unusual compensated suspension, but this was not repeated on the next order. As new this first batch of 10 were allocated to Leeds and Manchester, Robert Weatherburn had pressed Johnson to introduce the Belpaire boiler on the Midland in 1875, when he took up an appointment with the company, having observed the satisfactory outcome of the application of this type of firebox to boilers of engines built by Messrs Kitson & Co for the German Government and used on the Alsace and Lorraine Railways at Metz. However it was not until after Pollitt had introduced the Belpaire boiler on the Great Central line that Johnson permitted their use on the Midland. His reply to Weatherburn on being reminded that the Midland could have been the first to use them had his advice been taken, was "Yes, I remember Weatherburn, but I like to be sure and on the safe side before taking so important a step", a remark so typical of the man.

The next two orders for this type followed in 1902, with a further two orders in 1903, the last year of Johnsons reign, as listed below:

Order No	Locomotive Nos	Year
O/2135	2781–90	1902
O/2250	810–19	1902
O/2458	820–29	1903
O/2601	830–39	1903–4

On these later orders the bogie wheels were reduced to 3ft 3½in diameter and had four point suspension, the distance from the leading driver to the centre of the bogie being increased to 10ft 8½in and from the centre bogie to front buffer 7ft 1in as against 6ft 10in on the first order. This was to accommodate the longer boiler barrel of the new boiler.

Even larger, 4,500gal double-bogie tenders were fitted to those orders up to the fifth engine of O/2458, while the remainder had 4,100gal tenders of the same type. The length over buffers for all those listed was 59ft 6¼in with a total wheelbase of 47ft 4⅛in, working weights being 53 tons 4cwt for the engine and 52 tons 12cwt 3qtr for tenders of 4,500gal capacity and 47 tons 14cwt 1qtr for those of 4,100gal capacity. All the later batch had the new type G8 boiler with Belpaire firebox, a 6in longer barrel, and having a total heating surface of 1,528 sq ft of which the 262 tubes of 1¾in diameter gave 1,383sq ft and the firebox 145sq ft. The grate area remained at 25sq ft. All but three of these locomotives later had boilers with superheaters fitted. These engines were allocated to Kentish Town, Nottingham, Leeds and Manchester, and were reserved for the heavier long-distance-express passenger trains.

The second of the final classes of Johnson's time were to become perhaps the most famous of all, the Midland compounds, the first of which commenced working on November 26, 1901, and was immediately christened an "ugly brute" by the running department staff at Derby. However they soon revised their opinions when the performance of the first two locomotives built was made known.

The introduction of compounds to the Midland was not done without a great deal of soul searching by Johnson. He was not, as we have noted before, a man to jump on the band wagon of every new development, but waited patiently on the bye-lines until he felt that the time was ripe, and with his length of experience in all branches of engineering his was the almost perfect mechanical judgement.

Curtain raiser to the Midland compound had been the rebuilding by W. M. Smith, to his own compounding system, of one of William Worsdell's two-cylinder compounds on the North Eastern Railway. Smiths system involved one high-pressure cylinder placed between the frames and two low pressure cylinders placed outside. This could be worked on starting as a three-cylindered simple engine but by the use of non-return valves, and a spring loaded regulating valve, the cylinders could be made to work compound, steam from the high pressure cylinder being utilised again in the low pressure cylinders.

The first order for compounds was O/2109 and the numbers of the engines were 2631-5 the first two being officially dated January, 1902 although both were turned out before the end of 1901 (see Plate 49). The remainder were turned out in July, September and November, 1903. The first two had one inside high-pressure cylinder 19in diameter and 26in of stroke and two outside low-pressure cylinders 21in diameter and 26in stroke, and the valves were operated by three sets of Stephenson's link motion operating a piston valve for the inside cylinder and slide valves for the outside cylinders. Separate reversing gear was provided for high- and low-pressure systems, and the leading coupled axle was driven from all three cylinders, the inside crank being set at 135deg to the outside cranks 90 deg. A reinforcing valve was fitted on the side of the smokebox by means of which high-pressure steam could be admitted to the low-pressure cylinders to provide extra power such as when starting, this valve being operated by the driver. The driving wheels were 7ft diameter set at 9ft 6in centres and the bogie wheels 3ft 6½in diameter at 6ft 6in centres, the centre of the bogie being 11ft 6in in front of the leading coupled axle. The boiler of 2631 was a G8½in type with Belpaire firebox, introduced specially for the compounds, having a total heating surface of 1,598sq ft of which the 261 tubes of 1¾in diameter provided 1,448sq ft and the firebox 150sq ft. Grate area was 26sq ft and the boiler was pitched 8ft 6in above rail level, and set to work at 195psi maximum pressure, the barrel being 11ft 7in long, and 4ft 8in minimum diameter. The tender held 5 tons of coal and 4,500gal of water and was of the double bogie type weighing 52 tons 12cwt 3qtr in working order, whilst the engine weighed 59 tons 10cwt 1qtr divided as follows: bogie 20 tons 12cwt 3qtr, driving 19 tons 11cwt 2qtr, trailing 19 tons 6cwt. There was some slight variation in weights between the first five engines, those given applying to the first engine only. No 2632 was identical except that the boiler carried Serf (Serve) corrugated boiler tubes, 2¾in outside diameter with internal ribbing, and the heating surface was tubes 1,569.8sq ft + firebox 150sq ft totalling 1,719.8sq ft.

The last three of the first order, built in 1903, differed somewhat from Nos 2631–2 in that they had only one set of reversing gear operating all three sets of valve gear, and the running plate was not raised over the cylinders as with the originals, and they were somewhat lighter, the engine weighing 58 tons 9cwt in working order. No 2635 was also fitted with Serf tubes but these were replaced by the orthodox type, as were those on 2632, in 1904. Of these early compounds the first two were put to work on the line north of Leeds up to Carlisle, and the other three in the London area.

For those interested in a more detailed account of these fine locomotives there are two excellent books on the subject, *The Midland Compounds* by D. F. Tee published by the Railway Correspondence and Travel Society and a fuller account *The Midland Compounds* by O. S. Nock published by Messrs David & Charles, both of which can be recommended to those interested. Turning to the other end of the scale, so far as size is concerned, one further batch of 0-4-0ST shunting engines was turned out in 1903 to O/2517. These were Nos 1139A–43A which were built during November and December of that year. These were identical to Nos 1134A–8A previously described as built in 1897, except that 1139A, as 1523 (1907) acquired an all-over cab extending beyond the rear buffer beam above waist level, the back plate being provided with two round windows as in the front plate for working in the Swansea area. The remainder had more orthodox back weatherboards fitted to O/2786.

The last engines of Johnson design built for the Midland during his turn of office were a new form of his standard 0-6-0 goods tender engine, the first of which, No 2736, emerged from the Derby shops in January, 1903. These had larger H class boilers set at 175psi and with a total heating surface of 1,428sq ft, of which the 258 tubes of $1\frac{7}{8}$in diameter provided 1,303sq ft and the firebox 125sq ft, the grate area being 21.1sq ft. The boiler barrel was 10ft $5\frac{5}{16}$in long and 4ft 8in outside diameter and the distance between tube plates 10ft $10\frac{5}{8}$in. The firebox was 7ft long × 4ft $\frac{1}{2}$in wide outside. These boilers had twin Ramsbottom-type safety valves plus a lock-up safety valve in front situated over the firebox enclosed in an oval casing, and the cab side sheets were extended for a greater distance beyond the cab front plate than heretofore, giving them a new and distinctive appearance. With 5ft 3in diameter driving wheels on a standard 16ft 6in wheelbase and 18in diameter × 26in stroke inside cylinders with slide valves between operated by Stephensons valve gear engine weights in working order were: leading 13 tons 15cwt 2qtr, driving 16 tons 18cwt, trailing 13 tons 2cwt 3qtr, totalling 43 tons 16cwt 1qtr. Total wheelbase was 38ft $9\frac{1}{4}$in and length over buffers 50ft $9\frac{1}{2}$in.

The first order for these, O/2328, for engines 2736–40 and 240–44 was fulfilled between January and May, 1903, and a further order O/2530 for 10 further engines of this design, Nos 245–54, but having larger $18\frac{1}{2}$in × 26in cylinders, was also delivered by the Derby shops the same year, these being built between July and December. All subsequent engines of this type had the larger size of cylinders until the introduction of the larger Class 4 freight engines in 1911.

Johnsons final fling in design would have raised many eyebrows had they ever seen the light of day. The first to be described took the form of an outside-cylindered eight-wheel coupled goods engine, and would of course have been the first of this type to work on the Midland. These engines, for 10 were to be built to O/2694 of December 5, 1903, were somewhat similar to the North Eastern Class T engines of this type. The outside cylinders driving onto the third pair of driving wheels were to have been 20in diameter with 26in stroke and the driving wheels themselves 4ft 7in diameter. The driving centres were to be 6ft + 5ft 6in + 6ft, and the total wheelbase, with a 3,500gal tender, was to have been 42ft 3¼in. Weights were tentatively set at 15tons 5cwt on leading and trailing wheels and 15 tons 10cwt on intermediate and driving wheels giving a total engine weight of 61 tons 10cwt. Most of the drawings were completed for this locomotive including general arrangement, frame arrangement, pipe and rod arrangement etc, but the whole scheme was squashed in favour of more small engines.

The second design was for a double-bogied four-wheel coupled (or 4-4-4) inside-cylindered tank engine of quite large proportions compared to anything around at that time. The inside cylinders were of 18in diameter with a stroke of 26in having inside admission slide valves between, driven by Stephensons valve gear. Driving wheels were to be 5ft 7in diameter at 8ft 6in centres, the leading and trailing bogies having 3ft 1in diameter wheels at 6ft centres being centred 10ft ½in in front of the leading driver and 9ft 6in behind the trailing driver respectively. The boiler pitched 8ft from rail and working at 175psi was provided with encased twin Ramsbottom safety valves, carried 258 tubes of 1¾in diameter (firebox end) giving 1,302.9sq ft of heating surface which together with the firebox 125sq ft gave a total of 1,427.9sq ft, with a grate area of 21.13sq ft. Boiler dome was on the middle ring and distance between tube plates was 10ft 10⅝in the barrel being 5ft 1¼in diameter outside and 10ft 5 5/16in long. Firebox was 7ft long × 4ft ½in wide outside. Height to the top of the flowerpot chimney was 13ft 3 9/16in. Both driving wheels and trailing bogie wheels were braked. The side and bunker tanks held a total of 2,000gal of water and there was room for 2½tons of coal. Total wheelbase was 34ft ½in and length over buffers 41ft 2¾in.

However in the event neither design was built although five of the second design were ordered to O/2651 in September, 1903, but this was cancelled, and it was left to Johnson's successor to provide further food for thought in designs which "never were", as will be recounted later in our story (*see Fig 1*).

Samuel Johnson gave up his post at the end of 1903 and retired to Nottingham where he was tragically knocked down by a runaway horse and trap, and died shortly afterwards on January 14, 1912 at the age of 80. During his long and active life he had brought a certain poetic beauty into his locomotive designs which together with his genius for producing a machine of great precision and reliability would have endeared him to today's "quality and reliability" advocates, as well as to the artistically minded "pro-Victoriana" champions, for quite different reasons.

His successor was Richard Mountford Deeley who took office at the beginning of 1904. Strangely enough history repeated itself so far as the Derby Works were concerned because shortly before Johnson ceased to

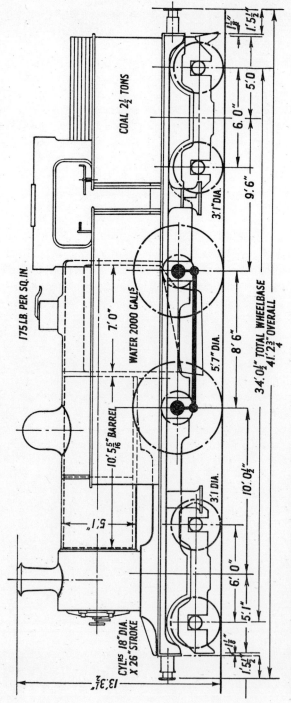

Fig 1   *Proposed double-bogied passenger tank engine.*

occupy the position of Locomotive Superintendent a bold plan for the further long term enlargement of the Derby Workshops on a grand scale, to eventually double its size, was being worked out. By June 1902 a plan of the proposed extension had been drawn up and was ready for submission but unlike Kirtley's plans brought to fruition by Johnson, these proposals were never carried through and the only part of them ever to appear in physical form was the power station across the canal, although even that was removed from the site shown on the plan, being built in the middle of what was to be a new smith's shop extension, running parallel to the present one and of the same length, but on the other side of the canal. The original proposed site for this power station was to be opposite the mess rooms on the far side of the Derby Canal which is now filled in and abandoned.

The main reasons why this great extension was never carried forward were that, in order to build the new shops and sidings to serve them, the line of the canal had to be diverted in a long circular sweep, following the line of the River Derwent to a position opposite the present Chaddesden sidings, from where it was intended to follow a straight course to the canal bridge on the main London Road; and secondly the cost of the £84,075 was somewhat prohibitive.

The new shops were to be as follows:

(a) A new locomotive stores building 120ft × 500ft long to be erected right across the end of the machine and erecting shops farthest from the clock tower comprising three bays with a three ridged roof supported on cast iron columns.

(b) A vast new erecting shop 350ft wide and 625ft long, being four times the size of the present one, comprising six bays each with room for 30 engines placed across the bays, ie side by side, giving overall accommodation for 120 locomotives at a time. This shop was to be built alongside the new loco stores on the opposite side to the machine and erecting shops, extending beyond these shops by some 90ft. This shop was to be served by a new complex of sidings running from Etches Park and entering the new shop on the south side.

(c) A new smiths shop 60ft wide × 400ft long as previously mentioned.

(d) A new power station 90ft wide × 200ft long, also mentioned previously.

(e) A new complex of shops to be built in the large area of ground between the iron foundry and the river on a lower level and comprising:

   (i) A paint shop 200ft wide and 300ft long having 12 roads.

   (ii) A pattern shop 100ft wide and 300ft long.

   (iii) A pattern store 100ft wide and 250ft long.

(iv) A millwright's shop 150ft wide and 300ft long served by four
      lines of sidings.
(v)   A saw mill 75ft wide × 200ft long.
(vi) A timber store 75ft wide × 200ft long.

The last two were to be separate from the rest being end on to each
other, and the paint, pattern and millwrights shops were to be side by
side with the pattern store, end on to the pattern shop. This complex of
shops was to be served by a new line running from the south end of
Chaddesden sidings, crossing the Derwent and the canal by a new
bridge, continuing to meet the new service sidings running past the new
erecting shop from Etches Park. A branch of this new siding was to
leave this new line just after it crossed the canal and follow the canal
along the west bank serving the new shops, the bottom yard in general
from a direction at right angles to the existing sidings, and the new
power station, running between this and the new smiths shop extension
and terminating behind the offices in the space now occupied by No 1
roundhouse which it was proposed to demolish.

One further extension was to be a new engine shed and sidings provided adjacent to the west side of the Chaddesden sidings with space for
a further one if required in the future.

When the scheme was brought before the General Purposes Committee they queried the drop in individual engine earnings and the
whole scheme was referred to the Midland Board, who suggested that a
large scale reorganisation of the facilities of the workshops might achieve
the required result.

Deeley embarked on a vast plan of reorganisation bringing in a great
army of new machines and pensioning off the old outmoded machine
tools, and his successor, Henry Fowler, followed on with this great plan,
employing electrification as one of his chief ploys as will be recounted
later.

Before the close of this chapter mention ought to be made of the
opening of the Derby Railway Institute on February 16, 1894, the
ceremony being performed by George Ernest Paget, Chairman of the
Midland Board of Directors. This 'palatial" red brick building stands
on the site of some of the older Midland Company houses, and its construction was a culmination of an approach made to the Midland
Directors as far back as February 14, 1851, when a petition, signed by
423 employees was presented to them asking for the use of a free room
suitably fitted out for the activities of the Derby Railway Literary
Institution. This group had begun activities at a meeting in the *Brunswick Inn* one December night in 1850, when a few of the company's
employees agreed to form a Reading Society. A few weeks later they

decided to establish a reading room and a subscription library. Two cottages were provided in Leeds Place, off Railway Terrace, to serve in this capacity, and then in 1857 rooms adjacent to the new shareholder's room were given over to their use.

Finally the completely separate building, still in use today, was built, providing not only space for the library, now grown to 14,000 volumes, but also for a magazine and newspaper room, waiting room, three class-rooms, a lecture and concert hall to seat 500 persons, chess, card and billiard rooms and a coffee room.

Membership of the Institute was open to all railway employees on payment of a small weekly subscription, and it continued to function in this form until comparatively recently when it was converted to a British Railways Staff Association Club. The library closed through lack of support and its large collection was sold in 1963, only a reference library, now in the care of the Locomotive Works Manager, being re-tained.

CHAPTER ELEVEN

Deeley and Paget

(1904-1909)

THE NEW Locomotive Superintendent, Richard Mountford Deeley, was not, like his predecessors, an appointee from another company, but had worked his way up through the ranks after showing great promise as a pupil of Johnson many years earlier. His father had served at one time in the accounts office of the Midland Railway but Richard, who was born on October 24, 1855 spent his early years at Chester, where he received his grammar school education. In 1873 he became a pupil of E. B. Ellington, Managing Director of the Hydraulic Engineering Co in that city.

The following year he was selected to go to London to assist in the development of the Brotherhood three-cylinder hydraulic engine, and two years later, while still under 21, he was accepted as a pupil of Johnson, being given experimental work at which he so distinguished himself that in March, 1890, at the age of 35, he became chief of the testing department where the foundations of his notable research work and scholarly outlook on life were laid. He retained connections with this department when promoted first of all to the position of Inspector of Boilers, Engines and Machinery in March, 1893 where he had a big hand in the design of boilers for Johnsons later engines. On January 1, 1902, he replaced John Lane as Works Manager and exactly a year later took on the additional post of Electrical Engineer at a combined salary of £1,000 per annum. In July of the same year he was given a further post, that of Assistant Locomotive Superintendent in preparation for Johnsons' retirement at the year end, and on January 1, 1904, he succeeded Johnson at a salary of £2,000 per annum (*see Plate 36*).

Before passing on to discuss the locomotives turned out by Deeley we must introduce the other protagonist in the battle that was to follow, Cecil W. Paget, who had followed Deeley "up the tree" as it were, becoming Assistant Works Manager in January, 1902, and Works Manager on January 1, 1904 after holding the post in a temporary capacity from June 19, 1903. Cecil Paget had earlier been sent by the Midland Company in January, 1899, to supervise the construction of the Schenectady engines at their works along with John Smith who supervised the Baldwin engine contract. Cecil's father, Sir Ernest Paget, Bart., was then the chairman of the Midland Company, but his son was forceful enough personality on his own, not needing much of the backing his father could give him (*see Plate 35*). He was a tremendously enthusiastic worker and set about his task with vigour.

One other figure needs to be mentioned at this stage, this being Henry Fowler who had joined the Midland Company on June 18, 1900 at a salary of £350 per annum in the position of Gas Engineer & Chief of the Testing Department, from a similar position on the Lancashire and Yorkshire Railway at Horwich. He was to be in just the right place at the right time and reap the full fruits of the clash of personalities soon to develop between Deeley and Paget. Fowler became Assistant Works Manager on November 1, 1905 in succession to Paget (*see Plate 39*).

The first locomotives turned out by Deeley were simply further orders for Johnson's types already well established, but he also indulged in a great amount of rebuilding with larger boilers of many of the earlier passenger tender engine classes, the few exceptions being the Johnson singles and the American 2-6-0s, together with a few other Kirtley types.

In 1904 a further order, O/2726, was put in hand for ten 2781 class 4-4-0 passenger tender engines Nos 840–49, followed by O/2798 for engines 850–59, and O/2918 for the last batch of ten, Nos 860–69, all of which were completed by September, 1905 (*see Plates 23 & 72*). All of these had 3,500gal six-wheeled tenders fitted with water pick-up gear, for the Midland now had water troughs at Oakley, Melton Mowbray and Loughborough, soon to be followed by the introduction of troughs near Hawes Junction on the Settle-Carlisle line.

The first 10 of these 4-4-0s had the same G8 boilers as the earlier engines of the class, but the last two orders were fitted with a modified G8A boiler, having only 251 tubes of 1¾in outside diameter, giving a heating surface of 1,310.5sq ft which, together with the firebox heating surface of 145sq ft, gave a total of 1,455.5sq ft compared with 1,528sq ft on the G8 boiler. Grate area was 25sq ft. However the pressure of the new G8A class was raised to 200psi for the last order, the highest yet used on the Midland, but this was later reduced to 180psi when the engines were brought into the shops after May, 1912. The external dimensions of these boilers were identical, the barrel being 11ft long and 4ft 8in diameter inside, the centre line being pitched 8ft 3in above rail level. Total length over buffers was 54ft 11in and working weights of the latter orders were as follows: leading bogie 18 tons 3qtr, leading driver 18 tons 9cwt 3qtr, trailing driver 17tons, totalling 53 tons 10cwt 2qtr. The tender weighed 41tons 8cwt 3qtr giving a total weight of 94tons 19cwt 1qtr. The final engine of O/2798, No 859, was incidentally the last new engine turned out to carry the initials "MR" on the tender, for commencing with the first engine of the next order, No 860, the engine number was displayed in large gilt lettering on the sides of the tender, and in place of the brass numerals on the cab side appeared the Company's old coat of arms. The date plate was carried on the side frame below the smokebox as with the earlier engines.

A variation on the above theme was tried out on 2-4-0 139A as renumbered 64 in 1907. This carried the number on the tender side-panel between the letters "M" and "R" but this experimental form of numbering was not continued with.

Also in 1904, Deeley arranged for the delivery of two further batches of 0-6-0 goods tender engines which had been ordered in Johnson's time. These were Nos 255–64 built to O/2652 and Nos 265–74 built to O/2692, which were turned out of the shops between February and September, 1904. H-class boilers were fitted as built as with the previous two orders, with which they were almost identical. Only two further orders of this class were to be built the first being Nos 275–84 to O/2821 the first six being turned out in January and February, 1906, and the last four in December 1906 and January, 1907 (see Plate 71). The final order for 20 engines to O/3344 was filled between January and May, 1908, and since these were built after Deeley's great 1907 renumbering scheme to be described later, they took the numbers 3815–34. This last lot had a different boiler to the others, being built with a new H1 class, having 242 tubes of 1¾in diameter in vertical rows giving 1,222sq ft which with the firebox 125sq ft gave a total hs of 1,347sq ft. These all carried Johnson's characteristic "flowerpot" chimney.

One novel feature of the railway scene at this time was the building of the two steam-rail motor-coaches for the Morecambe and Heysham line, introduced largely at the instigation of David Bain who had come to Derby from the North Eastern Railway in 1902, in succession to T. G. Clayton, as Carriage and Wagon Superintendent. The coach work, 60ft long overall and divided into four sections, engine rooms, passenger and baggage compartments and a vestibule, was designed by Bain, the power unit, completely enclosed by the coach body, had a vertical multi-tube boiler operating at 160psi mounted on a 0-4-0 chassis, with 11in diameter outside cylinders of 15in stroke and Walschaerts valve gear built in the Locomotive Works. The driving wheels were 3ft 7½in diameter and they were turned out in June and July, 1904, to order 2741, being numbered M1 and M2, the carriage stock numbers being 2233 and 2234. Weight in working order was 36 tons.

These rail-motors went off to the Heysham line under their own steam and are recorded as having attained about 50mph maximum in service, being designed for a normal service speed of 30mph. In 1907 they were reboilered with loco-type boilers, and one remained in service until 1917, when No 2234 was converted into the General Superintendent's service car (*see Chapter 9*). Two steam motor-coaches were also constructed at Derby for the Northern Counties Committee of Northern Ireland (NCC) in 1905 to O/2915, the first of which was to be delivered to the NCC by June 1 of that year for use between Greenisland and Antrim (*see Plate 76*). The Midland Railway Company had purchased the former Belfast and Northern Counties Committee in 1903, and had changed its name to "Midland Railway" (Northern Counties Committee) hereafter referred to as NCC for short. Following this purchase a quite considerable number of locomotives was built at Derby right up until 1947, for this line.

These two steam motor-coaches were numbered 90 and 91 and had a J1 class boiler with shorter barrel and a firebox 3ft 7½in diameter × 3ft 7⅜in. The driving wheels were 3ft 7¼in diameter, the trailing 3ft 3in diameter and the carriage wheels 3ft 6in diameter. The outside cylinders were 9in diameter × 15in stroke at 6ft 5in centres. Boiler pressure was 160psi and the 139 brass tubes of 1¾in outside diameter provided 262sq ft of heating surface which, with the 51sq ft of firebox, totalled 313sq ft. Centres of wheels was 5ft 8in + 4ft 4in and trailing to leading carriage wheel 31ft 3½in. Centres of carriage bogie was 8ft and the length over buffers 60ft 5¼in. The tanks carried 500gal of water and there was bunker space for 11½cwt of coal. Accommodation was provided for six first-class passengers, 16 third-class non-smoking and 24 'smoking" third-class passengers.

These were however not the first order for the newly acquired line when delivered during May, 1905 for a group of four 4-4-0 two-cylinder compound tender locomotives Nos 63–6 was at the same time forwarded to the NCC having been ordered to O/2833 and O/2834 (tenders) in July, 1904 (*see Plate 75*). The driving wheels were 6ft diameter at 8ft 2in centres and the leading bogie, having wheels 3ft diameter at 6ft 6in centres, was centred 9ft 10in from the leading driving axle. The boiler, pitched 7ft 8½in from rail, carried 199 brass tubes 1⅞in od having 1,054sq ft heating surface, firebox 112sq ft, totalling 1,166sq ft. The two inside cylinders were 18in × 24in stroke (high pressure) and 26in diameter × 24in stroke (low pressure). Total wheelbase was 40ft 11in and length over buffers 49ft 7¾in. The old-fashioned-type tender with outside springs above footplate level carried 2,090gal of water and 6 tons of coal, and the working weight was 73 tons 15cwt 2qtr. The round topped boiler, pressed to 190psi had a barrel 4ft 3¾in diameter × 10ft 4¼in long.

The following year, 1905, saw the first of Deeley's modified compounds running, this being No 1000 turned out in October of that year, soon to be followed by the remainder of O/2889, Nos 1001–9, the last of which was put into service in the December. They were renumbered 1005–14 in 1907. These engines had a different look about them altogether, with the running plate raised slightly over the coupling rods and a larger cab which combined with it the curved rear splasher, whilst the cab roof extended backwards over the tender, a novel feature indeed. The new tender had high straight sides without coal rails and was on six wheels, (the need for bogie tenders having now disappeared) having capacity for 3,500gal of water and 7 tons of coal.

The most radical changes were in the mechanical parts however, for Deeley did away with the reinforcing valve, and also arranged for the compounding to be worked from the regulator. When this was opened partially hp steam was admitted to the auxiliary steam pipe through an auxiliary valve, thus supplying both lp and hp cylinders. Upon opening the regulator further the auxiliary valve was closed automatically and the engine began proper compound working. Also on these engines a larger firebox was provided having a grate area of 28.4sq ft and a heating surface of 152.8sq ft. The tubes added a further 1,305.5sq ft making a total heating surface of 1,458.3sq ft. Further the pressure was raised to 220psi, and this type of boiler was classified as a G9.

Working weights of the new locomotives were as follows: leading bogie 20 tons 14cwt, driving wheels 19 tons 15cwt, trailing wheels 19 tons 7cwt, totalling 59 tons 16cwt. The tender weighed 45 tons 18cwt 2qtr, giving a total engine and tender weight of 105 tons 14cwt 2qtr.

These first 10 Deeley compounds did excellent work, some being allocated to the London area where they were put to work on the expresses to Nottingham, Derby and Manchester, and some were allocated to work on the Scottish expresses.

In 1906 a further batch of 20 compounds were built to O/2998, being Nos 1010–29, (to be renumbered 1015–34 the following year), and these also differed somewhat from the earlier batch, having shallower front-end frames, an extended smokebox and an increase in overall length of 1½in, this difference being in the bogie wheel centres, which were increased from 6ft 6in to 6ft 7½in.

In 1906 arrangements were made for the sale of a batch of 50 Kirtley designed 0-6-0s to the Rete Mediterraneo Company of Italy to bolster up their failing and ailing stocks of motive power, the Midland locomotives being allocated Nos 3801–50. They lasted until about 1927, the first ones being withdrawn for breaking up in 1913.

This completes the list of locomotives built at Derby up to the end of 1906, and also makes a useful break for the following year Deeley drastically renumbered the entire locomotive stock of the Midland Railway. It must be admitted that over the years the list of locomotives had got very complicated, and it was extremely difficult to decide the type of locomotive from its number.

In Deeleys new list, where locomotives were grouped according to type, the 2-4-0 passenger locomotives were renumbered in the range 1 to 281 in order of building, followed by the 4-4-0 passenger engines, renumbered 300–562. The Johnson singles occupied Nos 600–694, and the large Belpaire 4-4-0s Nos 700–779. The first five compounds, formerly 2631–5, became 1000–1004 and the next 30 were renumbered from the range 1000–1029 to 1005–1034. The Beyer-Peacock 204 class 4-4-0Ts 204A and 205A became 1198–9, the Beyer Peacock WT became 1200–1205 (formerly 690A–95A) and the 780 class tanks became 1206–25. Johnson's 0-4-4 passenger tank engines took numbers 1226–1430 followed by the small yard shunting 0-4-0 tanks which became 1500–1527.

The few 0-6-0 WTs still extant took the numbers 1600–1604 followed by three 0-6-0 tank engines, formerly belonging to the Severn and Wye Railway, absorbed into Midland stock in October, 1895, which were renumbered from 1124A–6A to 1606–8. The Beyer Peacock 880 class of Kirtley's time became 1610–19 and were followed by the large group of Johnson's 0-6-0 side tank engines which became 1620–1959.

The large masses of 0-6-0 goods tender engines were renumbered 2300–2867 (Kirtley) and 2900–3814 (Johnson & Deeley). Interposed between this last group and the tank engines was the American 2-6-0 Moguls which became 2200–2239 the first 30 being those built by Burnham Williams.

Deeley had also introduced the smokebox door numberplate some two years earlier, which was a great improvement from both the shed staff's and the signalmen's point of view in identifying train locomotives for recording purposes. It was especially useful in the Midland roundhouses and sheds for the quick recording of details of locomotives in for repair, etc.

Further new locomotives were of course being turned out while the others were being renumbered and the first to emerge in March, 1907, was No 999, the forerunner of a class of 10 locomotives which Deeley had had designed in order to compare their performance with that of the compounds (*see Plate 73*). This first one was built to O/3139 and had a new type of boiler, a G9A, varying from the compound boiler only in the position of the boiler sludge hole, which had to be sited differently owing to the position of Deeleys valve gear and in its circular front tubeplate. Working pressure was 220psi and the boiler carried a total heating surface of 1,557.4sq ft, of which the 249 copper tubes of $1\frac{3}{4}$in diameter provided 1,404.6sq ft and the firebox 152.8sq ft. The grate area was 28.4sq ft and this engine was later to be fitted with Deeley's own design of superheater, made to O/3841, and based on the Swindon pattern, in May, 1911. It also had his own design of valve gear which dispensed with eccentrics entirely, the oscillation of the expansion link being derived from the opposing crossheads although the crosshead connection for lap and lead movement was like the Walschaerts gear. These two basic modifications regrettably rendered any fair comparison between this class and the compounds rather impracticable.

Other main dimensions were as follows: leading braked bogie wheels were 3ft 3½in diameter at 6ft 7½in centres: driving wheels 6ft 6½in at 9ft 6 1/32 in centres; the inside cylinders, later fitted with bye-pass valves following trials in 1911 with No 998 in an attempt to prevent big-end knock, were 19in diameter × 26in stroke, these being placed at 2ft centres. One other novel feature was the ball-and-socket joints provided in the gudgeon pins of the connecting-rod small-end. A standard tender of 3,500gal capacity was attached, having water pick-up gear fitted. Working weights were: engine 58 tons 10cwt 2qtr, tender 45 tons 18cwt 2qtr, totalling 104 tons 9cwt. As new this engine was allocated to Derby shed.

The rest of the class, Nos 990–98, built to O/3371, emerged two years later between April and October, 1909. These were of the same main dimensions and had the same type of boiler but set at the lower pressure of 200psi, to which 999 itself had been altered in April, 1907. No 998 was fitted with a Schmidt type superheater in May, 1910, to O/3649, and the remainder of the class so treated to O/3943 from 1912 onwards, the cylinders being enlarged to 20½in diameter. In trials between 998 (superheated) and 992 (saturated) on the London-Leeds route the average consumption of coal and water was 24.3lb per mile and 213lb per mile for the superheated engine and 31.2lb per mile and 270lb per mile respectively for the saturated one, showing a saving of 22per cent in coal and 21per cent in water consumption. Total monetary saving, when allowing for the fact that oil consumption went up by 75 per cent, was £58. 8s 11d per year.

One oddity was No 995 which carried steam reversing-gear between 1912 and September, 1922, and this engine also ran trials on the S&DJR in August and September, 1925, but was apparently not a success. The class was split equally between Kentish Town, Manchester and Leeds as new, later graduating to the Carlisle area.

In comparison with the compounds these engines were inferior performers, having a markedly higher coal consumption, and they had an early demise, being withdrawn between 1925 and 1928, one of the last two in service being the original 999 herself and the other 998. For details of runs see the *SLS Journal* for 1953 pages 288–9. Beginning in 1926 those engines surviving were renumbered in the series 800–809,

Nos 990 (800), and 994 (804) having already been scrapped, and strangely 992, although not broken up until March 25, 1928, was never given its new number 802.

Deeley obviously had many new ideas of his own as to the type of locomotive he felt was needed, and, concurrent with the building of 999, a new class of large 0-6-4 passenger tank engines was being erected in the Derby shops. These were to become nicknamed the "Flatirons" on account of their heavy and ponderous appearance, and they were brought out to take on some of the intensive local passenger work on the Midland system. Just about a year prior to the appearance of the first of these, No 2000, in April 1907, three standard 0-6-0 goods engines had been rebuilt with 6ft driving wheels, the largest fitted to a British locomotive of this wheel arrangement at this time. These were Nos 2049 (later 3326), 2056 (3333) and 2110 (3387) and they were provided with new frames, to O/2677B, and converted in June, September and July, 1906 respectively. The first two had already been rebuilt with H class boilers to O/2677, under which 575 0-6-0s were to be converted with this type. The boiler on these particular three was pitched 8ft ½in from rail and the height to the top of the flowerpot chimney was 13ft 3½in. These three large wheeled 0-6-0s were tried out on passenger trains, and from the results obtained the final form of Deeley's new tanks crystallised. Before this he had several alternative designs of large tank engines drawn out in diagram form for his perusal. Simple bogie tank engines of the 2-6-4, 4-4-4 and 4-6-2 wheel arrangements were looked at, and also two forms of 2-4-4-2 compound tank engines were drawn out, but all were turned down in favour of the 0-6-4 tanks. Twenty locomotives, Nos 2000–2019, were built to O/3187 and a further 20, Nos 2020–39 were constructed to O/3258, all being completed by the end of 1907 (see Plate 70).

The main dimensions were as follows: driving wheels 5ft 7in diameter placed at 8ft + 8ft 6in centres, and the bogie wheels 3ft 11in diameter at 6ft centres, the bogie being centred 9ft 6in behind the trailing driving axle. The inside cylinders were 18½in diameter having a stroke of 26in, and the boiler as built was the H1 class round-topped variety having a total heating surface of 1,347sq ft and working at 175psi, although all were later rebuilt with G7s superheated boilers having Belpaire firebox. The long side-tanks extended right to the end of the smokebox and held 2,250gal of water, most of the engines being provided with water pick-up apparatus and the bunker carried 3½tons of coal. Fully loaded the weights were as follows: leading 18 tons, driving 18 tons 10cwt, trailing 18 tons 12cwt 2qtr, bogie 20 tons 2cwt 3qtr, totalling 75 tons 11cwt 3qtr. With bogie-brake an extra 12cwt 1qtr was added to the bogie weights. The connecting rod small ends and the knuckle joints of the leading coupling rods were provided with spherical bearings to provide some angular freedom, and the leading axle was fitted with Cartazzi axleboxes slightly modified by Deeley, giving 1¼in side play. The trailing bogie was given 2¼in side play each side of the centre line.

Of the first batch Nos 2000–2004 went to Trafford Park and 2005–11 to Heaton Mersey, these not being fitted with the water pick-up gear. These engines were powerful, but became somewhat unsteady and oscillated at anything above moderate speed. When the Midland took over the London Tilbury and Southend Line in 1912, six of them, Nos 2004, 2011, 2013, 2024, 2034 and 2035, were fitted with Westinghouse brake equipment to O/4328 and sent to work on that line. They proved to be not as successful as the engines already working the traffic on that line, and were returned a few years later. Then under LMS ownership, two of the class suffered derailments with trains in a short space of time, and they were thereafter forbidden to work passenger trains bunker first. They were withdrawn from service between 1935 and 1937 after one had been modified by the addition of a Stanier bogie with side bolsters without much success. The troubles with the 0-6-4T also caused the abandonment of a proposal to built some 0-6-2 tank engines which were actually started in 1928, but which subsequently emerged as 2-6-2 tank engines.

The above two Deeley designs proved somewhat unsuccessful, but the other class which appeared, also in 1907, were an undoubted success. These were the five 0-4-0 outside cylindered side-tank locomotives, Nos 1528–32, built to O/3031 between August and December of that year. These were for shunting in works and colliery sidings and had 3ft 10in driving wheels on a 7ft 6in wheelbase and 15in diameter × 22in stroke outside cylinders, and were mainly the work of James Edward Anderson, who did the preliminary designs in 1905. He will be mentioned later but as the successor of J. W. Smith in the position of Chief Locomotive Draughtsman in August, 1906, when the latter accepted the position of Manager of the Great Central Railway Works at Gorton, Manchester.

These shunting locomotives were to last for many years, and were to be later joined by five of Johnsons older saddle-tanks which were "rebuilt" to this form with new frames, cylinders and motion and new boilers, becoming in fact almost new engines. This work was carried out during 1921 and 1922 to O/5528. These engines all had the J2 type of round-topped boiler working at 160psi and carrying 141 tubes of 1¾in giving 697sq ft of heating surface which with the firebox 64sq ft equalled a total of 761sq ft. The grate area was 10.5sq ft, and working weight with 650gal of water in the tanks and 10cwt of coal in the bunker was 32 tons 16cwt 1qtr. Two of these rather attractive locomotives were theoretically at least "sold out of service" to the Staveley Coal and Iron Co in December, 1923, and they did good work for that company for many years under the standing agreement with the Midland Company.

Mention should be made here of Deeley's scheme for classifying loco-motives according to their power as part of the newly introduced traffic control system. In Johnson's time a classification of locomotives had been arranged and although the class number did nothing to indicate loading ability, these numbers were used to indicate to depot staff the maximum loads which each class could take.

Deeley's system of classification originated with goods engines early in 1905, each engine carrying a classification number, from 1 to 4 in ascending order of power, displayed 2in below the engine number on the cab side. This system was later replaced by what was to become the standard system, where the small brass figure denoting the classifica-tion was mounted higher on the cab side, level with the centre of the top radius of the cab side-sheet look out. Goods engines were dealt with first and the passenger engines the following year.

The goods engines were classified as follows:

Class 1 All double-framed goods engines, *except* those with boilers set to
      160psi or more *and* No 2462 (18in × 24in cylinders and 150psi).
      Single-framed goods engines 3055 and 3092.
Class 2 All other 0-6-0s of both varieties except Class 3 below.
      The American 2-6-0s.
Class 3 0-6-0s 3765 onwards.

The passenger engines were classified as follows:

Class 1 All 2-4-0s.
      All 4-2-2s except 685–94.
      4-4-0s 300–27.
Class 2 All 4-4-0s 328–562, 4-2-2s 685–94
Class 3 All 4-4-0s 700–79.
Class 4 All 4-4-0s 990–1044.

All tank engines and the various miscellaneous locomotives not covered by the above were not classified at this time.

For the NCC the Derby Works had built four different types of boilers during 1905–7, including two spares for the two-cylinder com-pounds 63–6, and two boilers for the narrow gauge compounds. Then in 1907 order O/3385 for a further 2 two-cylinder compound 4-4-0s like Nos 63–6, was placed in October of that year. These were numbered 67 and 68.

For the S&DJR two further 4-4-0 passenger locomotives Nos 77 and
78, were built to O/3310 in 1907. These had 6ft driving wheels and
18in × 26in stroke inside cylinders, and were generally similar to Nos
69–71 mentioned earlier. The round-topped boilers carried uncased
Ramsbottom safety valves set to operate at 175psi. The leading bogie
wheels were 3ft 1in diameter at 6ft axle centres, and the driving wheels
at 8ft 6in centres carried loaded weights of 16 tons 11cwt 2qtr and
15 tons 6cwt 1qtr respectively. The leading bogie, centred 10ft ½in in
front of the leading driver, carried 15 tons 10cwt 2qtr. The 2,950gal
tender, with space for 3½ tons of coal, weighed 36 tons 13cwt 2qtr in
service order, total weight of engine and tender thus being 84 tons 1cwt
3qtr. As new they went to Bournemouth on the fast passenger train
workings through to Bath and back daily.

In 1908 the final Midland order for 4-4-0 compound locomotives was
placed. These were built to O/3410, bearing the numbers 1035–44, the
first, 1035, being completed in November, 1908, and the last of the
order in March of the following year. There were few variations between
these and the previous order completed in 1906, except in heating surfaces, that of the tubes being raised slightly to 1,320.2sq ft making the
total 1,473sq ft.

Following on the superheating of the 990 class, beginning in May,
1910, the Class 3 4-4-0s also began to be supplied with superheated
boilers beginning with 700 in September, 1913, as also did the Class 2
4-4-0s commencing in February, 1912 with No 494. (These are referred
to later in Chapter 12.) The rebuilding of the Class 3s involved the
fitting of larger cylinders, superheated boilers, new front end frames
for Nos 700–709 only, and Deeley pattern cabs. The first of the compounds to be superheated was 1040 which was rebuilt to O/4211 with an
old G9 boiler rebuilt in superheated form in July, 1913, and the whole
of the class were so treated between that date and January, 1928, when
the last No 1022 was dealt with.

While discussing the reboilering of locomotives a mention should here
be made of the various rebuildings undertaken with the 0-6-0 freight
tender engines. Shortly after the appearance of the later 0-6-0s with H
class boilers in 1903, the Derby Works embarked on a vast programme
for reboilering the small-boilered engines to Class 3 by fitting H class
boilers. Engines in the ranges 3130–89 and 3190–764 were the only
ones dealt with to O/2677A and O/2677 respectively. From 1905 new
frames were also fitted to some of these rebuilds, although if the old
frames were in good condition for adaptation they were retained.

Three orders for rebuilding Kirtley 0-6-0s should be mentioned, the
first issued being O/3007 of July 25, 1905 which provided for the reboilering of six of the old double-framed goods with H class boilers set

at 175psi and having 1,428sq ft of heating surface. These were Nos 2451, 2454, 2472, 2567, 2579 and 2589 rebuilt between July and October of that year. The second order was O/3335 of July 27, 1907, issued to cover the rebuilding of 20 of the same type of locomotive with second-hand D class boilers from stock. The range to be covered was 2844–63, but of these only the following were actually rebuilt: Nos 2846, 7, 9, 2852, 3, 8, 2861, 2 and 3. First to be done was 2862 in January, 1908 and the last of the nine 2847 in June, 1909. The last order for trial rebuilding was O/3336 to cover the 25 Kirtley 0-6-0s 2805–29 of which seven only were done. These were Nos 2806, 2813, 8, 9, 2821, 2 and 8 and were provided with second-hand E class boilers from stock. These attempts to improve the basic Kirtley 0-6-0 were obviously thought to be not worth the expense and no further engines were done.

All the engines rebuilt to O/3007 later had G6 boilers set to work at 160psi, as did all the engines with D boilers except 2861 and 2862 and four of the engines with the E class boilers, which reverted to B class boilers again, these being 2806, 2818–9 and 2828.

Mention can here be made of the odd items of work undertaken by the Derby shops at this time in addition to the normal building and rebuilding of locomotives. In 1892 the Midland had introduced carriage warming as part of the passenger amenities on the special carriages for the Manchester suburban services. Prior to this the foot warmer had been the only means of heating except on the Pullman cars which had had an oil-fired hot water heater. The Derby shops were therefore soon busy fitting the carriage warming equipment to those locomotives used on this particular type of train. The majority were fitted with a hot water heating system developed by Johnson and Clayton, and this work was continued for many years. Other systems, such as the PLM, were tried and in 1901, 15 engines were fitted with this type to O/2292, being Nos 167, 168, 169, 65–9, 208–9, 2213, 2215, 2599, 2600 and 64 and all of these, except 2215, were also fitted with automatic steam regulators.

The fitting of water scoops proceeded apace following the introduction of more water troughs on the Midland main lines.

During 1905 4-4-0 passenger engine 232 was fitted with J. T. Marshall's valve gear to O/2948 for trial purposes but the gear did not acquit itself well enough to merit an extension of the gear into other engines and was later removed.

At the end of the same year O/3053 was issued to cover alterations to four Midland and Great Northern Joint Railway 4-4-0 tank engines to enable them to work as Auto-cars with certain of the original Midland Pullman cars of 1874. Wire operated communication gear was fitted and the four were coupled as listed overleaf.

M&GN Tank Engine No	Pullman Car No
10	5
19	1
40	2
8	10

Engine 40 was later attached to Car No 10 and Car No 2 to Engine 8 then during 1906 all the engine numbers were altered to correspond with the car numbers. These engines were painted in MR crimson lake and the sets were put to use on the Hemel-Hempstead–Harpenden and Higham Ferrers–Wellingborough branches where they remained in use until 1912 and also on the Derby–Ripley and Derby–Wirksworth branches. All were sold to the Government in the first war after returning to their home territory. Three of the Midland's 0-4-4 passenger tanks were lent to the M&GN in exchange for these tanks, these being Nos 142–4. They were used on the then newly opened Mundesley & Cromer line, still retaining MR numbers and red livery but "M&GN" initials, in brass lettering, was fixed to the side tanks.

The new type of underhung live steam injectors were being fitted to a large number of engines from early in 1906 onwards, mainly under O/3087 and O/3088, the first covering Belpaire boilered engines of the 700 class and three of the compounds, and the latter order covering new and rebuilt passenger and goods engines with H class boilers.

One little known proposal of Deeley's was the scheme to rebuild Johnsons fine single wheelers as 4-4-0s with Belpaire boilers. The old leading bogie was to be retained as were the front part of the frames, but new rear-end frames were to be provided, the two being joined between the trailing bogie wheel and the leading driving wheel. The drawings for the frames were quite well advanced and two order numbers were issued in 1906, O/3128 to cover engines 2601–5 and 19–23, these to have 7ft diameter driving wheels; and O/3241 to cover engines 25–32, 1853 and 34, these to have 6ft 6in diameter driving wheels. Generally these engines would have closely resembled the 700 class 4-4-0s except for the position of the leading bogie which was centred 11ft 6in in front of the leading driving wheel. On smaller rebuilds the inside cylinders were to be the originals, 18½in diameter × 26in stroke, and the boiler pressure 200psi. Total wheelbase was 46ft 10½in, the driving wheels being at 9ft 6in centres, and the length over buffers 55ft 11⅜in, the original 3,250gal tenders being used again. Weights in working order were to be: bogie 18 tons 18cwt, driving 19 tons 3cwt and trailing 18 tons 15cwt, the total engine weighed 56 tons 16cwt, and tender 37 tons.

The larger engines, with the 7ft driving wheels and 19½in × 26in cylinders were on the same coupled wheelbase, the bogie placed 11ft 6in in front of the leading driver, having 3ft 3in diameter wheels at 6ft centres. Working pressure in both cases was 200psi, and the working weights were to be: bogie 18 tons 18cwt, leading driver 19 tons 12cwt, trailing driver 19 tons 7cwt. The original 4,000gal bogie tenders were to be fitted and total weights were to be engine 57 tons 17cwt, tender 50 tons 13cwt 3qtr. Length over buffers was to be 60ft 11¼in and total wheelbase 51ft 7½in. However, these rebuilds never took place, and the singles lasted generally until the 1920s, but had they been rebuilt we might well have seen some of these taken over by BR in 1948. The 990 class were coming along and further orders of compounds, and many of the other 4-4-0s were being rebuilt with Belpaire boilers so possibly the expense of this particular rebuilding programme was not thought justified, and the orders were cancelled in June 1912.

The class 2 4-4-0s were further rebuilt from 1909 onwards with either saturated or superheated G7 boilers to orders 3544A (Nos 328–57) and 3544B (358–77), and all except 20 of the remainder, Nos 378–562, were similarly rebuilt to further orders.

Perhaps the most interesting order at this time was O/2965 "One Rotary Valve for Mr Paget". This order was placed in April, 1905, while Paget was still the Works Manager working under Deeley. Paget had many revolutionary ideas of his own for he was the mechanical experimenter *par excellence*! After much experiment the design for a locomotive was evolved by Paget using his rotary valve this being viewed with displeasure and suspicion by Deeley who saw his authority circumvented by this son of the Midland chairman. This design was for a 4-6-0 passenger tender engine employing the rotary valve developed in the interim period up to 1907, and the draughtsman charged with most of the design work was James Clayton, a man whose talents have been very much underestimated, and to whom both Deeley and Johnson owed a great deal (*see Fig 2*).

He at first came to work privately for Paget in the autumn of 1904 in a small office near Derby station where he would be visited each evening for discussions on various points as the design progressed. Clayton came originally from the Albion Motor Co and was not taken on by the Midland until after the completion of the first designs.

In the design there were two sets of cylinder blocks provided, each consisting of a pair of opposed cylinders in each block with rotary valving. The middle pair of driving wheels was driven by the middle set of cylinders on the front block and the outside set of cylinders on the rear block. The leading and trailing axles were driven respectively by the outside set of cylinders of the front block and the inside set of cylinders of the rear block. The rotary valves had no lead; all liner ports opened to steam cut off 75 per cent stroke, three ports opened to steam at 59 per cent cut off, two ports at 42 per cent cut off and one only at 25½ per cent. The liner travelled a peripheral distance of 6⅞in to cut off completely with $\frac{7}{32}$in cover. In reversing the valve rotated through 117deg theoretically but 120deg was allowed to compensate for losses in the gearing (provided by David Brown & Sons of Huddersfield). The cylinders were 18in diameter and 12in stroke and, in order to accommodate these between the 1$\frac{1}{16}$in thick frame-plates, the latter were placed outside the driving wheels, with 5ft 6½in between them.

The special boiler all of which was above footplate level and had four safety valves set to 180psi, had a corrugated firebox of the marine type totally enclosed within the boiler barrel. This was developed further incidentally for use on a standard 0-6-0 goods locomotive with this type of firebox, drawn down by James Anderson in June, 1905, before he became the Chief Locomotive Draughtsman. Grate area was 150sq ft, by far the largest ever proposed on a Midland engine up to that time! The firebox carried 175sq ft of heating surface and the 212 steel Servé tubes, of 2¾in outside diameter and pitched at 3½in centres, provided a further 2,290sq ft of heating surface giving a grand total of 2,465sq ft.

The massive boiler barrel was 6ft 9in diameter outside at the front end and 6ft 10⅝in diameter at the firebox end. The corrugated firebox, with two fireholes, was 4ft 7¾in minimum inside diameter, and was made of $\frac{11}{16}$in thick steel plate with an 1$\frac{3}{16}$in thick copper back plate The boiler was pitched 8ft 4in above rail level and the height to top of chimney was 13ft 7in. The six driving wheels were 5ft 4in diameter at 8ft 3in + 8ft 3in centres and the leading bogie, carried on 3ft diameter wheels at 6ft 3in centres, was pivoted 8ft 5in in front of the leading driving wheel, giving a total wheelbase of 28ft ½in. Total length over buffers including special tender of 3,500gal capacity was 61ft 3in. A quadrant controlled reversing lever was provided to operate the gearing on the rotary sleeve-valves. In order to completely balance the motion all the solid forged crank-axles had four cranks, the outer cranks set at 180deg to the inside pair on the leading and trailing axles, and at 90deg to each other in order on the intermediate driving axle. Driving forces were carefully arranged to balance out on leading and trailing axles by the use of large open forks passing from the piston rod around the crank-axle on each side and ending in a guide respectively in front of and behind the leading and trailing axles. A connecting rod was then used between the guide pivot and the crank in question. These forks were placed about the two inside cranks on the leading axle and the two outside cranks on the trailing axle.

Unfortunately there is no known record of the weights of this proposed locomotive, but had it been built, and permitted to run by the

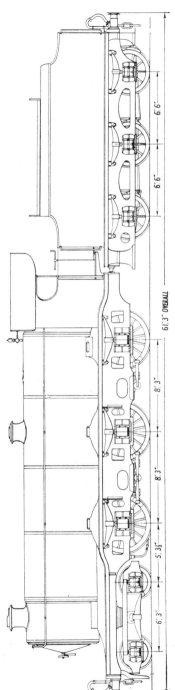

Fig 2 *Paget's proposed 4–6–0 tender engine, an alternative scheme to his 2–6–2 design, which was never built.*

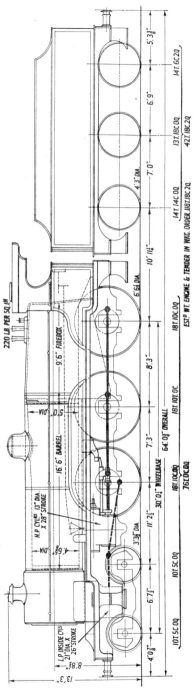

Fig 3 *Deeley's abortive scheme for a 4–6–0 4-cylinder compound express passenger locomotive.*
(Distance between trailing bogie wheel and leading driving wheel is given as 11' 2½". This should be from centre line of bogie pivot.)

Civil Engineers Dept, being persevered with through the inevitable teething stages, it would no doubt have revolutionised locomotive design and practice, and may even have eventually terminated the Midland's small engine policy which was often greatly criticised by those to whom the policy made no sense. Perhaps cost was a factor that figured largely in the decision not to proceed with this very unorthodox design, yet the rotary valve project was not dropped entirely for a further design was developed to replace the 4-6-0. This was a 2-6-2 tender engine, embodying the same revolutionary cylinder and sleeve valve designs, and which was actually built to O/3306, during 1908 (*see Plate 74*). The driving wheels were again 5ft 4in but the leading and trailing pony truck wheels were 3ft 3½in diameter. Total engine wheelbase was 31ft 4in divided as follows: leading truck to leading driver 7ft; leading driver to driving 8ft 8in, driving to trailing driver 8ft 8in, trailing driver to trailing pony truck 7ft. An unorthodox boiler was used having a firebox without water legs, but with a firebox furnace formed from 6in-thick firebricks for side and back walls with a 9in-thick crossbridge of firebrick at the front. The boiler had a heating surface of 1,948sq ft and firebox heating surface of 70sq ft, totalling 2,018sq ft. Grate area was 55¼sq ft. Working weights were as follows: leading pony truck 9 tons 10cwt, leading 18 tons 14cwt, driving 18 tons 8cwt, trailing 18 tons 12cwt, trailing pony truck 9 tons 6cwt, totalling 74 tons 10cwt. The tender built to O/3373 and having a 3,500gal tank and holding 7 tons coal, weighed 42 tons 18cwt 2qtr. The engine carried the number 2299.

That this locomotive design was proceeded with at all beyond the drawing board stage was made possible by the fact that Paget was promoted to the position of General Superintendent of the company in April, 1907 thus becoming Deeley's chief, whilst Henry Fowler stepped into his shoes, as Works Manager, the following month. One earlier appointment should be mentioned here, that of James Edward Anderson to the position of Chief Locomotive Draughtsman on August 20, the previous year at the princely salary of £300 per annum. Anderson had been taken on as a draughtsman on April 27, 1903 at £3. 15s 0d per week and so impressed Deeley that he became Chief Draughtsman when J. W. Smith left for the GCR, and was also left in charge of the Locomotive Works in the absence of Henry Fowler. Earlier he had applied for the position of Chief Locomotive Draughtsman on the GCR in February, 1906, but would not accept less than £450 per annum and therefore was not appointed.

Anderson served his apprenticeship on the Great North of Scotland Railway and later worked for both Messrs Sharp Stewart & Co and Messrs Dübs & Co before becoming a leading draughtsman in the

Glasgow and South Western Railway Company's design office. His last appointment before joining the Midland Company was with Messrs Robert Stephenson & Co Ltd of Darlington where he was assistant to the Chief Draughtsman. He therefore had a wide grounding in the arts of locomotive engineering and brought a lot of experience onto the Midland scene. He was awarded the CBE in March, 1920, for services rendered during World War I.

So now the stage was set for the battle of personalities about to commence. Anderson had become a kind of mediator, getting orders both from Deeley as Locomotive Superintendent and Paget as General Superintendent. The building of Paget's engine was largely financed by himself apart from the final £2,000, and construction proceeded apace in 1908, whilst Deeley was quietly fuming on the side lines, seeing valuable workshop capacity taken up by the manufacture of this engine, while his own brave scheme for a 4-6-0 four-cylinder compound engine remained dormant. Sandham Symes, then Anderson's assistant, sketched out the design for this particular engine in November, 1907, and, as schemed, it was a scaled up version of the 4-4-0 compound except for the introduction of 8¾in diameter piston valves for all cylinders, and outside valve gear for the low pressure cylinders. This locomotive merits a detailed description for it, too, would have revolutionised the Midland engine policy, had these large compounds been built, and proved as successful as their smaller sister engines. The driving wheels were to be 6ft 6½in diameter on a wheelbase of 7ft 3in + 8ft 3in. The leading bogie, centred 11ft 2½in in front of the leading driving wheel had 3ft 3½in diameter wheels on a 6ft 7½in wheelbase, total wheelbase being 30ft ¼in. The inside high pressure cylinders located above the trailing bogie wheel, were 13in diameter and 28in stroke at 2ft ctrs, and the outside low pressure cylinders were 21in diameter × 26in stroke at 7ft ctrs, driven by outside valve-gear piston valves centred between the bogie wheels.

The boiler set to work at 220psi, had a firebox 9ft 6in long at top of the ring, a 16ft 6in barrel of 4ft 6⅝in inside diameter on the front rings, the first ring being tapered from 5ft inside diameter. Heating surfaces were tubes 1,804.58sq ft, firebox 165.5sq ft, total 1,970.08sq ft and grate area was 30.1sq ft. Tractive power (or "effort") was 25,700lb or 11.471 tons, and adhesive power 33,688lb. (15.04 tons) with sanding. The boiler was pitched 8ft 8½in above rail level, and height to top of chimney 13ft 3in. Weights were bogie 20 tons 10cwt, leading driver 18 tons 10cwt, driving 18 tons 10cwt, trailing 18 tons 10cwt, totalling an estimated 76 tons in all, the tender weighing a further 42 tons 18cwt 2qtr, being the same as eventually fitted to the Paget locomotive. Total wheelbase was 54ft 8½in and length over buffers 64ft ¾in (see Fig 3).

But Deeleys *pièce de resistance* never was built while Paget's locomotive was completed in January, 1909, and made steaming trials soon afterwards. Immediately she struck a snag with the differential expansion taking place between the sleeve valves and their liners, which broke in consequence. On one occasion the speed of 82mph is said to have been reached, but this has never been officially confirmed. She worked several test trains down to London and up to Manchester, and on one occasion she seized up at Syston whilst being drawn clear of the curve upon which she had become stuck and the valve gear had to be disconnected before she could be dragged away. The cause of the seizure was working the pistons without steam which caused them to crack in several places.

Being financed by Paget himself, his pocket became strained by the cost of the various modificatons necessary to keep her running yet at this distance in time it seems a great pity that the money was not forthcoming to modify the sleeve valves which were the chief cause of all the trouble. Charles Taw, then the new Works Foreman in the No 9 erecting shop at Derby, insisted that if he was given time, and a little more money, he could get her working perfectly satisfactorily, but in the event the finances failed, and she was laid up in the paint shop under a tarpaulin sheet, a shrouded mysterious shape to visitors, until broken up finally in April, 1920 for scrap during one of Paget's many absences! A full account of this locomotive, written by James Clayton appeared in the *Railway Gazette* in 1945.

It was to Cecil Paget that the Midland Company owed a great debt for the introduction of his revolutionary scheme of train despatching. The coal traffic on the Midland lines had become a great hindrance to the operating people, for it is said that these coal trains frequently remained in loops alongside the main line for many hours, and in fact on a number of occasions the engine crew booked on and off duty without turning a wheel, waiting throughout their whole turn for the signal to proceed.

Following a visit to America by Paget to see their system in operation, he returned and backed up by his father, introduced the scheme of permissive block working. He eventually became the General Superintendent of the company on April 5, 1907.*

He was also responsible for introducing the premium apprentice system into the Derby Works, and furthermore he undertook a thorough re-organisation of the stores system for tools and equipment. One Easter holiday he began in the No 8 Erecting shop by organising a gang of labourers to clear out all the benches and cupboards of tools, not only belonging to the company but to the workmen also. These were laid

*BTHR Mid 15/101

out at the end of the shop, classified and put into the stores. His attitude when faced by inactivity was summed up by his words "Look here . . . if you don't carry out my wishes I've got a lot of power and I'll use it!"

Other changes evidenced Paget's advancement to General Superintendent. Over the years many piles of old papers had accumulated in various parts of the offices at Derby. These soon disappeared and the offices of not only the chiefs, but the heads of the various sections and the general staffs were redecorated, until with the more pleasing appearance of their surroundings there came a very noticeable decrease in the number of absences due to minor ailments. In fact, this was all part of a tidying up throughout the whole system, and this included tidying up the railborne traffic as well. Before the new train despatch system was instigated Paget lived for months in an inspection coach, parked suitably at the various congested spots, watching the working of traffic at these places and thereby formulating his remedy at first hand. In the coach kitchen he did his own cooking, and friends testified to his expertise in the culinary arts!

Deeley, as we have said had many pet schemes of his own, one of which has already been mentioned. Others were an eight-coupled goods engine having 4ft 7in coupled wheels with outside 20in diameter × 26in stroke cylinders and $10\frac{1}{4}$in diameter piston valves, weighing an estimated $61\frac{1}{2}$ tons (*see Fig 4*), 2-4-4-2 and 2-8-2 compound tank engines, 2-6-2 tank engines, a 0-6-2 shunting tank engine and a 2-6-4 bogie tank engine. Most of these were sketched out by Anderson before he became Chief Draughtsman and James Clayton, another member of the design staff already mentioned.

The eventual break between Deeley and the Midland Company has been the subject of many fanciful stories, not least the one concerning the alleged removal of the nameplate from Deeley's door by a workman in the chief's presence after which he is alleged to have stalked off over the latticed footbridge never to be seen again. Tales such as this abound in the lore of such places as the Derby Works. Some have a grain of truth and others are pure invention, the tale related above being most likely the latter.

In fact Deeley's departure was of a more amicable nature, although it must be admitted that the events previously related in this chapter had somewhat soured him. When called into the Director's meeting to be informed of the decision to dispense with the position of Locomotive Superintendent and to evolve two new posts covering his former duties: those of Chief Mechanical Engineer and Chief Motive Power Superintendent, Deeley offered his resignation informing the Directors that in his opinion with the creation of these two new posts, it would be better if two new men were appointed.

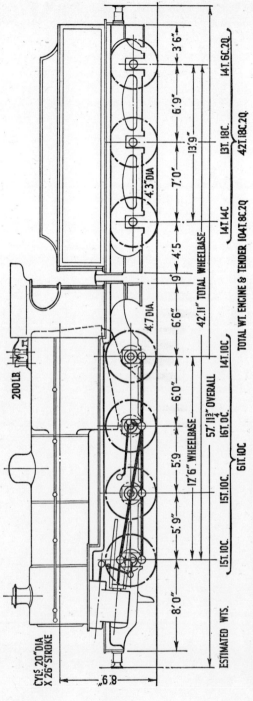

Fig 4 *Deeley's o–8–o mineral engine as proposed in 1907.*

After some discussion, Deeley's offer was accepted and the Midland Directors accorded him a handsome retirement pension for the rest of his life. He fully recognised the serious position that the Midland traffic had got into which clearly merited splitting the appointment. Thus Deeley resigned from the service of the Midland Company on August 13, 1909,* and devoted the rest of his life to science becoming involved first of all in a study of lubricants. In his 80th year he published a treatise on meteorology, a subject in which he had been greatly interested for a number of years. This was in 1935, and six years later he published a family history of the Deeley family. He died on June 19, 1944, aged 90.

*BTHR Mid 15/101

K

CHAPTER TWELVE

Fowler and Anderson

(1910-1922)

WITH THE DEPARTURE of Deeley, the stage was set for Henry Fowler to make his entrance. In January, 1910, he was promoted from Works Manager to become the first (and incidentally the last) CME the Midland had. James Anderson (*see Plate 37*) was given the position of Works Assistant (formerly known as Works Manager) in addition to his duties of Chief Locomotive Draughtsman, and he served in both capacities until the last day of July, 1913, when S. J. Symes was promoted to Chief Draughtsman in his place. These three were to continue in office until the formation of the London Midland and Scottish Railway in 1923, but that is far ahead in our story.

Sandham John Symes was born on February 25, 1877 and served his apprenticeship at the Inchicore Works of the Great Southern and Western Railway Company in Dublin. In February, 1894 he became an apprentice draughtsman and early in 1903 was put in charge of the erection of new engines in the works.

It is recorded that he was "painstaking and reliable" and his work was "always done in most accurate manner". He left to gain further experience with the North British Locomotive Co at their Atlas Works in Glasgow where he was a draughtsman for five months up until the time he left to join the Midland Company. This firm too recorded a similar tribute to his painstaking care. He joined the Midland Company as a draughtsman on January 4, 1904, and was appointed to the salary list at £145 per annum in March the following year (*see Plate 38*).

One disappointed party in all this was James Clayton who, along with Symes, had been one of the two chief assistants to Anderson and, in consequence of his greater experience and longer service, he had expected to become the new Chief Locomotive Draughtsman. He was one of those rare genuine nice fellows who would never attempt to advertise himself in order to gain recognition and possible promotion from his chief, and because of this, no doubt, Symes, who was a more forceful personality perhaps, was given the post.

Following Symes appointment, Clayton left the Midland Company after completing work on the S&DJR 2-8-0s and went to work for the SE&CR in March, 1914, as their Chief Draughtsman at Ashford. One of Clayton's protégés, Herbert Chambers, was however later to make his mark in the pages of our story as will be recounted in due course.

A brief biographical note on the new CME, Henry Fowler, may be of interest at this point. He was born at Evesham in Worcestershire in 1870 and finished his education at Mason's College, Birmingham, between 1885 and 1887. As previously recounted he left the L&Y to join the Midland in 1900 as gas and experimental engineer in which position he continued until his appointment as Works Manager in 1910. Henry Fowler was a strict teetotaller, extremely energetic being involved in football, cricket and hockey. He could keep goal or wicket with equal facility. In his spare time he devoted much of his time to the Boy Scout movement, being also keen on cycling and the collection of coins and medals. So far as his employment is concerned, he was extremely particular about boilers and fireboxes, being happy if he could put on a boiler suit and tinker about. He was easily irritated, but this did not last for long, and his usual reply when faced as he was on one occasion by an estimate of six months for a new cylinder pattern was "I want it in three". And that was the end of the discussion.

His tours of the Derby Works, while the manager there, were usually made by bicycle, he being easily recognisable in his strawyard hat. He would ride around the shops inside and out and if he chanced upon someone committing a misdemeanour he would remonstrate with him and then instruct the offender to "clock off" and come back on the morrow, punishment indeed in those days of small wages!

One particular morning tour is well remembered for on this occasion, as he rode into the machine shop, his front wheel became jammed in the crane lines throwing him off the machine. The amusement of the workmen was hard to suppress, but, picking himself up, Fowler brushed himself down and continued his tour, but at a more leisurely pace!

In later years he was closely connected with St Andrew's Church, in particular with the bellringers, a favoured appointment for the few. An invitation to one of his Sunday afternoon tea parties also became a mark of approbation, assuring the guests of his interest in their future.

For his services with the Ministry of Munitions during World War I he was given the CBE in 1917 and was knighted in January the following year, His Majesty the King bestowing both awards personally.

Henry Fowler became Director of Production at the Ministry of Munitions in June, 1915 and was then appointed Superintendent of the Royal Aircraft Factory, South Farnborough in September of the following year, being further promoted as Assistant Director of Aircraft Production in January, 1918. He returned to the Midland Company on May 31, 1919 at a much enhanced salary of £3,000 per annum advanced a year later to £3,500 per annum.

To Fowler partly belongs the credit along with Mr Dalziel, for the introduction of electricity into the Derby Works, for in May, 1910, O/3716 was issued for the construction of the new electric power station which was erected adjacent to the tube shop, but on the other side of the Derby Canal.

The specifications for the station were drawn up by Dalziel under Fowler's overall guidance and provided for an installed capacity of about 3,000kW, the normal load when first opened being 1,900kW. A connecting bridge over the canal carried the coal conveyor belt having a capacity of 15 tons per hour. Two turbo-generators of the disc and drum type running at 3,000rpm were provided, each of 1,250kW capacity. The air-cooled generators themselves were of the revolving field type, two pole, 50 cycles, 460V, three phase. Three 400kVA transformers raised the line pressure from 460V to 6,600V for transmission to the carriage and wagon works. For the locomotive works cranes and auxiliary power station supply two 150kW rotary converters were used for a 440V dc supply.

Steam was supplied by three Stirling superheated boilers set at 170psi with an evaporation rate of 20,600lb per hour each with feed at 80degF. These were of the five-drum type with three steam and two mud drums. Heating surface was 6,021sq ft and grate area 109sq ft.

The main cables to the various shops ran overhead on the walls and in and on the roofs of the shops, all being suitably boxed in, all being provided to O/3729 issued on June 8, 1910.

Apart from the electrical machines and conveyors the majority of the other plant was manufactured in the Derby Works, the whole installation being superintended by Mr Dalziel, Fowler's electrical assistant.

To prepare for the use of electricity in the works a large batch of orders, Nos 3730–52, were issued also on June 8, 1910, for the electrification of shop-plant and the installation of electric lighting in the various shops and offices to replace the gas type, which had been in use since the works were first erected.

The basic reasons behind this move to electrification were all economic. The existing steam engine plant was inadequate and a number of the boilers would soon require replacement, and in addition the cost of coal, wages and boiler repairs for the Locomotive, Carriage & Wagon and General Stores Superintendent's Departments was £20,000 per annum.

What electric power was required before the works power station would be completed and in action, could be obtained from Ilkeston via the Nottinghamshire Electric Power Company at a little over ½d per unit, thus making a saving of £7,000 per annum.

The first move was to electrify the cranes, by this time too slow in

action, followed by the motorising of shafting to reduce the existing
excessive load on the main engines. Two 50-ton capacity electric cranes
were ordered for the erecting shop from Cowans Sheldon & Co at
£985 each, the third overhead crane in No 1 bay being electrified at a
cost of £320.

Turning to locomotive matters once again, more experiments took
place with valve gears durring 1910–11, two engines 382 and 387 being
fitted with Isaacson's and MR modified Stephenson's respectively for
comparison purposes with 379 with the standard gear.

The standard valve-gear showed up best in coal consumption figures
at 34.8lb per mile compared with 35.0 and 35.3lb per mile respectively
for the Isaacsons and the modified gears, although water consumption
was slightly higher.

One interesting design prepared in September, 1910, was for an
inside-cylindered 2-6-0 tender engine with 5ft 3in driving wheels, 20in
× 26in cylinders and a G7s boiler working at 160psi. Total engine
wheelbase, with standard driving wheel spacing, was to be 22ft 9in and
working weights were: engine 54 tons 10cwt, tender 42 tons 18cwt
2qtr (full), totalling 97 tons 8cwt 3qtr.

However this was yet another proposal which never saw the light of
day for following the appointment of Henry Fowler. a very lax period
for new construction in the Derby Works ensued, and from 1910 to May,
1917 only two locomotives were built there for the Midland in 1911,
plus two for the NCC and six for the S&DJR in 1914.

The new Midland engines were a further development of the standard 0-6-0 goods tender engine, being the first to carry what was to
become the standard Midland G7s type superheated boiler. No 3835
emerged from the works in October, 1911 built to Derby O/4000, and
3836 in November, 1911 to O/4001 (see Plate 78). The chief difference
between these was in the superheaters which was of the Schmidt type
with Midland type element fixing on 3835 and of the Swindon double-
pass type on the other. One other difference was in the inside cylinders
the former having 20in × 26in and the latter 19in × 26in. Piston valves
were fitted having inside admission operated by Stephenson link
motion through rocking shafts. The standard wheelbase was again
used, the driving wheels being 5ft 3in diameter. On 3835 the G7s
boiler, set at 160psi, but later raised to 175psi in May, 1917, carried
148 tubes of 1⅝in diameter and 21 tubes of 5¼in diameter which, with
the 21 element superheater and the firebox heating surface of 125sq ft
gave a total of 1,483sq ft. Weights in working order were: engine 49
tons 2 cwt; 2,950gal tenders, ex-4-4-0s 386 and 388, with 4 tons coal
capacity, 39 tons 2qtr, totalling 88 tons 2cwt 2qtr.

These engines were originally fitted with steam reversing gear, but this was later removed in 1922. As built they went to Saltley shed and were employed on both freight and passenger duties for a trial period. The extensive building programme undertaken for this type starting in 1917, will be described later. Between June 24 and August 2, 1912, these two prototypes were employed on an extensive series of coal and water consumption tests alongside two of the saturated engines Nos 3817 and 3818, on the route from Toton to Brent via Syston and Melton.

Trains of loaded wagons equal to 600 tons were worked from the Toton end and 50 or 100 empty wagon-trains worked back. On trial the joints between the superheater elements and the header on both engines were a source of trouble, and 3836 steamed badly on its fourth trip, it also having been provided with new valves and liners after the second trip.

From the results 3835 came out best and was used as the standard performer. On the last two up trips she consumed .0632lb of coal per ton mile compared with .0658 for 3836 and .0756 for the saturated engines. Water consumption was also better at .554lb per ton mile compared with .590 and .691 respectively. These figures indicate increases of 4·12 per cent and 19.6 per cent on coal consumption and 6.5 per cent and 24.7 per cent on water consumption, considerable savings.

For the Northern Counties Committee two further U class superheated 4-4-0 two-cylinder locomotives, Nos 69 and 70 were built to O/4369 (engines) and O/4370 (tenders). These had 6ft diameter driving wheels at 8ft 2in centres and a leading bogie on 3ft diameter wheels at 6ft 6in centres pivoted 9ft 10in in front of the leading driving wheel. The inside cylinders were 19in diameter × 24in stroke and were driven by 8in diameter piston valves operated through inside Walschaerts valve gear. The boiler pressed to 170psi, had a barrel 10ft 4¼in long and the firebox was 5ft 4in long. It carried a heating surface of: tubes 876.0sq ft, superheater elements 275sq ft, firebox 110.5sq ft, totalling 1,261.5sq ft. Grate area was 18.0sq ft.

Actual weights in working order were as follows: bogie 16 tons 16cwt, driving 16 tons, trailing 15 tons, totalling 47 tons 16cwt. The 2,090gal tender with coal rails and space for 6 tons of coal, weighed a further 27 tons 16cwt (with 3 tons 5cwt of coal on board). Total wheelbase was 40ft 11in and length over buffers 49ft 7¾in.

Also in February, 1914, appeared the first of a new type of mineral tender locomotive with a 2-8-0 wheel arrangement, designed largely by James Clayton for the S&DJR for working freight trains over the Mendips with their harsh ruling gradients (*see Plate 80*). These were the largest size of locomotive ever built by the Midland (with the exceptions only of the "Lickey Banker" and Paget's experimental engine). Unique for the MR at this time was the use of outside cylinders on a goods locomotive and these were 21in diameter × 28 in stroke at 6ft 8in centres. Outside admission short travel piston valves, 10in diameter with a lap of ⅞in and having ⅛in inside clearance, were provided, operated by Walshaerts valve gear. The 4ft 7½in diameter driving wheels on a wheelbase of 17ft 6in, were spaced at 6ft + 5ft 6in + 6ft centres and the leading pony truck, with 3ft 3½in diameter wheels, was placed 8ft 3in in front of leading driving axle. A G9AS compound type boiler, set to work at 190psi by two Ramsbottom safety valves, and having a circular front tube plate carried a total heating surface of 1,618.75sq ft, of which the 148 solid drawn tubes of 1¾in outside diameter provided 1,180sq ft, the 21 superheater tubes of the Schmidt pattern 290.75sq ft, and the firebox 147.25sq ft. The grate area was 28.4sq ft and the boiler was pitched 8ft 10in above rail level. The boiler barrel was 4ft 7⅞in outside diameter and 11ft 11in long, the distance between tubeplates being 12ft 3¾in. As built all the wheels, including the pony truck, were braked, and steam operated reversing gear was originally fitted although this was later replaced by the screw type. The six wheeled 3,500 gal tenders, with space for 7 tons of coal, were provided with tender cabs for the protection of the driver and fireman, since it was not possible to turn them at Bath until a longer turntable was provided in 1934. It was unfortunate that the chimney cap, dome cover and cab ventilator fouled the roof of the engine shed at Radstock and the engine had to be modified to clear this obstruction. In all six of these engines were built to O/4209 between February and August, 1914, the tenders being built to O/4210, and the locomotives were numbered 80–85.

It is of interest to note that a heavier locomotive for S&DJR mineral traffic had been proposed as early as March, 1907, when two preliminary designs for outside cylindered 0-8-0 tender engines weighing respectively 61½ and 59½ tons in working order, had been drawn up. The general appearance of these designs was very much like the eventual 2-8-0 just described, although with regard to the working weight of the latter, whilst being some 10cwt heavier in all, the leading pony truck carried 8 tons 14cwt 2qtr, thus reducing the driving axleloads to 12 tons 18cwt, 13 tons 16cwt, 15 tons 16cwt and 13 tons 15cwt 2qtr respectively as against the heavier weights for the 0-8-0s. Outside cylinders were to have been 20in × 28in and 19½in × 26in respectively. Standard Midland details were used throughout including the somewhat undersized Class 4F axleboxes.

As an interesting footnote, this basic design of 2-8-0 tender locomotive was re-hashed for consideration as a goods engine for the Midland in July, 1920, but with a maximum axle weight of 17 tons plus, the design was not submitted to the Civil Engineer on account of the excess weight.

One other locomotive was turned out in September, 1914, the only one to be designed in the General Drawing Office since the arrival of Billinton as the first Chief Locomotive Draughtsman, and this was the four wheel battery-electric locomotive No 1550, constructed for work at the West India Docks to O/4301 of July, 1913.

It was constructed on a modified wagon under-frame on an 8ft wheelbase, the main structure being angle iron and wood, and was powered by two Dick Kerr nose-suspended electric traction motors of 22hp each, driven by a dp battery consisting of 108 cells of the 21 plate tl type with a capacity of 300 ampere hours.

Wheels, axles and drawgear were basically of the standard wagon type, and the rated capacity of the locomotive was six loaded wagons drawn at about 7mph. Control was by the series-parallel method and rheostatic braking was provided operated from the main controller. Length over buffers was 19ft 11¼in.

Access to the yard where the locomotive was to work was by means of a hydraulic lift which precluded the use of steam, and No 1550 performed its task with very few failures for over 50 years, being re-numbered BEL1 by BR, and it was finally withdrawn from service in July, 1964, and sold the following November to Messrs A. King & Sons of Norwich.

Somewhat of a compensation for the lack of new orders for the shops were the various schemes for rebuilding existing locomotives. The biggest order by far was the rebuilding of the 483 Class 2 4-4-0s with new frames and cylinders, and G7 boilers with Schmidt superheaters. In fact when rebuilding was complete, what was virtually a new engine emerged from the shops, and the first one so treated was 494 (ex-153) in February, 1912, "rebuilt" to O/3942 of June, 1911. In all 157 Midland engines and five S&DJR engines were so rebuilt as follows:

Quantity	Order	Date	No Range
40	O/3942*	June 21, 1911	483–522
40	O/4116†	July 29, 1912	523–62
25	O/4311*	July 31, 1913	403–27
2	O/4337*	October 15, 1913	S&DJR 70 & 71
32	O/4476*	April 22, 1914	428–82 + S&DJR 67–9
20	O/5664* (superseding O/4476)	January 9, 1922	328–482

*With 3,250gal tender   †With 3,500gal tender

Standard dimensions, apart from the tenders, were as follows:

Driving wheels 7ft ½in diameter at 9ft 6in centres, bogie 3ft 6½in diameter wheels on a 6ft wheelbase and centred 10ft 2½in in front of the leading driving wheel, making a total wheelbase of 22ft 8½in. The G7s boiler, to dimensions in Appendix III, carried 148 small tubes of 1¾in diameter and 21 large tubes of 5⅛in diameter carrying 21 superheater tubes, giving a heating surface of 1,045sq ft + 313sq ft of superheating surface and 125sq ft of firebox heating surface and making a total of 1,483sq ft. Grate area was 21.1sq ft. Weights in working order were: bogie 18 tons 18cwt 2qtr, driving 17 tons 10cwt, trailing coupled 16 tons 19cwt 1qtr. The total engine weighed 53 tons 7cwt 3qtr. The tender weight varied from 39 tons 16cwt 3qtr for 3,250gal type and 41 tons 4cwt for the 3,500gal type.

Mention of the other orders for the rebuilding, superheating etc of other classes has already been made in the previous chapter, and this work no doubt kept the shops functioning at a reasonably economic level over this period of few new work orders.

Apart from new locomotives, the Derby Works were supplying new cylinders and boilers to the Highbridge (S&DJR), Melton Constable (M&GNJR) and Belfast (NCC) Works for rebuilding the locomotives of these particular railways for which the Midland was responsible.

At the same time Fowler was continuing Deeley's policy of rebuilding the various types already in existence, usually at the expense of Johnson's graceful lines. His chief additional feature was the introduction of bogie brakes, the cylinders having opposing pistons, on a larger proportion of locomotives, whilst his predecessor had only fitted them to the 990 class simple and compound express engines and the Johnson 0-4-0 ST engines between the coupled wheels. These bogie brakes remained until the advent of Stanier who had them all taken off in view of the strain they imposed on the bogie pivot and the thought that braking would affect the ability of the truck to properly guide the locomotive.

Tender cabs also began to appear in great numbers prompted not only by the desire to protect enginemen but by the blackout imposed in 1914 at the commencement of World War I.

Somewhat before that however, the London, Tilbury & Southend Railway became absorbed into the Midland system on January 1, 1912, and the Derby Works felt immediate effects from this. They had had quite a strong locomotive policy of their own under the Locomotive Superintendent Robert Harben Whitelegg, but control of locomotive power passed to Fowler in August, 1912. Many engines were reboilered and quite a number, in run down condition, were shopped immediately. All the boilers were numbered in sequence as fitted to the engines at that time. In time they were supplied with various standard fittings and became somewhat Midlandised.

Following this amalgamation the old LT&SR apple green livery disappeared gradually as the standard Midland crimson lake was applied as and when repainting became necessary.

During World War I (1914–18) the Derby Works played an important role in the munitions field. One shop in the works, staffed by girls, was responsible for the renovation of 18-pounder used brass cartridge cases which were afterwards refilled and used again, one coming in no less than five times. Weekly output was 130,000 and in all over 7m were treated.

Other work included the manufacture of 6in and 8in Howitzer cradles, limbers and carriages, fuse parts, cradle bodies for 60-pounders, axletrees, stampings and castings of all kinds, flanged plates for guns, bomb cases, breech bolts, gun jacket forgings, loading derricks, dray lamps, acetylene flare lamps, and special machinery for the Railway Transport Expeditionary Force. Work was also done for other companies including ten locomotive boilers to O/5237 of September, 1919, for the LB&SCR. These were untubed and unmounted.

Towards the end of the war some work was also done for the infant Royal Air Force at Farnborough, including forged fly wheels, the machining of aluminium high compression pistons and the original engine test beds for Rolls Royce Ltd of Derby, which were machined in the works.

After the cessation of hostilities one of the 6in Howitzers, incorporating a Derby made cradle and carriage, was placed on show in the works yard alongside the 7ft 9½in diameter driving wheels from *Princess of Wales*.

During 1917 81 Kirtley 0-6-0 goods tender engines, Nos 2707–11 and 2713–88, were loaned to the Railway Operating Division for use in the war in France and Flanders, of which 61 went overseas in May, nine in August and eight in November. The remaining three, Nos 2783, 2784 and 2785 went to work on the London and South Western Railway, the first two being allocated to Eastleigh, and the last to Salisbury. They remained at work on that line until February, 1920, when they were returned to service on the Midland.

One of those goods engines sent overseas, No 2717, was captured by the Germans on November 30, 1917, whilst on the Peronne–Cambrai line, and it was used as an enemy machine gun post among other duties, receiving the number 01251. It was repossessed in November, 1918, by Colonel McMurdie and Colonel Speir, of 13th CRT.

Only one of those sent overseas was not put back into service again after the Armistice, this being No 2765 which was broken up in December, 1920.

As mentioned previously there was rather a lull in locomotive building at Derby between 1910 and the end of 1916, during which only 12 new engines were turned out, but in May, 1917, the first of a new batch of the Class 4F 0-6-0 goods tender engines No 3837, emerged from the works. This had 20in diameter × 26in stroke cylinders as built and the G7s boiler carried 175psi working pressure. Fifteen were built to O/4991 during the rest of 1917 and further orders were fulfilled up to the end of the Midland period as follows:

Order	Eng. Nos	Year Built
O/5064	3852–61	1918
O/5127	3862–71	1918
O/5168	3872–86	1918–19
O/5233	3887–3901	1919
O/5308	3902–16	1920
O/5335	3917–36	1920–1
O/5469	3987–4006	1921
O/5530	4007–26	1921–2

It will be noticed that Nos 3937–86 are missing. These were built by Sir W. G. Armstrong Whitworth & Co to O/5432 during 1921–2. Although these engines suffered from a poor front end design and undersized axlebox bearings they were later to become a standard design for the LMS.

Of the above many of the earlier engines had second-hand tenders off the American Schenectady 2-6-0 goods engines or 2-4-0 and 4-2-2 passenger engines, but new 3,500gal tenders were fitted to engines 3877 onwards.

It is worthwhile recording that in 1917 the Midland Railway had 1,495 0-6-0 goods tender engines, 21 per cent of the total for the whole country and representing almost 50 per cent of the whole of the company's locomotive stock. The nearest rival to this figure was the North Eastern Railway with 777.

Also in 1917 the first of the Johnson 0-6-0s in the series 2900–3019 began to receive G6 Belpaire boilers mounted on either the original frames or on new frames provided in the period from 1909, and between 1917 and 1928, 113 engines were rebuilt thus 68 having new frames. In addition 97 engines from the range 3020–3129 were rebuilt with G6 boilers, 27 also having new frames.

The other class of 0-6-0s of the series 3190–3764 were also re-boilered starting in 1916, with a Belpaire version of the H boiler classified G7. some engines were rebuilt directly from B boilers and others from H type boilers, but all had new frames unless previously provided with them. In December, 1925, this rebuilding ceased.

One additional rebuilding scheme involved the fitting of three of

Deeley's Class 3 0-6-0 goods tender engines with G7s superheated boilers to O/5774 of July 31, 1922. Engines 3792, 3806 and 3828 were also converted in January, 1923, but the experiment was short lived and all three had been restored to their original unsuperheated form by June, 1929.

Only two other classes were built for the Midland before the 1923 amalgamation, and the first to be described is the famous "Lickey Banker" or "Big Bertha" as she was known in the shops. Designs for a special type of locomotive to do the banking work up the 1 in 37.7 between Bromsgrove and Blackwell had been prepared as early as March, 1911, and some very interesting proposals were put forward, a few of which will be here described.

Proposal 1 was for a 2-10-0 side tank locomotive with 4ft 7in driving wheels, 3ft 3½in diameter leading pony truck wheels, outside cylinders 21in diameter × 26in stroke at 6ft 9in centres, driven by piston valves and driving onto the middle pair of driving wheels. A special two ring tapered boiler, working at 200psi, with the dome on the first ring, was to be fitted having a heating surface of 1,393sq ft (tubes) +130sq ft (firebox), and with 25sq ft of grate area. Total weight working with 1,500gal side tanks full and 3 ton rear bunker full of coal was to be 90½ tons with the maximum load of 17½ tons coming on the centre driver.

Proposal 2, and perhaps the most interesting, was for an articulated 2-6-6-2 tank engine. The two pairs of horizontal outside cylinders, 18in diameter × 26in stroke, were placed between the pony truck and leading driving wheel and were arranged to drive the trailing axle. The driving wheels were 4ft 7in diameter at 5ft 6in centres and the leading pony truck was centred 8ft 3in in front of the leading driver, having 3ft 3½in diameter wheels. The distance between the trailing driving wheels on each truck was to be 12ft 9in, giving a total wheelbase of 51ft 3in (*see Fig 5*).

A special superheated boiler, pitched 8ft 9in from rail and having a 10ft 3in long firebox and a 13ft long barrel of 4ft 8in diameter, was set to work at 170psi and the heating surfaces were to be tubes: 1,393sq ft, firebox 162sq ft, total 1,555sq ft, grate area 32sq ft. Total weight was to be about 122 tons with a maximum of 17 tons 18cwt on the trailing driven axle and 8½ tons on each pony truck.

Proposal 3 was for a rigid framed 0-6-6-0 tank engine with coal space and water space for 1,000gal placed behind the cab. The total wheelbase was to be 25ft 11¼in equally divided and two sets of 16in diameter × 26in stroke inclined cylinders, front and rear, were provided, at 6ft 9½in centres and driving onto the third set of driving wheels. The superheated boiler, set to work at 170psi, had an 8ft firebox and a barrel 11ft 11in long and 4 ft 8in diameter. The tubes were to provide 1,393sq ft

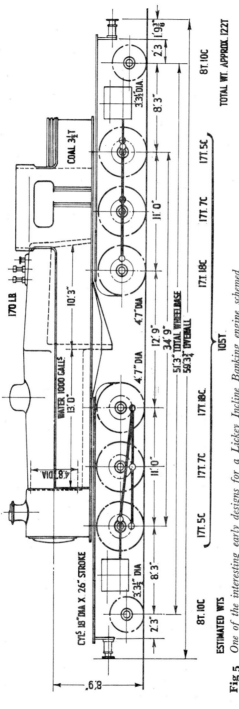

Fig 5 One of the interesting early designs for a Lickey Incline Banking engine schemed during Fowler's time as CME in 1911.

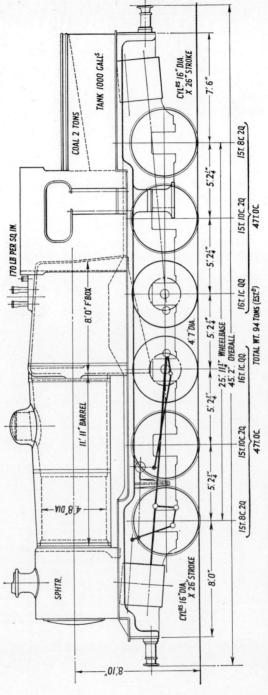

Fig 6 *A further scheme for a Lickey Banker with superheated tapered boiler, two pairs of cylinders and flangeless driving wheels.*

of heating surface and the firebox 130sq ft, giving a total of 1,523sq ft, and the grate area was 25sq ft. Leading and trailing axleboxes were of the Cartazzi type allowing a total side play of 1¼in for a 6 chain curve. Estimated weight in working order was to be 94 tons with a maximum 16 tons 1cwt on the inside driving wheels (*see Fig 6*).

Proposal 4 drawn in February, 1912, provided the basic design for the engine actually built for this work almost eight years later. On December 29, 1919, No 2290 made its bow to the public, being the one and only "Decapod" tender engine in Britain at that time (*see Plate 82*). The order, O/4482, was placed on May 13, 1914, but owing to the war, the work was not completed until 1919.

Four-cylinders, two inside and two outside, being 16¾in diameter × 28in stroke, were provided all driving onto the centre pair of wheels, with two sets of Walschaerts valve gear driving a pair of 10in diameter piston valves having a ⅞in lap, mounted one on top of each outside cylinder, these being inclined at an angle of 1 in 7. The five pairs of 4ft 7½in diameter driving wheels were on a 20ft 11in fixed wheelbase equally divided. The special superheated boiler, No 4886, was classified G10s, having a firebox 10ft long outside, and a barrel 14ft long and 5ft 3in outside diameter. The distance between tubeplates was 14ft 4¾in and the 147 1⅞in diameter solid drawn steel tubes and 27 5⅜in od superheater tubes provided 1,560sq ft whilst the 27 sets of superheater elements provided 445sq ft of heating surface respectively. The firebox added a further 158.25sq ft making a total of 2,163.25sq ft, and the grate area was 31.5sq ft. The four safety valves were set to operate at 180psi. Total wheelbase was 46ft 3¾in and overall length, including six wheeled 2,050gal tender on 2,350gal tender frame, with space for 4 tons of coal and having a tender cab like the S&DJR 2-8-0s, was 61ft 0⅝in. Working weights were: engine 73 tons 13cwt 1.6qtr, tender 31 tons 11cwt 2qtr, totalling 105 tons 4cwt 3.6 qtr. Maximum axleload, on the centre driving axle, was 15½ tons. A further special boiler, No 5395 was built to O/5738 and put on in December, 1922 to replace the original one, which was put under repair, these two boilers were fitted alternately for the rest of "Big Bertha's" life.

In 1921 to O/5475 she was provided with a powerful headlight, the current for which was supplied by a steam turbo-generator fitted below the running plate in front of the cab on the left hand side. Both these items were supplied by the British Thompson & Houston Co Ltd. She retained this equipment until finally withdrawn from service as No 58100 in May, 1956, when it was transferred to her successor, BR standard 2-10-0 No 92079. In spite of the fact that "Bertha" had only worked up and down the 2 mile stretch of the Lickey incline for most of her existence, apart from a short test period on coal trains to London, she managed to accumulate a total mileage of 838,856 in her 36 years of existence.

The only other engines to be described, which were built under the auspices of the Midland Railway for themselves, were five 0-4-0Ts built to O/5528 but nominally "rebuilt" from earlier Johnson saddle tank engines. Of these, numbered 1533-7, the first two were rebuilt from Nos 1501 and 1512 in July and August, 1921 respectively, whilst the remainder were rebuilt from Nos 1521, 1526 and 1527 in February, March and May 1922. They were identical to the five new engines, Nos 1528-32, built in 1907 to O/3031 and mentioned previously.

Three further orders which were filled remain to be described, two for the S&DJR, and one for the NCC. In 1914 two of the 4-4-0 tender engines belonging to the S&DJR were rebuilt to O/4337 with G7s type boilers, these being Nos 70 and 71, followed by Nos 67-69 similarly treated to O/4476 in 1921. These were shown officially in S&DJR records as new engines.

The order for the NCC was for two 4-4-0 tender engines to O/5648 of November, 1921, having 6ft driving wheels at 8ft 2in centres and 3ft bogie wheels on 6ft 6in centres placed 9ft 10in in front of the leading driver. Two inside cylinders of 19in diameter and 24in stroke were provided with 8in diameter piston valves. Boiler pressure was 170psi. Six wheeled tenders of 2,090gal capacity were provided to O/5650. The engines were re-numbered 72 and 73 respectively, and rebuilt by the NCC as U2 class engines in February and December, 1937, respectively, but were not named like many others of the class.

Electric welding was first introduced into the works in the shape of a Quasi-Arc No 3 size welding set purchased for use in No 1 Shop in January, 1919.

Mention should also be made here that in June, 1918, it was agreed to provide an ambulance room at the foot of the slope near the mess rooms, in accordance with Government regulations, at a cost of £500.

Looking to the future we should remember that new blood was being infused into the Midland set-up all the time, and promising newcomers were being groomed to play their part in the next chapter of our story. These were men such as George Sydney Bellamy, ex-pupil, already works Inspector by June, 1920, and destined to become Works Superintendent at Derby. There was Herbert Chambers who had entered the service of the Midland Company in April, 1899 as a machine-shop apprentice with a remuneration of 5s 7½d per week. He was later to become the first Derby Chief Locomotive Draughtsman of the LMS in succession to Symes, and later still Locomotive and Personal Assistant to the CME at Euston.

Other men there were who, although they did not rise to such great heights, were to leave their individual stamps on many aspects of affairs in the locomotive department at other levels, men such as D. W. Sanford, F. G. Carrier, P. D. Lucas, W. L. Armin to name but a few. All were to play their parts in the exciting yet difficult days which lay ahead for those of the "Derby mold".

So ends the first great chapter in the history of the Derby Locomotive Works. Up to the end of 1922 a total of 1,570 new engines had been built, and from fragmented beginnings the great complex of workshops was now on the eve of being threatened by competition for the first time in the shape of the various workshops inherited by the vast new railway system, the London, Midland and Scottish Railway, into which the Midland Company and all its several parts was to be absorbed.

L

CHAPTER THIRTEEN

The LMSR & Midlandisation
(1923-1931)

AT THE OUTBREAK of the Great War in 1914 a "Railway Executive Committee", consisting of all the General Managers of the principal railway companies, was set up by the government to take over the control of the railways, but the Railways Act of 1921 was the instrument by which the systems were returned to their owners who were duly compensated for war losses. Most important of all was the provision for the amalgamation of all the numerous independent companies into four main groups, of which the London, Midland and Scottish Railway Company was one. This group embraced not only the Midland but such rivals as the London & North Western Railway, Lancashire & Yorkshire Railway and the North Stafford Railway together with lines in the north and smaller lines in the south.

So the Derby Works became an important centre within the new organisation, and for the first time they were not the only works available for the building and repair of locomotives, and a considerable element of competition was introduced. On the January 1, 1923, the LMS took over 10,316 locomotives of 393 different types, and the immediate policy was to select and develop standard types and to eliminate policy was to select and develop standard types and to eliminate the many variations as quickly as possible.* Fourteen of these standard types emerged between the amalgamation and the advent of William Arthur Stanier as CME in 1932. The first CME was George Hughes, who had been well established in a similar post on the Lancashire & Yorkshire Railway since 1904, taking up the same position when the amalgamation with the London and North Western Railway went through on January 1, 1922, some 12 months before the big "grouping". Sir Henry Fowler, the CME of the Midland, became assistant to Hughes and later succeeded him in October, 1925. James Anderson, the Works Assistant was appointed the first Superintendent of Motive Power for the entire LMS and Sandham J. Symes, the Chief Draughtsman, moved up the ladder to take over from Anderson in charge of the Derby Works as Works Manager.

Symes had joined the Midland in 1904 as previously stated, and had become Chief Locomotive Draughtsman on July 1, 1913, in succession

*A Modern Locomotive History by E. S. Cox. Journal of Inst. of Locomotive Engineers No 190.

to Anderson. As Works Manager he was very much respected. He had about him the air of a perfect gentleman, and would always remove his hat on entering any of the workshops "out of respect for the men who work here" he would say.

The term "Midlandisation", coined by E. S. Cox,* expresses well the general policy in the early years of the LMS and through low repair costs and a generally lower coal consumption the decision eventually produced a stock of 2,925 locomotives, having a range of standard parts which showed immediate financial benefits. Four classes of Midland engines were adopted for standardisation these being the compound 4-4-0s, the superheated Class 2 4-4-0s, the 0-6-0 Class 4 tender engines and the 0-6-0 Class 3F tank engines. The Derby Works produced none of these standard engines in 1923, but filled two orders for a total of 13 locomotives.

The first, O/5649, was for three 0-6-0 superheated goods tender engines of the V class, for the NCC numbered 71–73 and quickly renumbered 13–15. They had 5ft 2½in diameter driving wheels at 7ft 5in + 7ft 10in centres and inside cylinders 19in diameter by 24in stroke, inclined at 1 in 9 to the horizontal, driven by 8in diameter piston valves. Working pressure was 170psi, and the heating surface was originally 1,158.5sq ft comprised of tubes 838.6sq ft, of which the superheater provided 230.3sq ft, and firebox 109.9sq ft, the elements adding another 210sq ft. The grate area was 18.6sq ft. The boiler was provided with a 10ft 7$\frac{11}{16}$in long barrel, the diameter inside the smallest ring being 4ft 3$\frac{3}{8}$in, and this was pitched 8ft 5$\frac{1}{16}$in from rail. There were 127 1$\frac{3}{4}$in diameter ordinary tubes and 18 superheater tubes.

A six wheeled tender of 2,090gal water capacity and 6 tons coal capacity was provided, with outside springing above the footplate. Total wheelbase of engine and tender was 34ft 6in and length over buffers 46ft 11$\frac{3}{4}$in. Working weights were as follows: leading 15 tons 12cwt, driving 16 tons 12cwt, trailing 15 tons 11cwt, tender 28 tons 17cwt 1qtr, totalling 76 tons 12cwt 1qtr.

The tenders were incidentally constructed to O/5650, the next in series, as was usually the case with the Derby order system.

These three engines were completed by March, 1923, and the works then commenced the construction of the batch of ten 4-4-2 unsuperheated tank engines for the London, Tilbury & Southend line, the first of which only remained in the erecting shop for 11 days and was completed in May, 1923 (*see Plate 83*). These engines, Nos 2110–19 were built to O/5871 placed in February 5, 1923 and were officially the "rebuilding" from No 1 to No 3 power class of existing tank engines,

A Modern Locomotive History by E. S. Cox. Journal of Inst. of Locomotive Engineers No 190 (1946).

even though the original engines were not withdrawn until 1930–5.

They were basically the LT&SR design of 1909 but somewhat "Midlandised". The outside cylinders, 19in diameter × 26in stroke, drove the 6ft 6in diameter coupled wheels placed at 8ft 9in centres. The leading bogie, centred 10ft 6½in in front of the leading driver was carried on 3ft 6in diameter wheels at 7ft centres, whilst the trailing pony truck, also on 3ft 6in diameter wheels, had its axle centred 8ft behind the trailing driver.

Class 3 boilers, Nos 5526–35, pressed to 170psi, were fitted, and with 1,800gal side and back tanks and room for 2¾ tons of coal, the working weights were: bogie 20 tons 10cwt, driving 19 tons, trailing 18 tons 10cwt, pony truck 13 tons 10cwt, totalling 71 tons 10cwt.

So far as express passenger locomotives were concerned the first year of amalgamation saw only the production of 21 new Hughes four-cylinder 4-6-0s at Horwich and it seemed for a while that the Derby produced compound 4-4-0 might have had its "nose pushed out". It was fortunate therefore that, in the dynamometer car trials on the Settle–Carlisle line towards the end of 1923, a compound in pristine condition No 1008, was matched against a well run-in LNW Prince 4-6-0, with a Midland 999 class Deeley 4-4-0 simple thrown in for good measure. The compound showed up surprisingly well on the heavily graded line with heavy test trains and showed a considerable saving in coal consumption over that of the Prince.

These results proved that the correct decision had been taken in June, 1923, when O/5938 was placed for 20 new superheated compounds Nos 1045–64, having driving wheels of 6ft 9in diameter but being otherwise similar to the Midland engines except for a ¾in increase in the diameter of both high and low pressure cylinders. This order was completed by the Derby shops between February and July, 1924, and was followed by another O/6066 for 20 further engines to work on the Northern Division, to be numbered 1065–84, which were delivered between July and December of the same year although only 1065–9 actually went to the Northern Division. These were basically the same as the first batch, but had shorter chimneys to clear the lower loading gauge in Scotland, and were provided with Ross Pop in place of Ramsbottom safety valves, although retaining the lock-up valve behind.

A further batch of 30 compounds, this time with left hand driving positions, was constructed to O/6293 between May and December, 1925. These were numbered 1085–1114, and in the light of experience gained with the working of the previous batch which had proved to run less well with the larger cylinder, the size was reduced back to 19in and 21in for high and low pressure respectively, but the reduced size of driving wheels was retained (*see Plate 81*).

The new compounds were dispersed to many parts of the new LMS system, some going to Camden, Rugby, Longsight and Kingmoor while the remainder of the first two orders were retained on the Midland Division. Of the third batch most were also kept on the Midland lines except for Nos 1110–14 which went to former LNWR sheds. They were however well received on some of the former lines of the other absorbed companies although in Scotland they were well liked. Compared with the LNW and Caledonian 4-6-0s they had very real advantages in coal consumption rates burning 34lb per mile as against 44 and 52 respectively, the lb/drawbar hp per hour figures being 4.06, 5.07 and 5.19 respectively.

A further series of comparison tests carried out in November and December, 1924 proved decisively the superiority of the performance of the Midland compound over other existing designs. They were LNWR Claughton four-cylinder simple 4-6-0 No 2221, Caledonian superheated 4-4-0 simple passenger No 124 and three compounds, Nos 1065 and 1066 with 6ft 9in coupled wheels and 1023 with 7ft coupled wheels. The route chosen was the hard graded line from Leeds to Carlisle with both 300 and 350 tons trains and the results proved that, while there was very little difference in the average drawbar hp between the Claughton and the compounds, the former consumed 29 per cent and 21 per cent more coal per ton mile than the latter for the 300 and 350 ton trains respectively while the Caledonian engine consumed 42 per cent more on the lighter trains.

The steaming of the compounds was regarded as satisfactory throughout the tests whilst the Claughton was quite the reverse, and in efforts to keep time the enginemen allowed the water to go very low in the glass in order to conserve the steam pressure. The Caledonian engine steamed well with the lighter train but the general performance was stated to be "not satisfactory". The conclusions were that while the Claughton proved itself a very free running engine it had heavy coal and water consumption and also a very poor steaming boiler. The Caledonian engine steamed well but engine performance was not satisfactory. The compounds were regarded as giving the best and most economic performance, and were therefore selected for future building programmes.

One other design which the Locomotive Committee of the new company decided to propagate, was the "big goods" Class 4F 0-6-0 tender engines, introduced by the Midland way back in 1911. By the end of 1922, 197 were in service, and from 1924 a big programme of construction was put in hand, not only in the company's workshops at Derby, Crewe, St Rollox and Horwich, but also at private builders

works, until by 1941, a further 575 had been built. The Derby orders
for the years 1924–27 were as follows:

Order No	Locomotive No	Year Built
O/6213	4027–56	1924–5
O/6438	4207–26	1925–6
O/6460	4227–46	1926
O/6473	4247–66	1926
O/6486	4267–86	1926
O/6632	4287–4301	1926–7
O/6841	4407–36	1927

Right hand drive, Midland style, was retained on the first order, but
thereafter the Derby built engines were to the future LMS standard
left hand drive. These had shorter chimneys and domes, Ross Pop
safety valves and a new pattern of straight sided tender. Nos 4432–6 had
Owen's double beat regulator valve.

Concurrent with the building of the last mentioned order for the 4Fs
the Derby Works were undertaking the construction of a further batch
of Class 3 4-4-2 passenger tank engines for the LT&S lines to O/6751,
these being numbered 2125–34 (later BR 41943–52). They were similar
to those built to O/5871 and were turned out between May and July,
1927.

Elsewhere on the new system the former works of the Lancashire and
Yorkshire, London & North Western and North Stafford Railways
continued to turn out a few lots of locomotives already on order at the
amalgamation and Horwich built a further 41 Hughes 4-6-0s and ten
Lancashire & Yorkshire designed "Baltic" tank engines, while St
Rollox continued building the Caledonian design of 4-6-0 until 1926.
One new Hughes design emerged from the Horwich Works in 1926, the
first of the 2-6-0 mixed traffic tender engines No 13000, soon to be
nicknamed "land-crabs" from their ungainly appearance. The design
was ruined in many eyes, by the substitution of the Midland design of
3,500gal tender in place of the wider 4,000gal tender of the L&Y design
which was to have been fitted, and no doubt would have been, but for
the death of the old LMS Chief Draughtsman J. R. Billington, a
Lancashire & Yorkshire man, and the succession of Herbert Chambers
a Midland man, to the post. George Hughes too was on the brink of
retirement, and the weight of Midland men in key positions no doubt
forced the issue.

The new Chief Draughtsman, Herbert Chambers, as has been mentioned earlier, served his apprenticeship on the Midland Railway and
passed through all the principal workshops at Derby including a period

of practical footplate training as a pupil fireman. He then went into the locomotive drawing office and after a number of years experience applied for, and got, the appointment of Senior Locomotive Draughtsman with Beyer Peacock & Co Ltd, Manchester in May, 1911. In August, 1913, he returned to the Midland Railway Drawing Office and was put on the salary list in October the following year. When the LMS was formed he was made Chief Locomotive Draughtsman of the Midland Division, in subjection to the L&Y man at Horwich, but only briefly!

With Hughes' retirement the torch passed to Derby, and now, in 1927, Chambers was to be both Technical Assistant and Chief Locomotive Draughtsman of the LMSR soon to become involved in the detailed design of the Royal Scots, but that is anticipating our story.

In March, 1935 as successor to Chambers as Chief Draughtsman (Headquarters), Derby, came T. F. "Tommy" Coleman, an ex-North Stafford man, who had been apprenticed at Kerr Stuart & Company, engineers and locomotive builders of Stoke-on-Trent from 1900 to 1906 when he entered the service of the "Knotty" at their Stoke Works as Works Plant Draughtsman. Later he went into the locomotive and carriage and wagon drawing office at Stoke where he was made Chief Draughtsman upon the formation of the LMS in 1923. In September, 1926, he took the same position at Horwich and then in October, 1933, he became assistant to Chambers and Chief Draughtsman at Crewe. Some of these career details may seem tedious to the reader, but they give an insight into some of the old loyalties, apt so often in railway circles to influence important and less important decisions in favour of one "school" or another.

On the subject of works organisation, things were beginning to move again. Prior to 1926 the practice at Derby Works was to allow for 10 per cent of the locomotive stock to be out of use under repair at any one time. This was common practice in the majority of railway locomotive shops in this country, the chief factor being the insufficiency of spare boilers to enable one to be quickly substituted for the old boiler on a locomotive under repair, thus cutting down the time the locomotive was in the shops, since it will be appreciated that the time to repair a boiler could be $5\frac{1}{2}$ weeks on average.

Following a re-appraisal of the whole repair system, a larger stock of spare boilers was created and this cut down the number of locomotives in the shops from between 260 and 300 to between 60 and 65, giving some idea of the improvements gained. The average time to repair a locomotive under the new system was reduced from 25 to 20 days, and with the works at that time being responsible for the maintenance of 3,000 engines the figure of 10 per cent out of commission dropped to about 2 per cent, a quite considerable improvement as will be appreciated. Shop space and storage space could thus be cut down and utilised more efficiently for the quicker repair of the smaller number of engines now coming into the works.

It is perhaps of interest here to briefly describe the shopping of a locomotive. After reaching the Derby running shed in steam the engine would be handed over to the works when dead, uncoupled from its tender and stripped of all its lagging, external pipework, brick arch and firebars. The smokebox would then be emptied and the superheater elements removed, all on the first day. The locomotive was then ready for the stripping pits in the Erecting Shop where, in an average time of $1\frac{1}{2}$ days, the engine would be stripped of its wheels, motion, cab, boiler, etc, leaving just the bare frame and chassis usually complete with running plate, to move up the shop into its allotted position, where it would be examined for any frame cracks, damage, mis-alignment, etc, and where the horn guides would be reground, rivets replaced and the cylinders and valve ports attended to and remachined if necessary. In some cases cylinder liners would have to be fitted for the first time, or renewed as necessary. All the other parts were meanwhile being examined in the respective shops, and repaired or renewed.

The replacement boiler, from stock, was next fitted to the frame, the engine makers' plates being altered to show the date when the new boiler was fitted, and the old smokebox and cab reassembled in place, together with any splashers, tanks, etc. Pipework and injectors were then fitted and next came the re-erection of the motion, refitting of axle-boxes, wheeling of the engine, fitting of coupling and connecting rods, and reuniting with the tender, which had been similarly stripped down, repaired and reassembled. The paint shop was the final port of call, where from three to six days were allowed, according to the class of engine. She was then ready to be run-out onto the motive power depot for steaming trials, weighing, testing of brakes and a trial run before going back to her home depot and into regular revenue earning service once again.

The output of the Derby shops, under this new system, was 20 general repairs per week, the average number of engines dealt with per day being four in and four out, any variation being balanced up on the half day's work on Saturday mornings each week. Regarding the makers plates carried by the engines it was realised early in 1928 that the changing of these plates would go on indefinitely and cost a great deal of money. It was therefore decided that all the 4-4-0 passenger tender rebuilds were to show the original date of superheating, and all others were to carry a plate showing the date of building, except for the Class 3F 0-6-0s which were to show the date of rebuilding from Class 2F to

Class 3F. Plates already cast for 1928 were used up on the Class 2F 0-6-os and the 1F and 3F 0-6-oT engines then being fitted with G6 Belpaire boilers.

An essential part of the new system was the Central Order Office to provide for the systematic progressing of the various documents introduced which comprised in the main the works order, materials list, drawing slips, detail specifications, operation layout sheets and requisitions. Thus the shopping procedure at Derby was geared up to a higher pitch of efficiency, as in due course were all the other works on the new system.

A word now about liveries, ever a complex issue, and made even more complicated by the reluctance of certain camps to comply with requests from the Derby headquarters which they rightly regarded as distinctly "Midland biased"! The committee co-ordinating design approved, on December 10, 1923, a series of recommendations regarding the repainting and renumbering of engines. In line with the decision to plump for the "old Midland crimson lake" colour for coaching stock it was ordered that passenger engines be painted the same crimson colour and freight engines be painted black without lining as hitherto adopted.

It was also decided, in line with former MR policy, that "the Company's engines be not named in future, but that those engines which already bear a name continue as hitherto". All passenger engines were to bear the Company's "coat of arms" on the panel plate or on the bunker side in the case of tank engines, and all goods engines were to have the initials "LMS", without stops, in a corresponding position. Engine numbers were to be on the tender or tank sides, as well as being shown on a cast-iron plate on the smokebox door. Building plates were to be retained, and changed to show rebuilding dates, and engine classification plates were to be fitted to the cab side "in a conspicuous position about the height of the drivers head."

In December, 1927, the instruction to place engine numbers on the sides of the tenders was countermanded, and the numbers were in future placed on the cab side with the letters "LMS" on the tender side-sheets in all cases, while tank engines were to carry their numbers on the bunker. A change to black livery was made in March, 1928, for all passenger engines except the Royal Scots, Claughtons, Standard 4-4-o compounds and the L&Y Class 8 4-6-os. The Prince of Wales class were to have been red also, but this decision was countermanded the following December "in the interests of economy". However one concession to taste was made in that black passenger engines were to be lined in red. The red engines were lined in yellow with black edging.

The first true LMS designs to appear were those for the Royal Scot 4-6-os built by the North British Locomotive Co and the two-cylinder

2-6-4 tank engines of the 2300 class built at Derby. Both designs embodied many improvements brought about by experience with other types, and utilised long travel valve gear, unheard of before in the Derby office, larger bearing areas and a higher working pressure of 200psi for the tank engines and 250psi for the Scots.

The design offices of the LMS were by this time becoming centred on Derby being housed in the old locomotive drawing office under the clock tower in the Locomotive Works. Herbert Chambers was by now the Chief Draughtsman as we know, with Arthur Eugene Owen, an ex-Furness Railway man, as his assistant and responsible for most of the design work. At that time the office was divided neatly in half, under two Scots, Jock Henderson and Buff Campbell, but there were many others, not of the Midland school, now housed together under one roof with many varying lines of thought about how the various parts of the new design for the 2-6-4T should be done, since due to pressure of work the design for the Royal Scots was being done at the North British Locomotive Co under the direction of Chambers and other senior designers from Derby.

As to the other design, the new tank engines were supplied with two outside cylinders 19in diameter × 26in stroke and 5ft 9in diameter driving wheels on the standard wheelbase, acceptable to the then Civil Engineering Department of 8ft + 8ft 6in, the leading pony truck and trailing bogie wheels being a common 3ft 3½in diameter, the pony truck axle being 9ft in front of the leading driver, and the trailing bogie, on a 6ft 6in wheelbase, was centred 9ft 9in behind the trailing driver, giving a total wheelbase of 38ft 6in, with a length over buffers of 47ft 2¾in.

The G8AS boiler, the same as that fitted to the Class 3 4-4-0s and a superheated version of a 1902 Midland boiler, was pressed, as previously stated, to 200psi and had an 11ft long barrel of 4ft 8in outside diameter. It was superheated with 21 1½in od elements, the large tubes being 5⅛in od and the 146 ordinary 1¾in od. Heating surfaces were: tubes 1082.5sq ft, superheater 266.25sq ft, firebox 137.55sq ft, totalling 1486.30sq ft. The grate area was 25sq ft and the tractive effort, at 85 per cent boiler pressure, was 23,125lb. The coal bunker held 3½ tons of coal and the tanks 2,000gal of water. Weight, light, was 69 tons 8cwt and loaded 86 tons 5cwt.

The first order for 25 engines was O/6807 of March 3, 1927, and the first emerged from the Derby Works on December 11, 1927, as number 2300, the remainder, Nos 2301–24, being delivered between the end of that month and June, 1928. One of these engines, No 2313, was specially named *The Prince* in honour of a visit to the Derby Works by the Prince of Wales, (later the Duke of Windsor), when the engine was nearing completion in February, 1928. The name was painted on the side tanks and retained for a number of years (*see Plate 84*). This class were fitted with brakes on both the pony truck and trailing bogie and also byepass valves, but these were removed later during Stanier's "reign". They also had water pick-up gear, arranged to pick up in either direction of travel, delivering into a dome in the bunker tank.

For light passenger work a new series of modified Class 2 4-4-0 passenger engines but with left hand drive was designed, being developed from the old Midland Class 2s which, despite selective improvements, were now considered to be rather indifferent performers by that day's standards, and a partial redesign was undertaken, whereby the original cylinder diameter of 20½in, was reduced to 19in, the stroke remaining the same at 26in, while the cylinder block was redesigned to improve the steam passages and the boiler pressure increased from 160 to 180psi. The coupled wheels were reduced from 7ft 0½in diameter to 6ft 9in diameter at 9ft 6in centres, and the leading bogie, again on 3ft 6½in wheels, was centred 10ft 2½in in front of the leading driver. The boiler set at 180psi carried 146 ordinary tubes of 1¾in outside diameter and 21 superheater elements of 1½in outside diameter enclosed in 21 large tubes of 5⅛in outside diameter giving heating surfaces of: tubes 1033.7sq ft, superheater 252.7sq ft and firebox 123.8sq ft, totalling 1410.2sq ft. The grate area was 21.2sq ft and the tractive effort at 85 per cent boiler pressure, was 17,729lb. The six-wheeled tender of 3,500gal water capacity and holding 4 tons of coal, weighed 41 tons 4cwt in working order, and the engine 54 tons 1cwt 2qtr.

Fifty of these engines in all were ordered to O/6901 (30) issued on May 19, 1927, and O/7080 (20) issued on February 18, 1928, respectively. Of the first order, which were to have been 563–92, three locomotives, numbers 575, 576, and 580, were sent to the Somerset & Dorset Joint Line, by now jointly vested in the Southern and LMS Companies, as their numbers 44–46, while 572 was experimentally fitted with Owen's double-port exhaust valves, and was renumbered 601. The second order covered engines 572 (replacement for 601), 593–600 and 602–12. The first engine of O/6901 came out on the March 29, 1928, and the remainder of the orders were filled by December, 1928. Those engines sent to the S&DJR eventually came back into LMS stock on January 1, 1930 as numbers 633–5.

One last design to be mentioned in this section of the book, and also built at Derby, is the diminutive little 0-6-0 Dock Tank engines, classed as "2F", which were designed under the supervision of T. F. Coleman at Horwich, shortly after he arrived from Stoke, the former North Stafford Railway headquarters. Incidentally Coleman was later to replace Herbert Chambers as Chief Draughtsman of the LMS at the Derby headquarters.

These tanks of his were rugged little engines, admirably suited to their work in dock and other areas where on tight curves in depots with restricted space they came into their own, being on a very short 9ft 6in wheelbase, equally divided. Ten were constructed to O/7137 issued on May 30, 1928, and they emerged from the Derby Works during December, 1928 and January, 1929, five being sent to Scotland and the remainder to the Birkenhead and Fleetwood depots, their running numbers being 11270–79 (*see Plate 87*).

They had outside cylinders 17in diameter and 22in stroke, and the valves were actuated by outside Walschaerts valve gear. The driving wheels were 3ft 11in diameter and length over buffers was 27ft 6in, the overhang being 9ft each side of the driving wheels. The saturated G5 boiler carried 194 tubes 1¾in outside diameter giving a heating surface of 923sq ft and the firebox added a further 85sq ft. Grate area was 14.5sq ft and the tractive effort at 85 per cent boiler pressure (160psi) was 18,400lb. The tanks carried 1,000 gal of water and the bunker 1½ tons of coal, the weight in working order being 43 tons 12cwt divided thus: leading 12 tons 18cwt, intermediate driving 15 tons 14cwt and trailing 15 tons 0cwt. These were regarded as a standard design of locomotive by the LMS.

Apart from new engine building, of course the Derby Works was now getting drawn into the LMS system in a more general way, and one of the marks of this was the decision to bring ex-LNWR 'A' Division Prince of Wales class engines into the Derby Works for repairs. O/6199 was issued for this on April 4, 1924, and covered the shopping of 30 locomotives. This was supposed to be an exchange arrangement with the Crewe Works who were shortly to build some of the Midland 4F 0-6-0s under the new building programme, and were therefore sent 20 of those already built but ready for repairs to familiarise the erecting shop hands with these strange machines. In the event it appears that only 20 Prince of Wales were actually shopped, and of these only six were renumbered and outshopped in LMS livery, the remainder, not requiring a repaint, were merely touched up and sent on their way, Derby no doubt being glad to get rid of them!

A similar event occurred in 1927, when under order O/6805 of January 4, 25 LNWR 0-6-2 tank engines from the Western Division were sent to Derby for repair to help out the Crewe Works, who were at that time in the throes of organising the complex "belt" system for engine repairs. Ten further locomotives, due for withdrawal, were sent to Derby for scrapping, to provide boilers and other spare parts, especially in view of Derby's recently instituted boiler exchange system as mentioned previously. Other types of non-Midland pre-grouping engines were to be shopped in the next few years.

On the subject of boilers generally the works boiler shop was busy producing new boilers not only for the various old Midland classes still being rebuilt with Belpaire fireboxed boilers, but also repairing other boilers from various parts of the system, not only for ex-Midland and LMS engines, but for other odd engines as well. The shop was also rebuilding saturated boilers to superheated form for the compounds, etc, and providing boilers to the NCC for both their standard 5ft 3in gauge and narrow gauge locomotives. There was also the provision and maintenance of the multitude of stationary boilers on the various parts of the Midland division to be looked after.

The other shops were of course very busy, particularly the iron foundry where new cylinders were wanted in quantity, together with the multitude of smaller cast-iron items, the production of the smallest and the least important of which was the ideal first grounding in the founders art for the apprentices of that day. In the chair foundry orders flowed in, three orders alone, Nos 6556–8 issued on November 13, 1925, requiring the production of a total of 8,340 tons of cast-iron chairs of three different types.

In 1926 the coal strike badly affected the supplies available for railway purposes, and later this became a general strike throughout the country. An attempt to keep the wheels turning, should the large reserve stocks be exhausted, was made by fitting up some of the mainstay locomotive stock with oil-burning apparatus. The first order to be issued for the Derby shops was O/6664 in May, 1926, to cover the Class 2P and 3P 4-4-0 engines 527 and 765, extended by the end of the month to cover 362, 364, 479, 480, 484, 487, 492, 499, 500, 555, 557, 558 and 559. All but 480 had twin 8ft long circular tanks fitted, but this particular locomotive had a square tank. Further orders were issued as follows:

O/6666	50 sets of oil fuel burning apparatus
O/6670	144 tanks for oil fuel
O/6671	10 compounds to have oil fuel apparatus (Rectangular tanks 9ft long)
O/6675	30 further compounds to have oil fuel apparatus
O/6682	25 further compounds to have oil fuel apparatus (these were not fitted)
O/6684	20 No 2 Class passenger engines to have oil fuel apparatus

This was not incidentally the first time that oil burning apparatus had been fitted to Midland locomotives for in 1921 a number of locomotives had been so treated including 28 Class 3 4-4-0s, 20 Class 2 4-4-0s, 1 0-6-0T and the Lickey Banker. In addition six sets of equipment for Class 2 4-4-0s had been sent to Highbridge.

A few other odd orders are of passing interest, like O/6829 which covered any work undertaken at Derby for the Royal Scots being built by the North British Locomotive Co and included the provision of the Royal Scot cast brass nameplates, "letters to be polished on a red background". Many were the standard items of equipment of basically Midland design, in particular boiler fittings, that were manufactured in the works and supplied by them to the other railway and private contractor workshops then constructing new locomotives for the LMS.

In January, 1928, the CME Department, brought out their scheme for the distinctive numbering of all the tenders on the LMSR system, to permit the easy exchange of tenders between engines and recording of same. Various methods of identification had been adopted by the different pre-grouping companies, but henceforth each tender was to carry its own individual number. The practice at Derby had for long years been to identify the tender with a particular engine whose number appeared on the cast plate on the tender back-plate. Now it was at last possible to ring the changes on tenders to speed repair work and it was no longer necessary to send an engine back into traffic with its original tender. A brief summary list for Midland Division stock only may here be of interest:

Water Capacity (Gallons)	Total Number of Tenders	Distinctive Numbers
1,850	1	77
2,000	217	83–299
2,050	1	343
2,200	239	395–634
2,330	68	692–759
2,350	57	763–819
2,500	2	856 & 857
2,750	55	1173–1227
2,900	2	1353 & 1354
2,950	185	1385–1569
3,250	723	1884–2606
3,500	693	2691–3175 and 3326–3533

In addition to the above there were 15 spare assorted tenders, 10 water carrying tenders and 50 spare tender tanks. This ordered list, linking individual engine with tender, soon became extremely disordered with tender "swapping" and the use of second-hand tenders for new engines and vice versa soon made the keeping of accurate records a complex matter. In the final years of steam on British Railways this caution was thrown to the winds and the final linkings were in many cases never officially recorded, but that is far ahead in our story.

At the end of April, 1928, S. J. Symes became personal assistant to Sir Henry Fowler, and his place as restyled "Works Superintendent" at Derby was taken by H. G. Ivatt who had been the Assistant Locomotive Superintendent in the former North Stafford territory based at Stoke until this closed. He was the son of the celebrated CME of the Great Northern Railway, H. A. Ivatt, and no doubt inherited some of his father's mechanical genius. Nevertheless he carried this to his own high level of achievement in the practical engineering field, particularly in later days in Scotland as Mechanical Engineer there and eventually as CME of the LMS to which position he succeeded on February 1, 1946. His preoccupation with strict maintenance control and regular examinations carried out on locomotives between shoppings, gave rise to very real savings on repair expenditure, the minimum being done commensurate with virtually assured mileage to the next repair.

As Ivatt's Assistant Works Superintendent came R. A. Riddles, an extremely talented man destined to become the innovator of several designs of locomotives including the BR standard steam locomotive fleet, but that too is later in our story.

Further large orders of 2-6-4T engines of the 2300 class were built during the years 1929–34 as follows:

Order	Locomotive Nos	Year built
O/7120	2325–34	1929
O/7224	2335–54	1929
O/7237	2355–74	1929
O/8027	2375–84	1932
O/8241	2385–94	1933
O/8338	2395–2424	1933–4

The majority of these were almost identical to the first order, but Nos 2395–2424 were built with side-windowed cabs with full-length doors and a window, providing a completely enclosed driving position for the first time ever on the LMS. These were known as "limousine cabs". Bogie brakes were not fitted to these particular locomotives.

As mentioned previously three of the Class 2P 4-4-0 light passenger engines had been sent to the Somerset and Dorset Joint Line when built in 1928, and part of the next order for this type to be recorded was in replacement for these. Twenty-three further 4-4-0 locomotives were constructed in the Derby shops in 1929–30, to O/7403, these being numbers 613–32, 575, 576 and 580, followed by the last order for this type to be built at Derby, O/7854 for engines 661–85, issued on April 9,

1931, and filled between December, 1931 and April, 1932. The remainder of the locomotives of this type, to make up a class total of 138
engines, were constructed at Crewe in the former LNWR works.

A new design of tank engine for light suburban passenger work, but
of smaller size than the 2300 class, was being looked at in the Derby
drawing office in the late 1920s and various schemes had been got out,
including 0-6-2 and 0-6-4 tanks based apparently on the designs already
running on the adjacent ex-North Stafford lines, some of which ran
regularly into the Derby station where they could be observed from the
windows of the drawing office "eyrie" under the clock tower.

In 1928 the drawing office removed to a separate building adjacent to
the main office block and nicknamed "The Stables" where scheming
continued. Midland influence still pressed hard and the various designs
produced all clearly showed from what quarter their origins came.
From the time of Deeley various conceptions of ideal tank engines for
different purposes had been drawn, including an interesting 2-8-2 compound tank engine with two high-pressure inside-cylinders 13in diameter × 26in stroke having 8in diameter piston valves below, and two
low-pressure outside-cylinders 20in diameter × 26in stroke operated by
10in diameter outside piston valves. Boiler heating surface would have
been 1,458.3sq ft and working pressure 220psi. The driving wheels were
to have been 5ft 6in diameter spaced at 7ft, 6ft and 6ft centres and the
leading and trailing bissel trucks were to have 3ft 3½in diameter wheels
centred 9ft in front of and behind the leading and trailing driving wheels
respectively.

One other design proposal for a 0-6-2 passenger tank engine actually
reached the stage of an order, O/7107, being placed for 25 in April,
1928, but before work had progressed very far this was cancelled. This
would have been a most useful design for light passenger work in the
London area and elsewhere, having two inside-cylinders 17½in diameter × 26in stroke and 5ft 3in driving wheels, on the standard wheelbase of 8ft + 8ft 6in. The trailing pony-truck on 3ft 3½in diameter
wheels, was centred 8ft behind the trailing driver. A G6s (superheated)
boiler, set to work at 200psi was to have been provided and the side
tanks extended to the centre of the boiler barrel, level with the dome.
The rear bunker was to have provided space for 3 tons of coal, and working weights would have varied from 68 tons 15cwt with condensing
gear, 53 tons of which was on the driving wheels, to 68 tons without
condensing gear but with exhaust steam injector with 52 tons 8cwt on
the drivers. Tractive effort at 85 per cent boiler pressure worked out at
21,482lb.

Other preliminary designs were for the 2-6-2T variety, and this was
the configuration eventually chosen. The first order for 25 was O/7467,

68 The Iron Foundry as it was in 1895. This shop remained largely unchanged in appearance for over 60 years until converted into a sub-fabrication shop when foundry work was transferred elsewhere.

69 A general view of the boiler shop assembly bay as it was in 1895.

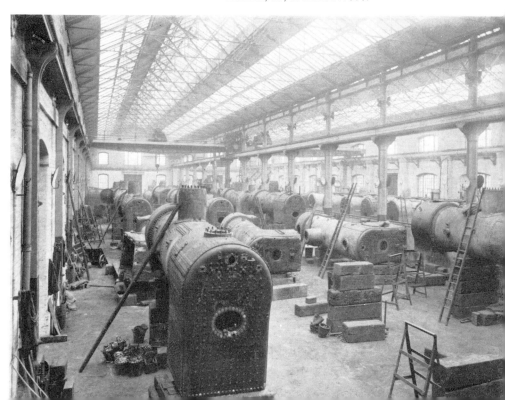

70 Deeley's 2000 class 0–6–4 tank engines known disaffectionately by the running staff as "flat irons". No 2000 was built in April, 1907.

71 Deeley 0–6–0 No 279 as built in February, 1906 with H class boiler.

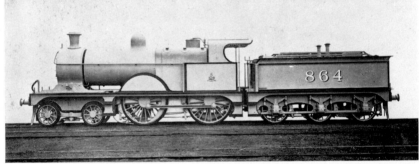

72 One of the Deeley "Belpaires" 4–4–0 No 864 shown as built in July, 1905 with G8A boiler.

73 No 999 the first of Deeley's 990 class of Class 3 4–4–0 built in March, 1907 to compare their performance with the compounds and fitted with Deeley's valve gear.

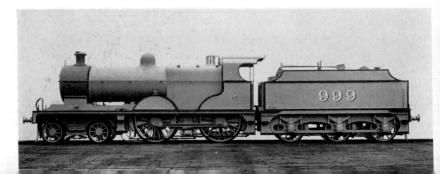

74 Paget's experimental 2–6–2 No 2299,
financed largely by himself and completed
in January, 1909. After much trouble with
the valves, it was broken up in April, 1920.

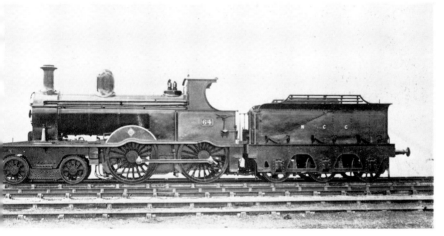

75 NCC two-cylinder compound 4–4–0
No 64 as built in 1905. Later named
Trostan.

76 MR (NCC) rail motor coach No 90
built at Derby in 1905.

77 The paint shop in the halcyon days of steam. A view taken in March, 1914 showing locomotives in various stages of repainting.

78 The first of Henry Fowler's "big goods" Class 4F 0–6–0s. 772 were built in all over a period of 31 years. No 3835 was completed in October, 1911.

79 S&DJR 4–4–0 No 68, built at Derby in January, 1896, with H class boiler. Later rebuilt with G7s boiler in 1921.

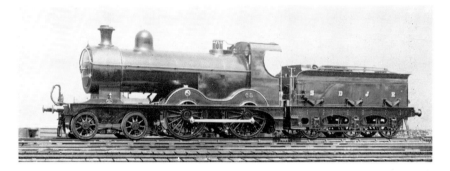

80 S&DJR 2–8–0 No 84, turned out in April, 1914, one of a batch of six built specially for working freight trains over the Mendips and the largest size locomotive class built by the Midland, shown as running later without tender cab.

81 No 1094 one of the LMS standard versions of the three-cylinder compound 4–4–0 developed from the original Midland design. No 1094 was built in July, 1925.

82 The famous 0–10–0 Lickey banker No 2290 stands complete in the erecting shop on November 27, 1919, ready to leave for the paint shop.

83 The first LT&SR 4–4–2T No 2110 to be built at Derby, ready to leave the erecting shop on May 9, 1923 after only 11 days in the shop.

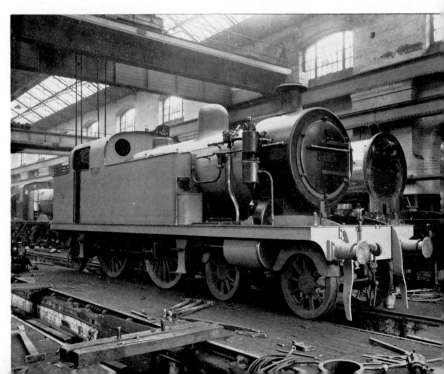

84 Fowler 2–6–4T No 2313 named *The Prince* in honour of the visit of the Prince of Wales to Derby Works in 1928 whilst the engine was being completed.

85 The first of Fowler's 2–6–2Ts, seen in original condition in March, 1930, when almost new. These engines had very small boilers, short travel valves and inside steam pipes. They were not a success even after outside steam pipes were added later.

86 Stanier's three-cylinder 2–6–4 tank engine No 2536, last of a class of 37 built at Derby in 1934 for the London Tilbury and Southend line.

87 The smallest standard locomotive of the LMS. 0–6–0 dock tank No 11270 was designed at Horwich and built at Derby in 1928, one of a class of ten such locomotives.

88 The final 1932 version of Johnson's original 0–4–4T, built as No 6400 in December, 1932 and shown here as renumbered 1900 and with Stanier chimney in 1946.

89 The first of C. E. Fairburn's design of 2–6–4 tank engines built at Derby and shown here as new in shop grey for photographing in March, 1945.

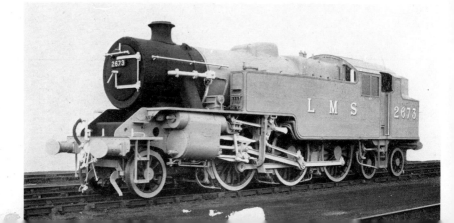

90 One of the 5ft 3in gauge NCC 2–6–4Ts No 50 being wheeled in No 3 bay of the Derby erecting shop in April, 1949

91 One of the Derby built Royal Scot class locomotives being wheeled in the erecting shop in July, 1930.

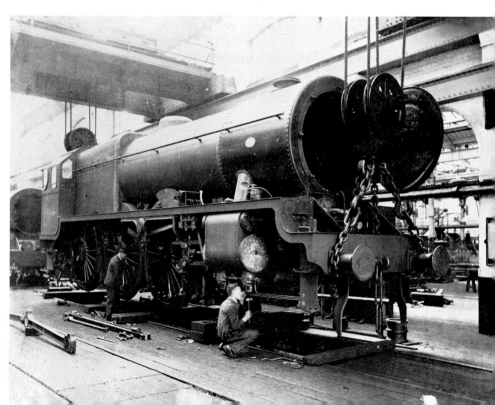

92 The *Royal Scot* built at Derby as No 6152 in June, 1930, which exchanged names and numbers with the original No 6100 for the North American tour in connection with the Chicago World's Fair in 1933. Shown here with presentation bell and commemorative plaque and smokebox nameplate in November, 1937.

93 The second of the original pair of re-built Claughtons turned out in November, 1930, No 5902 was later renumbered 5501 and renamed "St. Dunstan's".

94 Derby's first diesel, No 1831 was converted from a Johnson 0–6–0 tank engine in 1932 and fitted with a Paxman six-cylinder diesel engine and hydrostatic transmission.

95 0–6–0 diesel shunter No 7080 with Jackshaft drive, the first of a long line of diesel shunting locomotives built at Derby over the next 21 years, as built in May, 1939.

96 The celebrated locomotive No 10000, forerunner of today's main line diesel-electric fleet, completed at Derby in December, 1947 just before nationalisation.

97 An aerial view of the worst fire in Derby Locomotive Works which occurred on April 19, 1950. The extent of the damage can be clearly seen.

98 The last steam locomotive to be built at Derby. Standard Class 5 4–6–0 No 73154 in the works yard in June, 1957.

99 Steam makes its final official exodus from No 8 erecting shop as No 75042 leaves under its own power on September 20. 1963.

100 The last steam locomotive to undergo light repairs to a damaged front end in No 8 shop early in 1964. No 92102 was ushered in and out as quickly as possible.

[*A. B. Larmer*

101 Derby built BR Standard Class 5 4–6–0 No 73008 passing through Kirkby Stephen at speed with a Perth-London express in 1951.

102 BR/Sulzer Type 4 2,300hp diesel-electric ICo-Col locomotives under construction in No 8 erecting shop in 1960.

103 BR/Sulzer Type 2 1,160hp diesel-electric Bo-Bo locomotives under construction in No 3 (new work) bay of the erecting shop in 1960.

104 Works open day on August 29, 1964 in connection with the Works Horticultural Society's annual show when the public are invited to freely tour the workshops and examine the various exhibits.

105 BR/Sulzer type 2 diesel-electric Bo-Bo locomotive No D7667, the 1,000th diesel locomotive turned out by the Derby Works in December, 1966, shown with a group of chargehands.

issued on August 2, 1929, the first 20 to be non-condensing and the last five of the condensing type for use on Midland Division London area suburban trains working into Moorgate station and replacing the older Johnson 0-4-4 tank engines (*see Plate 85*). They were turned out between March, 1930 and January, 1931.

Main features of these engines were the parallel boiler of the G6s type, a superheater version of the Belpaire boiler used for reboilering the Class 2 0-6-0s, straight-topped side tanks and cabs similar to the early 2300 class engines.

The two outside-cylinders, driven by piston valves operated by Walschaerts valve gear, were $17\frac{1}{2}$in diameter and 26in stroke. Working weights were: condensing 71 tons 16cwt, non-condensing 70 tons 10cwt.

The driving wheels were 5ft 3in diameter on a standard wheelbase (8ft + 8ft 6in) and the leading and trailing bissel trucks with 3ft $3\frac{1}{2}$in diameter wheels were centred 8ft 9in in front of the leading driving wheel and 8ft behind the trailing driving wheel respectively, the total wheelbase being 33ft 3in. The length over buffers was 41ft $11\frac{3}{4}$in and height to chimney top 12ft $5\frac{3}{4}$in. The side and rear tanks carried 1,500gal of water, and the bunker 3 tons of coal. Tractive effort at 85 per cent boiler pressure was 21,486lb. Power class was 3P.

The running numbers of the first 25 were 15500–524,* and further orders were built as follows:

Quantity	Order	Locomotive Nos	Year Built
25	O/7575	*15525–49	1931
10	O/7753	15550–59	1931
10	O/8052	15560–69	1932

These engines proved to be rather poor performers, being under-boilered for their size, and with the same major fault as the Class 4F 0-6-0s, a thoroughly bad front-end design. It seems a pity at this distance in time, that the same cohesive force of design used on the 2-6-4 tank engines could not have been applied to this smaller version. In the event they pottered about rather ineffectively and were often used on the lightest branch services such as the Harrow–Stanmore auto trains.

In 1930 the works had its first taste of building what could be called the new generation of first-string express locomotives hitherto built entirely elsewhere on the system, when they constructed 20 Royal Scot-class locomotives, Nos 6150–69 to O/7580, the first being turned out in June, 1930 (*see Plate 92*). Much controversy has centred around the designing of the locomotives and many have accused Sir Henry Fowler of lifting the design from the Southern Railway Lord Nelson class.

*Note Nos 15521-39 were fitted with condensers and Weir steam-driven feed pumps.

M

This is demonstrably untrue and it is worth while at this point in our story to dispose of this myth once and for all.

The facts seem to be that the LMS authorities were impressed by the superior performance of the GWR 4-6-0 No 5000 *Launceston Castle* during her trials on the Crewe–Carlisle road in October, 1926. J. E. Anderson, now Motive Power Superintendent, had attended these trials and was most impressed, and brought influence to bear on the formulation of the new design of express engine now being considered in place of Sir Henry's abortive Pacific schemes. He was decidedly in favour of a non-compound three-cylindered locomotive.

Approaches were made to the GWR authorities for a set of Castle class drawings for consideration in the design stages, but this was firmly but politely turned down. Among other approaches made, a request to the Southern Railway Company was granted and a set of drawings for the Lord Nelson class 4-6-0s was sent to the North British Locomotive Co at Glasgow who were not only to fill the first order for the "Scots", but were to be responsible for the overall design under the direction of Herbert Chambers and some senior staff from Derby who made regular visits.

Chambers had got himself somewhat of a bad name among some of the old diehards in the Derby office who mistook his zeal for work as a young man pushing too hard, and he found life somewhat hard going. There was of course liaison between Chambers and Clayton and Holcroft of the SR and no doubt the design of the "Scots" came up at their regular meetings in connection with the ARLE which still was endeavouring unsuccessfully at this time to produce a range of standard locomotives.

Little variation from the basic design eventually formulated is shown on the three preliminary design schemes all drawn up by "Jock" Henderson in the Derby office, two being dated November 26, 1926 and the third January 4, 1927. This latter, which shows a 14ft 6in long boiler barrel, 6in longer than the previous two was adopted and it seems that this sketch DS-4220/2 set the seal on the basic design.

The boiler design came from the Midland 0-10-0 banking engine together with GWR style steel stays, humped grate and four-door ashpan. The cylinders and valve gear, including cylinder bye-pass valves, were current Derby practice, as were the bogie brakes.

The four-bar crosshead and four-bars for the inside motion came from the compounds, whilst the outside motion came from the 2-6-4Ts, as did the valve sizes and settings.

The boiler with 5ft 9in outside diameter carried 27 superheater flues of 5⅛in diameter and 180 small tubes of 2in outside diameter giving a heating surface of 1,892sq ft to which the superheater added 399sq ft and the firebox with a grate area of 31.2sq ft added a further 189sq ft of evaporative area making a total of 2,480sq ft. Working pressure was 250psi. The coupled wheelbase was 15ft 4in the driving centres being 7ft 4in and 8ft, and the diameter of the driving wheels 6ft 9in. The leading bogie with 3ft 3½in diameter wheels on a 6ft 6in wheelbase, was centred 8ft 11in in front of the leading driver. The three cylinders, one inside, were of 18in diameter and 26in stroke. One interesting feature in connection with the driving arrangement was that the inside cylinder was arranged to drive the leading driving axle, and the outside cylinders the middle pair of driving wheels, the cranks being set at 120deg. The piston valves were actuated by three independent sets of Walschaerts valve gear, and the last 14 Derby-built engines had an improved type of piston valve-head incorporating six narrow rings.

3,500gal six-wheeled tenders were provided initially, of Fowler straight-side design and holding 5½ tons of coal. These were later exchanged for 4,000gal curved-sided tenders holding 9 tons of coal. Tractive effort was 33,150lb at 85 per cent of the boiler working pressure. Working weights were: engine 84 tons 18cwt, tender 42 tons 14cwt, totalling 127 tons 12cwt.

The Derby Works followed up the original and staggering North British order for 50 engines with this further batch of 20, numbered 6150–69 as stated, and a highly creditable performance was achieved in the works on this particular order. The production programme provided for the frames for the first engine to be laid down on May 5, 1930, the completed engine to leave the erecting shop for the paint shop on May 23, and to be ready for traffic, after painting, by May 31. These dates were kept to, the engine being ready to leave the erecting shop within a few minutes of the scheduled time (*see Plate 91*).

This was undoubtedly a prestige order for Derby, and H. G. Ivatt, then Works Manager, was extremely pleased to win this work for the shops. It should be mentioned however that the boilers for these engines were built at Crewe to order B349 (Nos 8119–28) and B350 (8129–38), although they were numbered in the Derby series for some reason.

This achievement was proof that the progressive system, brought into use throughout the works a few years earlier, was working very well. It was virtually certain in every department reorganised under the system that work scheduled to be completed by a definite day or hour would have been disposed of when that time arrived.

The most convincing argument in favour of the new system was that fewer engines were in the shops at any one time, thus enabling more to be kept in traffic, whilst at the same time the various shops were maintained at a high level of activity without the former congestion at bottlenecks in various parts of the works.

Upon the appearance of these engines the LMS distributed a small handbook on the class in which they justified naming the locomotives thus: "It was felt that added distinction and interest would be attached to these locomotives if they were named, and also it would be in line with the former traditions of some of the original constituent companies. Many of us remember the enthusiasm of our youth, maintained into later life, that we had in looking for the names of locomotives on our railway journeys, and we can remember the names of many famous locomotives, which if they had only a number, would have had no individuality for us."

The names chosen were of famous regiments in the British Army, together initially with names of well known pioneer locomotives of the past, although these latter were gradually replaced by further regimental names. As a matter of interest "Royal Scot" was chosen for the fact that as the 1st Foot (the Royal Regiment) it was the oldest regiment in the British Army, taking precedence of line regiments and dating from 1633.

The Derby engines were all eventually named as follows:

6150	The Life Guardsman	6160	Queen Victoria's Rifleman
6151	The Royal Horse Guardsman	6161	The King's Own
6152	The King's Dragoon Guardsman	6162	Queen's Westminster Rifleman
6153	The Royal Dragoon	6163	Civil Service Rifleman
6154	The Hussar	6164	The Artist's Rifleman
6155	The Lancer	6165	The Ranger (12th London Regiment)
6156	The South Wales Borderer	6166	London Rifle Brigade
6157	The Royal Artilleryman	6167	The Hertfordshire Regiment
6158	The Loyal Regiment	6168	The Girl Guide
6159	The Royal Air Force	6169	The Boy Scout

It was a Derby-built engine that had the distinction of representing the LMSR on a North America tour in May, 1933. She was No 6152, which exchanged numbers and names with 6100, and was fitted up for the trip to Chicago with statutory electric headlight and bell together with a floodlit nameplate "The Royal Scot" affixed to the smokebox door (see Plate 92). An LMS eight-coach train was shipped with the locomotive to Montreal aboard the ss Beaverdale, and the tour began on May 1, covering the lines to Ottawa, Toronto, Hamilton, Buffalo and thence over the New York Central line to Utica, Albany and Boston. The rest of the tour included New York, Philadelphia, Baltimore, Washington, Pittsburgh and Indianapolis, reaching Chicago on May 25, in time for the opening of the World's Fair on June 1.

After the Fair, during which over two million people visited the show train, the tour continued to Denver, Salt Lake City, Los Angeles, San Francisco, Seattle, Vancouver and Calgary. During the trip, between Pueblo and Denver, a 6,100ft summit in the Colorado Mountains was negotiated and between Calgary and Vancouver the Rocky Mountains were passed through, both without the use of banking assistance. The locomotive and train arrived back at Tilbury on December 5, 1933.

After the tour 6152 retained the name *Royal Scot* and a special name-plate commemorating the tour was affixed to the leading splashers, on each side, the presentation bell also being retained.

As with all the other engines of the class 46100, as she had been renumbered in June, 1948, was rebuilt in June, 1950 with a class 2A taper boiler, giving improved steaming performance and having a total heating surface of 1,862sq ft a reduction from the 2,081sq ft of the original engines. No 46100 was honourably retired from active service on British Railways in November, 1962, being the first of the class to be withdrawn. She was not however destined for the breakers yard, but was restored in 1963 to LMS maroon livery as No 6100 (albeit in-correctly) and purchased by Mr Billy Butlin for display at his Skegness holiday camp.

Hard on the heels of the "Scots" came the Patriot class, a smaller three-cylindered engine adequately described as an enlarged Claughton boiler on a Royal Scot chassis, or almost so. Two of these engines, Nos 5971 and 5902 were "rebuilt" at Derby to O/7560 and emerged in November, 1930 (*see Plate 93*). Although these were virtually new engines, being replacements for two Claughton's badly damaged in accidents on the Midland Division, for book keeping reasons they were labelled "rebuilt Claughtons". These first two engines utilised the bogie and driving wheels, reversing screw and whistle, firebox, dragbox and frame stretchers only, the main frames being new throughout whilst subsequent engines utilised practically nothing from the old ones.

They had 6ft 9in driving wheels on a 7ft 4in + 8ft coupled wheelbase with a leading bogie on 3ft 3in diameter wheels at 6ft 3in centres pivoted 9ft in front of the leading coupled wheel. The cylinders, one inside and two outside were 18in diameter × 26in stroke, and a G9½ superheated boiler was fitted with a total heating surface of 2,100sq ft and a grate area of 30.5sq ft. A 3,500gal tender, with space for 5½ tons of coal, (with coal rails) was fitted and weights were: leading bogie 21 tons, leading coupled 19 tons 19cwt, driving 20 tons 1cwt, trailing coupled 19 tons 15cwt, tender 42 tons 14cwt, totalling (in working order) 123 tons 9cwt.

The remainder of the Derby built "Baby Scots" as they came to be nicknamed were turned out between February and May, 1933 to order 8179. Later in their history most of the class were rebuilt from their original parallel boiler to taper boiler form. They were subsequently given names and numbers as follows:

Original Number	Renumbered	Name
5971	5500	*Patriot* (formerly *Croxteth*)
5902	5501	*St Dunstan's* (formerly *Sir Frank Ree*)
5954	5520	*Llandudno*
5933	5521	*Rhyl*
5973	5522	*Prestatyn*
5916	5525	*E. Tootal Broadhurst* (renamed *Colwyn Bay* 1937)
5963	5526	*Morecambe and Heysham*
5944	5527	*Southport*
5996	5528	*REME* (not named until 1959)
5905	5533	*Lord Rathmore*
5935	5534	*E. Tootal Broadhurst*
5997	5535	*Sir Herbert Walker KCB*

Shortly after the arrival of the original Royal Scots the LMS lost the services of Sir Cecil Walter Paget who retired in 1929 at the early age of 54. As recounted earlier in our story, Paget had most certainly left his mark on the Midland Company, and to perhaps a lesser degree on the LMS. He did not have many years of retirement to enjoy however, for on December 9, 1936, he died at Kings Newton, near Derby, aged 61. He had won the DSO in 1916 and the CMG in 1918 and his funeral service in St Andrew's Church, Derby, was attended not only by many high ranking LMS Officers but also representatives of his own regiment, the Royal Engineers, together with family mourners and friends from many parts of the country. He was laid to rest in the little churchyard at Sutton Bonnington, near Kegworth, Leics.

Also completed at Derby during January, February and March, 1930, was a further batch of LT&SR design 4-4-2 tank engines, Nos 2151–60 built to order O/7406 issued the previous May. These were similar to those built to O/5871 mentioned previously and were later renumbered 41969–78 when taken over by BR. All were withdrawn between 1955 and 1960.

At the beginning of August, 1931, a decision was taken to separate the Locomotive Works and the Locomotive Drawing Office, which had over a period been gradually wooed away from the direct pressures of those in authority in the works. Now, under closer supervision by the Chief Mechanical Engineer, incursions into its sanctified precincts were to be made even more difficult to the fraternity from the shops. A grand removal scheme was undertaken on August 6/7, when all the various drawings, tracings, records etc, not to mention much of the bulky furniture, was transported into relatively palatial, almost new quarters on the ground floor of a two-storey block of offices on the London Road, adjacent to the Carriage and Wagon Works.

Here the majority of the staff re-assembled on the Monday leaving behind only a few in the old office to look after the old joint lines work etc, in charge of one Jimmy Doleman, the others being J. H. Mather, A. E. Mitchell, F. Slater and clerk J. W. Croxall. Doleman was quite a character always being immaculately dressed, and easily recognisable with his highly polished boots and bowler hat whilst on his regular evening perambulations calling at various "public establishments" en route, where he would stay for exactly the same time on each and every occasion. It was even said that one could set one's watch by him, always catching him at a particular spot to the very minute!

Other changes in office were taking place all the time of course, and at the top of the tree it was the turn of Sir Henry Fowler to lay down the rod of office at the end of 1930, and in his place as CME of the LMS came E. J. H. Lemon up till then in charge of the Carriage and Wagon side, while Hewitt Beames came from Crewe to be Lemon's deputy "in residence" at the Derby HQ. Here now at Derby was a further clash of loyalties, with Symes in charge of the works and Beames, a Crewe man "in office" as Lemon's "representative on site". "Sammy" Symes, as he was respectfully known by his close friends was, as we have observed, the perfect gentleman and his interest in design, even down to details, was lifelong. It followed therefore that there was very little give or take between the camps but fortunately the conflict formed by the Crewe–Derby–Horwich triangle was to last for only one more year, for Lemon was to be promoted to a Vice-Presidency in charge of Traffic and Operation, leaving the post of CME vacant, and seizing this opportunity to put an end to former HQ loyalties once and for all the Directors were to appoint an outsider to the position and thus nip further power struggles in the bud.

Two interesting schemes were got out during Lemon's tenure in office, whose lineage it is very difficult to trace. Neither of these designs took on flesh and blood as it were, but they deserve a mention in this chronicle as "might have beens". The first was for a large 4-8-0 goods engine with a G8X boiler having a total heating surface of 1,733sq ft comprising tubes 1,550sq ft and firebox 183sq ft to which the super-heater added 365sq ft. The grate area was 30.5sq ft and working pressure 190psi. The 4ft 8½in diameter driving wheels on an equally divided coupled-wheelbase of 17ft 3in were driven on the second axle by inclined outside-cylinders 21in diameter × 26in stroke. The leading bogie on common 3ft 3½in wheels at 6ft 6in centres, was pivoted 8ft 3in in front of the leading driver. A standard 3,500gal six wheeled tender, having 5½ tons coal capacity, and a wheelbase of 13ft, made up a total wheelbase of 52ft 6in. Tractive effort was calculated at 32,775lb and working weights were to have been: engine 81 tons 10cwt, tender 42 tons 14cwt. As a design this looked to be excessively lengthy, and the short stovepipe chimney did nothing to enhance its appearance. The other more attractive proposal was for a 2-8-0 goods engine, also with 4ft 8½in diameter driving wheels on the same coupled wheelbase, but with two 19½in diameter × 26in stroke cylinders driving onto the third axle. This had a G7¾ superheated boiler of more orthodox design. Working weights were to be: engine 70 tons 1cwt, tender 42 tons 14cwt (as with the 4-8-0). Tractive effort would have been 29,747lb at 85 per cent boiler pressure.

There were of course quiet times in the design office and schemes such as this were turned out in large numbers to be vetted by the Chief Draughtsman, and if suitable passed on for approbation at a higher level and clearance with the Civil Engineer. Possibly only a quarter of all the designs proposed were ever considered seriously with a view to putting them into production.

CHAPTER FOURTEEN

Progress under Stanier
(1932-1947)

IN JANUARY, 1932 William Arthur Stanier arrived on the scene as the new CME. Here was a considerable turning point in locomotive design policy for the LMS, yet the change was not purely towards GWR practice, from which company Stanier had come, being C. B. Collett's principal assistant (Collett being Chief Mechanical Engineer). Instead designs were hammered out by Stanier and his development team with an eye to everything best in current practice whether it be from the Swindon camp or established design practices on the LMS whilst at the same time being innovative in all aspects of locomotive design. It must be stated however that Stanier's adherence to certain Swindon practices such as low degree superheat, reduced small tube heating surface and domeless boilers with smokebox regulators involved heavy expenditure to put matters right later.

Born in 1876, the son of the GWR Chief Stores Superintendent, Stanier had been educated at Wycliffe College, Stonehouse, and at the age of 16 had entered the Swindon Works as an apprentice. Five years later he became a draughtsman, and in 1900 Inspector of Materials. He then became, in quick succession, Technical Inspector at Swindon engine shed, Assistant Divisional Locomotive Superintendent first at Swindon then at Paddington, followed by his appointment as Works Assistant at Swindon. Eventually in 1920, he became Works Manager, and then in 1923 took his last post with the GWR as Collett's principal assistant. Stanier came to the LMS at a time of great stress and was immediately charged with carrying out a big programme of locomotive construction and standardisation. To his great credit within eight years he was to renew practically the whole of the LMS "first string" locomotive stock.

Following Stanier's arrival a swift examination of the state of the locomotive stock was made with the result that only five further compound 4-4-0s, to the amended Midland design, were built at Derby, these being Nos 935-9 turned out in August and September, 1932 to O/8078. The reign of the small engine policy on the LMS was thus swiftly terminated and in a relatively short time by "direct" methods, the rooted objections raised by the Midland Divisional Civil Engineer to higher axleloads, on account of long standing restrictions on bridge loadings together with many of the petty clearance restrictions applied rigorously on the loading gauge were effectively swept aside.

In 1932 the Derby Works were responsible for one particular innovation, this being the conversion of one of Johnson's 0-6-0 side tank engines, No 1831, into the first diesel hydraulic shunting locomotive ever to run on the LMS system (*see Plate 94*) and in fact an early forerunner of a long stream of such shunting locomotives, to be built for use throughout the country, although later locomotives mostly were to be of the diesel electric type. This conversion, to O/8071 of February 2, 1932, was done to ascertain what economies might accrue from the adoption of a diesel type shunting locomotive in marshalling yards.

The engine was a six-cylinder, heavy fuel-oil, 4-stroke type of 400bhp running at 750rpm and supplied by Davy-Paxman & Co of Colchester. The hydrostatic transmission was provided by Messrs Haslam and Newton of Derby, the transmitter unit being capable of infinite speed variations in either direction of rotation, up to a top speed of 25mph. The driving wheels were 4ft 7in in diameter. Two driving compartments were provided, one at each end of the unit, with controls duplicated on either side of each cab, and the total weight of the vehicle in working order was 46 tons 12cwt. Once in service however the gearbox gave a considerable amount of trouble, and after several years of frequently interrupted service it was withdrawn in 1939 and converted into Mobile Power Unit No 3.

One result of Stanier's arrival was that the Derby Works ceased to build new locomotive boilers in 1932, the last order being the building of five spare LT&SR Class 2 boilers Nos 8292–6 to order 8101. Subsequently this work was concentrated at Crewe, who supplied all boilers for new locomotives built at either of the two works from that date. However the Derby boiler shop continued to meet the now even more demanding need for repaired boilers in order to maintain an economic stock of the various types for engines shopped at Derby and Bow.

At the end of October, 1932, H. G. Ivatt left his post as Works Superintendent at Derby and travelled north to become Mechanical Engineer for Scotland, and in his place came G. S. Bellamy from the Motive Power Department. He no doubt felt at home quickly, for his early years of training had been spent at Derby while still a young man, and following war service in the Royal Engineers, he had returned in 1919 as Works Inspector, the following year becoming the resident Midland Company Inspector at Newcastle-on-Tyne for locomotives under construction. Various other posts led on to him being appointed Assistant Superintendent of Motive Power in April, 1928, his last post before taking charge at Derby.

It should be mentioned that at this time the Derby Works Superintendent was responsible not only for the Derby Works but also for the repair shops at Carlisle, Leeds, Sheffield, Belle Vue, Birmingham, Bristol, Bow and Kentish Town.

The Derby Works were not initially involved in the building of Stanier's new fleet of higher powered main-line locomotives, but were given an interim order for 10 0-4-4 side-tank engines of a new design, originally numbered 6400–409 (*see Plate 88*). These were built to O/7860 issued on June 8, 1931, and are officially credited to Stanier but it is doubtful if he had much influence at all in their design, beyond the later change from a stovepipe chimney, probably a Beames influence, to one of Stanier's own approved design. Even that small refinement improved the look of the locomotives considerably to the aesthetic eye, although Stanier was never very fond of them and, but for urgent operating requirements, they might even at this late stage have been redesigned.

The first one emerged from the Derby shops in December, 1932, and these locomotives have rightly been described by E. S. Cox* as the "final fling of the Midland mystique". As a design they were merely an up-dated version of Johnson's tanks originally designed way back in 1874, but dressed up with a few of the modern accoutrements. The driving wheels were 5ft 7in diameter on an 8 ft coupled wheelbase. The trailing bogie with 3ft 3½in diameter wheels at 6ft 6in centres was pivoted 12ft behind the trailing driver, giving a total wheelbase of 23ft 3in and the two inside cylinders were 18in diameter and 26in stroke. The second-hand G6 saturated boilers held 194 tubes of 1¾in outside diameter which provided 967sq ft of heating surface to which the firebox, larger than on the original Johnson design, added a further 104sq ft. The grate area was 17.5sq ft and the tractive effort, at 85 per cent of the boiler working pressure, was 17,099lb. Weight in working order was 58 tons 1cwt, with 1,350gal of water in the tanks and 3 tons of coal in the bunker. They were classed as 2P and No 6400 ran out on December 3, 1932, all 10 being complete by the following January 14.

One sad page in the history of the works was the decision made by Stanier in 1932 to scrap all the historic locomotives then preserved at Derby with the sole exception of the Johnson single 118.

The collection was begun by the preservation of the old Kirtley designed double framed 0-6-0 2385, which had been built by Kitson & Co in August 1856. She was repainted in black livery, unlined, and renumbered 421, her original number. She was also fitted with the correct design of original makers plates which unfortunately carried the engine number 421 rather than the correct makers number 507.

*Locomotive Panorama Vol. I by E. S. Cox

She was joined in April, 1928, by the Johnson single 673, which was restored to Midland crimson lake livery, fully lined out, and bearing her original number 118. The following year the last of the Park North London 4-4-0 outside-cylindered passenger tank engines, 6445, was withdrawn and brought to Derby for intended preservation.

In 1930 two further locomotives were withdrawn from service with a view to preservation. These were No 1226, a Johnson 0-4-4 passenger tank, restored to her former Midland Railway livery and renumbered 6, and No 1, a Kirtley double framed 2-4-0 tender engine also restored to MR crimson lake livery and renumbered 156A.

All these were placed in the "museum" in January, 1931, and might have been preserved there to this day but for Stanier's aversion to anything historical taking up valuable space in the works. With a swift stroke of his pen he signed away their future and all went to the erecting shop to be dissected under the acetylene torch and loaded into wagons as scrap, a sad end for such noble representatives of locomotive classes of yesteryear. Only the "spinner" remained.

The loss of the Kirtley 2-4-0 however was later remedied by the preservation of 158A, also built in 1866, which was withdrawn from service in July, 1947, as 20002 and restored to MR livery. She now resides in a place of honour in the Leicester Museum.

The Northern Counties Committee had become absorbed into the LMS along with the parent company in January, 1923, and in 1933 an order for four 2-6-0 two-cylindered superheated tender engines was filled, these being built to O/8207 of November 16, 1932 and carrying running numbers 90–93. The design was derived from the 2-6-4Ts and had outside cylinders, driven by 9in diameter piston valves having $6\frac{3}{8}$in travel, 19in diameter and 26in stroke. The leading pony truck had 3ft diameter driving wheels and the driving wheels on a 16ft 6in coupled wheelbase, were 6ft in diameter, the total wheelbase being 25ft 6in. The Belpaire fireboxed boiler, with an LMS superheater and pressed to 200psi carried 21 large and 121 small tubes, and the total evaporative surface was 1,080.75 sq ft, the superheater adding a further 266.25sq ft. Grate area was 25sq ft and the tractive effort at 85 per cent boiler pressure was 22,160lb. These boilers were built at Crewe. Working weight of the engine was 62 tons 10cwt, and the 2,500gal tender, with 5 tons of coal, weighed a further 32 tons 19cwt. They were made Class W and were named as follows:

90	*Duke of Abercorn*	92	*The Bann*
91	*The Bush*	93	*The Foyle*

Further engines of this type were built by the NCC up to 1942, and in

1938 Derby Works built ten 3,500gal high-sided tenders of 7 tons coal capacity to enable the locomotives to work the fast passenger services between Belfast and Portrush without the need to stop for water.

At this juncture a further brief note on the workshops themselves would be in order. Generally speaking a considerable reorganisation had again taken place. Many shops had changed use and various others added to, but the most important change had been the introduction of the new progressive system referred to previously under which engine and tender repairs had been reorganised so that an eight day schedule was allowed for the complete renovation of a locomotive under repair.

Formerly, as has been stated, engine repairs were allocated to small groups of erectors who were responsible for all the work done in the erecting shop on that particular engine, and similarly for a tender. Under a changed system already in use for some time separate groups of men were appointed for each main part of the engine each under a chargehand who was responsible for the documentation and day to day running of his section. Splitting up engine repairs resulted in the following main sections:

Stripping and examination Injectors, carriage warming, etc
Frames and cylinders   Wheeling
Boilers and smokeboxes   Tender frames and tanks
Motion and axleboxes

Under this system the three bays of the No 8 erecting shop, the only one now functioning as such, could in 1932 hold 38 engines and 15 tenders at any one time, giving a possible total output of about 1,400 engines per annum. Five overhead electric travelling cranes, each of 50 tons capacity and with a 10-ton auxiliary, were provided, together with three smaller cranes, also with similar auxiliaries, of 35 tons capacity. A further two small cranes of 10 tons capacity were also supplied.

Elsewhere the wheelshop had been provided with a Nobel & Lund wheel lathe equipped with multiple tooling arrangements which obviated the necessity for changing tools, and having a cutting speed of 30ft per minute. Also provided was a Craven wheel centre turning machine, and a machine for re-turning big end journals without having to remove wheels from axles, thereby preventing damage to the wheel seats, a great improvement.

In the flanging shop the original 260 ton hydraulic flanging press had been joined by a further press of 500 tons capacity installed in 1913. This press, still in use, has three power rams, two of which operate the main table and a central ram which can either be used with the table or independently. The furnaces, used in connection with the presses, were well capable of reaching the required working temperatures of 700degC for copper plates, and 900degC for steel plates.

Innovations in the boiler shop since our previous tour had included the introduction of the oxy-cutting machine for platework, using piped oxygen from the nearby British Oxygen Company's Works; electrically driven stay-tapping and stay-drilling machines; a hydraulic riveting plant using electrically-heated rivets and pneumatic stay-drivers. By means of the new progressive system, whereby distinct operations were performed in specific positions in the shop, a reduction from 80 odd to 34 boilers only under repair at any one time had been achieved without affecting the overall output.

Reorganisation of the boiler mounting shop had resulted in men no longer being forced to work on the stagings formerly used, a number of pits having been provided to house the firebox of each boiler, access to the box being provided from below. Hand driven tube expanders had been replaced by electrically driven ones, and power tools for facing up seatings and fittings had been installed.

After fitting up the boilers, suitably mounted after having been allocated to a particular engine (thereby eliminating the necessity for carrying a stock of mounted boilers), they were moved to the boiler test pits where they were tested both hydraulically and under steam pressure supplied from an adjacent stationary boiler.

The tinsmiths shop was still producing a large variety of that class of work, including oil cans, oil feeders, hand lamps and head lamps etc, both for the Motive Power Department and for supply to depots throughout the company's system.

In 1928 the original equipment in the power station had been amplified by the installation of a 1,500kW turbine, along with water softening and ash-removal plants. In addition the coal bunkers and three of the five boilers were reconstructed with new grates increasing their evaporation capacities from 25,000lb to 50,000lb per hour. The total annual output of the station had risen to 13million units, such was the increased demand.

Outputs from the foundries were constantly being increased as a result of the use of new and improved methods. The chair foundry had two cupolas working on alternate days, each giving an output of 250 tons per week amounting to 12,000 chairs. In the general iron foundry the output was up to 150 tons per week from each of two cupolas the most complicated work undertaken being the casting of cylinder blocks. The brass foundry, producing all the brass castings used in both the Locomotive and Carriage and Wagon Works, employed Morgan Furnaces fired by oil gas tar, a by-product of the Oil Gas Works nearby, each furnace being capable of holding 600lb of molten brass at a charging.

The machine and fitting shop alongside the erecting shop, was organised into a variety of specialist sections as follows:

Axlebox—employing Kearn's axlebox machines.

Motion detail—employing a variety of fixtures for the various fitting operations.

Cylinder—employing cylinder boring drilling and planing machines.

Frame slotting—employing slotting machines capable of making four cuts at once through a set of 20 engine or tender frames each of one inch thickness.

Frame straightening

Brass fitting—employing Asquith Vertical machines displacing centre lathes formerly used. Fitting up and repairing boiler details.

Brass finishing

Tool room—employed in the manufacture of twist drills, cutting tools, gauges etc, required in the various shops throughout the works. Also measuring machines.

Marking off tables—employed in marking up the various castings, items of platework etc.

In addition separate sections were established where groups of all the main types of machine tools were available to do the work best suited to their particular features.

In the paint shop at this time were housed the full sized models of Stephenson's *Rocket* and the *Northumbrian* locomotive built for use during the Liverpool and Manchester Railway Centenary Celebrations held at Liverpool in 1930.

Regarding the area of the works, the shops and offices covered area was calculated at about 20 acres with a ground area of some 80 acres, and the total staff employed, including apprentices, amounted to 3,500.

On the locomotive front the works continued turning out tank engines for a number of years in fact right up to 1955, but the next type to emerge from the erecting shop was a cleaned up Stanier version of the Fowler 2300 class, but this time with three cylinders. These locomotives were designed specifically for use on the old London, Tilbury and Southend section to replace the older tank engines of that line in working the fastest passenger trains. Thirty seven, Nos 2500–536, were built in all, of which five were constructed to O/8425 and the remainder to O/8503, and they were turned out between April and December, 1934 (*see Plate 86*).

As a design they were a great success, except with shed and workshop staff who complained somewhat over the limited access provided to the inside cylinder. Setting the slide bars and valve gear and attending to the glands was not the easiest of jobs. In appearance, they were an attractive and neat design. The side tanks sloped towards the front and the bunkers tapered towards the rear buffer beam, and were set in below the rear spectacle windows to give clear vision front and rear. The cabs were also fitted with side windows, providing much more protection for the footplate crew. As to dimensions, the 5ft 9in diameter driving wheels were on the standard Midland wheelbase. The leading pony truck was centred 9ft in front of the leading driver, and the trailing bogie 9ft 6in to the rear of the trailing driver. The three cylinders, of equal size, were 16in in diameter and 26in stroke, all drove onto the second coupled-axle. The class 4C domeless tapered boiler, pressed to 200psi, carried 145 small tubes of $1\frac{3}{4}$in diameter and 12 large tubes of $5\frac{1}{8}$in diameter containing 12 superheater elements of $1\frac{3}{8}$in od. Heating surface was: tubes 1,011sq ft, superheater 160sq ft, firebox 137sq ft and the grate area 25sq ft. The boiler barrel was 11ft $10\frac{1}{4}$in long and 4ft 9in diameter increasing to 5ft 3in. Tractive effort, at 85 per cent boiler pressure, was calculated to be 24,600lb and weight in working order, with 2,000gal of water in the tanks and $3\frac{1}{2}$ tons of coal on board, was 92 tons 5 cwt. All later engines had boilers with 18-element superheaters, and three had domed boilers with a larger grate area of 26.7sq ft. Fortunately the first of these engines to be built is now preserved at Bressingham in working order.

Following these engines in December, 1934 and January, 1935, the works built 10 of Stanier's three-cylinder Jubilee class 4-6-0 express locomotives to order 8610. These were all eventually named as listed below:

5655	Keith	5660	Rooke
5656	Cochrane	5661	Vernon
5657	Tyrwhitt	5662	Kempenfelt
5658	Keyes	5663	Jervis
5659	Drake	5664	Nelson

This design, being a further development of the Patriot class, is almost too well known to merit description here, but suffice it to say that they had 17in diameter × 26 in stroke cylinders, two outside and one between the frames, 6ft 9in diameter driving wheels and they carried a 3A superheated taper boiler with total heating surface of 1852.4sq ft the boiler being pressed to 225psi. Rated tractive effort was 26,610lb.

These were to many most handsome engines, and were to be seen all over the LMS system, the Derby ones being allocated as built to Nottingham (3), Leeds (4), Kentish Town, Derby and Leeds in that order. The fine performance put up by No 5660 *Rooke* on trial has been well chronicled elsewhere, a tribute not only to Stanier's design but also to the quality of Derby workmanship. During a four-day period, beginning on October 12, 1937, she ran from Bristol to Leeds, Glasgow, back to Leeds and thence to Bristol again. Weight of the train including dynamometer car, was 305 tons, and perhaps the most outstanding part of the trial was the run from Settle to Carlisle, a distance of $73\frac{1}{2}$ miles covered in 72 min, a most remarkable achievement. Highest drawbar-hp recorded was 1,250 and average coal consumption 3.9lb per drawbar-hp/hr.

The next class built in the Derby Works was Stanier's version of the Fowler 2-6-2T which had been built in 1930–32. Improvements included side-window cabs, sloping tank tops and high-centred bunkers, giving clear vision to front and rear, and a Class 6A taper boiler with a single row of seven superheater elements having a total heating surface of 1,125.9sq ft and with a grate area of 19.2sq ft was fitted to No 121 onwards being domeless for Nos 121–44 and domed for the later builds. The earlier engines Nos 71–120 had Class 6 boilers with a total heating surface of 954.3sq ft and a grate area of 17.5sq ft. The same general layout was used as with the original class, with wheels at the same centres and the same size of cylinders. The orders are tabulated below:

Order	Locomotive Nos	Year built
O/8638	71–90	1935
O/8880	91–110	1935
O/8882	111–44	1935
O/9696	145–59	1937
O/9710	160–74	1937–8
New series		
O/46	175–84	1938

Further locomotives Nos 185–209, were built at Crewe in 1937–8.

In 1940, commencing with locomotive 169, a larger size of boiler was to be fitted to engines with the original class 6A boilers, when renewal became necessary. The new boilers, classified 6B, had an increased minimum boiler-diameter of 4ft 6in instead of 4ft 2in the boiler being $2\frac{15}{16}$in higher, and an increased heating surface of 1,246sq ft as against 1,124sq ft, the grate area remaining constant at 19.2sq ft. Only six locomotives were so treated however, the others being Nos 142, 148, 163, 167 and 203. The engines built to the first three orders originally

N

had domeless boilers in common with many of Stanier's other early designs. As new they went all over the system, a few even going very far afield to Scotland to work in the Northern Division, at Dumfries and Hamilton, but the majority being spread around the Midland and Western Divisions, where they were put to use mainly on local passenger trains, replacing many of the older superannuated engines of the pre-LMS era.

It was clear by this time that Stanier put a lot of faith in the usefulness of the 2-6-2 and 2-6-4 tank engines, and for many years the erecting shop at Derby abounded in this genus. In fact from 1927 to 1950, with the exception of 1944, not a year passed without a new tank engine emerging from the Derby paint shop.

Following up his successful three-cylinder 2-6-4Ts for the Southend line Stanier designed a two-cylindered version, with the same basic configuration, wheel diameters and spacings etc, the cylinders being 19$\frac{5}{8}$in diameter × 26in stroke. These were to become a basic standard design, and apart from detailed modifications, they continued to be built in this form and even with the advent of C. E. Fairburn in 1944 a few basic modifications enabled the building of this type to be continued for a further period. The Derby-built engines were as follows:

Order	Locomotive Nos	Year built	Boiler
O/8884	2537–44	1935	Domeless with 18 element superheater
O/9204	2425–44	1936	Domed with 18 element superheater
O/9206	2445–64	1936	Domed with 18 element superheater
O/9208	2465–94	1936–7	Domed with 18 element superheater
New series			
O/112	2618–27	1938	Domed with 21 element superheater
O/114	2628–37	1938	Domed with 21 element superheater
O/116	2638–52	1938–9	Domed with 21 element superheater
O/657	2653–62	1940–41	Domed with 21 element superheater
O/660	2663–72	1942–3	Domed with 21 element superheater

As regards the ubiquitous 0-6-0 goods tender engine of pre-grouping times, although Stanier had evolved two designs of standard 0-6-0 locomotive, intended to become part of his standard locomotive stock, together with a design for a 2-6-0 tender engine, developed from the 2-6-4 tank engines, which was placed on the building programme diagram in 1937, in the event the Operating Department said that they did not want the 2-6-0, but with 700 odd Class 4 0-6-0s in stock all they wanted were a few more of these. He therefore arranged for the construction of a further 45 of the Class 4F "big goods" to Fowlers design, of which Derby built three orders, for a total of 30 locomotives in all, as follows:

Order	Locomotive Nos	Year built
O/303	4577–86	1939
O/650	4587–96	1939
O/653	4597–4606	1940–41

These engines were little altered but for the provision of the Stanier design of chimney, the use of flat as against fluted coupling rods, and the elimination of piston tail rods. With the building of these final batches, the 4Fs totalled in all 772 locomotives built over a period of 31 years of which 192 had been turned out for the Midland, 5 for the S&DJR and 575 for the LMSR*

While the second batch was building, war was declared with Germany, and tentative preliminary plans for the use of Derby Works, along with other railway workshops throughout the country, in assisting the war effort were put into operation. The various workshops of the LMS at that time formed one of the biggest engineering organisations in the world, and these were gradually geared up to war production alongside their normal duties of maintaining locomotives and rolling stock, for the railways became the country's life-lines in the long struggle for peace that was to follow.

In common with other workshops, those at Derby had been reorganised both physically and administratively, but by the time the "great effort" was called for in April, 1940 only a trickle of Government orders was coming in, and new locomotive construction had been trimmed drastically. Inevitably this had led to the release of a number of skilled and semi-skilled men into the armed services and other industries more involved with war work.

Following the surrender of France the Government's demands became many and diverse and what had begun in quite a small way expanded rapidly and some of the Derby shops had to be considerably reorganised to cope with the influx of aircraft components.† Initially new wings for Hurricanes and Typhoon fighter aircraft and Horsa

*See article in SLS Journal Vol. 43 No. 504 page 196 (July 1967).
† The L.M.S. at War by George C. Nash. LMSR 1956.

gliders were a major requirement, and these were largely produced in the nearby Carriage and Wagon Works, but later into the works came main components, fuselages etc for the Whitley, Hampden and Lancaster bombers and Spitfire fighter aircraft. These often came straight from the battle field via RAF depots, and were stripped down, put on mobile trolleys and repairs speedily carried out down to the last inspection and coat of paint. Also produced were 25- and 17-pounder field guns for the army, searchlight projectors, tank seats, and turrets, Bailey bridges and bomb casings and in order to cope with this influx of work women were taken on in the Derby shops for the second time, and they proved to be fully equal to the task. Later still a number of Prisoners of War were set to work in the shops, under adequate supervision of course!

As the war progressed the urgent need for more motive power forced Stanier, often against his better judgement, to reprieve many of the old engines at the end of their economic life and have them put into good running order again for a further few years of war service.

It should be mentioned in passing that the repair facilities of the Derby Works were occasionally made available for the shopping of private company locomotives, which were given the necessary refurbishing before being returned to traffic. During 1940 two such locomotives were shopped at Derby for the Royal Arsenal, Chorley, Lancs., these being a former Lancashire and Yorkshire Railway 0-4-0 freight tank *Hannah* together with an ex-London & South Western Railway 0-4-0 freight tank which had a very interesting history.* This latter was the first engine built at the Eastleigh Works of the LSWR in September, 1910 being then numbered 101. It was sold in May, 1917, to the Ministry of Munitions for £1,350 and had a very chequered career. It arrived at the Derby Works on a low-loader lorry on June 17, 1940, with its cab and chimney removed and after repair was returned to Chorley and then apparently eventually sent to Grangemouth, Scotland, still being in existence as a stationary boiler in mid-1951.

In 1939 the first of a long line of LMS diesel electric shunting locomotives emerged from the converted bay of the old paint shop. This was No 7080, part of order 458, equipped with a six-cylinder English Electric 350bhp diesel engine driving the six coupled 4ft 3in diameter wheels through a jackshaft, and this locomotive went into service on May 25, of that year (*see Plate 95*).

These shunters, classified OF and weighing 55 tons 5cwt in working order, were the culmination of an extensive investigation into the possibilities of diesel traction for further use both in the form of shunting locomotives and main line passenger units.

*Locomotives of the LSWR by D. L. Bradley. Railway Correspondence & Travel Society.

One personality closely connected with this work and who can really be said to have "fathered" the introduction of diesel power on the LMSR was Thomas Hornbuckle, who had joined the Midland Railway as an electrical engineer under Johnson in 1901. He served an apprenticeship with Hornsbys of Grantham, who were at that time building Ackroyd Stuart hot bulb ignition oil engines. Hornbuckle had pioneered the introduction of a range of standard electric motors for use on the Midland and after appointments to various positions he ultimately became Chief Technical Assistant to the CME.

An official enquiry in 1932 eventually led to the trial of 11 prototypes of shunting locomotives from various makers and utilising various types of final drives and early in 1934 the Traffic Department, satisfied with the results so far obtained, asked for 20 more diesel shunters capable of dealing with the heaviest yard work. Since it was vitally important that these should be successful if the use of such locomotives were to be extended in the future, Hornbuckle recommended the purchase of 350hp 0-6-0 diesel electric types, leaving the development of a fully satisfactory diesel mechanical design for the future.

The order was divided between the English Electric Co and Sir W. G. Armstrong Whitworth and Co, and delivery of the locomotives was made between January and December, 1936.

It was unfortunate to a degree that the responsibility for the electrical part of the design passed in 1934 from the CME to the Electrical Engineer into which position C. E. Fairburn had just come from the English Electric Co. This decision effectively blocked the future development of mechanical transmission.

Hornbuckle recommended the use of a double reduction gear drive from the motors, having had experience of the failure of the drive on the diesel hydraulic from excessive pressure during low speed shunting, but the English Electric Co did not adopt this suggestion, merely increasing the reduction obtained from the single gear drive. After early troubles with the English Electric Co locomotives, both types gave satisfactory service, although the Armstrongs made the greatest impression on the Traffic Department and resulted in a further 30 locomotives with their design of jackshaft drive being ordered and built at Derby as detailed below.

Following these all future orders were to be built without the jackshaft, which enabled the coupled wheelbase to be reduced from 6ft + 9ft 3in to 5ft 9in + 5ft 9in, and coupled with the reduction in the size of driving wheels from 4ft 3in to 4ft ½in, the working weight was reduced to 47 tons 5cwt and they retained the double reduction gear, which was adopted as the future standard.

These locomotives were immediate winners, both economically and technically and the LMS led the rest of the country in the introduction of this type of traction. They remained a basic standard type, and are still doing valuable service on BR today. The Derby built orders up to 1948 were as follows:

Order	Locomotive Nos	Year built
O/458	7080–4(Jackshaft)	1939
O/486	7085–99(Jackshaft)	1939–40
O/1333	7100–09(Jackshaft)	1941
O/1334	7110–19(Jackshaft)	1942
O/3239	WD 70260–4 (Gear)	1944
Part O/3240	WD70265–73 (Gear)	1944–5
Part O/3240	7120–5 (Gear)	1945
O/1705	7126–31 (Gear) & 12045–48 (Gear)	1947–8

At the end of 1942, Stanier was appointed Scientific Adviser to the Ministry of Production and as such had to relinquish most of his work as CME of the LMS and C. E. Fairburn, mentioned above, took over the post as acting CME in October, 1942, until appointed permanently to that post in mid-1944. He held the position for only a comparatively short time however for he died in October, 1945.

Only one steam locomotive design is credited to Fairburn, that of a generally redesigned 2-6-4T based on Stanier's two-cylindered type. On these locomotives the "sacred" driving wheel spacing of 8ft + 8ft 6in was dispensed with for virtually the first time on a tank engine since Johnson's day, with very few exceptions.

These engines had 5ft 9in diameter driving wheels spaced at 7ft 7in + 7ft 9in centres, thus saving 1ft 5in on the length of the locomotive and enabling them to work round a five chain radius curve as against a six chain minimum curve for the earlier engines. All carrying wheels were 3ft 3½in diameter, the leading pony truck centred 9ft in front of the first driver, and the trailing bogie 9ft 6in to the rear of the third driving axle. The class 4C taper boiler, carrying three rows of superheater tubes and pressed to 200psi, gave a total heating surface of 1,596sq ft with grate area 26.7sq ft. The two outside cylinders were 19⅝in diameter × 26in stroke. Water capacity in the side and back tanks was 2,000gal, and there was room for 3½ tons of coal. Weight in working order was 85 tons 5cwt, a useful saving of some 12cwt on the Stanier version.

First to emerge from the Derby shops was 2673 at the end of March, 1945, and the 140 members of the class turned out by the LMS from Derby are tabulated opposite.

Order	Locomotive Nos	Year built
O/8277	2673-7	1945
O/8278	2678-87	1945
O/8467	2688-99, 2200-2	1945
O/8468	2203-2222	1945-6
O/672	2223-32	1946
O/675	2233-52	1946
O/678	2253-72	1946-7
O/1676	2273-92	1947
Part O/1678	2293-99	1947
Part O/1678	2187-99	1947-8

In 1943-4 the Derby Works were privileged to turn out some of Stanier's famous "Black Five" two-cylindered 4-6-0 tender engines, which, along with his 2-8-0s, were to become maids of all work during the war and after. These engines have been described too frequently to warrant details being given here. Suffice it to say that the outside cylinders of the standard form were $18\frac{1}{2}$in diameter × 28in stroke and the driving wheels 6ft diameter. The 3B boiler, pressed to 225psi, carried total heating surface of 1,998sq ft and the grate area was 28.65sq ft. Tractive effort at 85 per cent boiler pressure, was 25,455lb and weight in working order was: engine 72 tons 2cwt, tender 53 tons 13cwt, totalling 125 tons 15cwt. Details of the Derby orders were:

Order	Locomotive Nos	Year built
O/3836	5472-81	1943
O/4141	5482-96	1943-4
O/4888	5497-99 4800-06	1944
O/8283	4807-25	1944

Replacing Fairburn as CME came H. G. Ivatt, and on February 1, 1946, he set up his office at Derby with R. C. Bond as Mechanical Engineer and A. E. Robson as the Works Superintendent at Derby, replacing J. Rankin who had served in the position since the departure of G. S. Bellamy on April 30, 1941. Rankin had been an apprentice with Andrew Barclay Sons & Co Ltd of Kilmarnock, and joined the Midland Railway Company at Derby in 1920 becoming Works Inspector in February, 1923. From there he became assistant to the Works Managers at Crewe, Horwich and Derby in succession, and from September, 1939 to July, 1940 he was acting Works Superintendent at Derby during Bellamy's absence.

In the locomotive drawing office at Derby, changes had also taken place in the top position. A. E. Owen, in office as Chief Draughtsman since October, 1937, and formerly chief draughtsman of the Furness Railway Company was replaced by a Crewe man, George Reginald Nicholson, who took charge on November 23, 1942, during the thin years of the war. He had come from Chile and joined the LMS in 1932 at Horwich, as a draughtsman on the board. He moved to Crewe in October, 1933, his last post before coming to Derby. On March 25, 1945, he returned to Crewe in a similar position and was replaced at Derby temporarily by E. A. Langridge who served as acting Chief Draughtsman until the end of September, when J. W. Caldwell was appointed permanently. He was another Horwich man who had joined the Lancashire and Yorkshire Railway as a premium apprentice in January, 1918.

In overall charge of both the Locomotive and Carriage and Wagon drawing offices was T. F. Coleman as Chief Draughtsman, and he retained this position from the departure of Herbert Chambers to Euston on March 17, 1935 until his retirement at the end of July, 1949. Chambers himself died quite suddenly in September, 1937, aged 52 and his loss to the company was a very real one.

Ivatt's first design was a batch of ten 2-6-4 tank engines, for the NCC, of 5ft 3in gauge (*see Plate 90*). Two orders were built at Derby during 1946–7 as follows:

Order	Locomotive Nos	Year built
O/669	NCC 5–8	1946
O/1674	NCC 1–4, 9 & 10	1947

These were a development of the LMS 2-6-4T engines, but with 6ft driving wheels, and were classified WT by the NCC. The two outside cylinders were 19in diameter × 26in stroke and weight in working order was 87 tons 10cwt. Tractive effort, at 85 per cent of the boiler working pressure of 200psi, was calculated to be 22,160lb.

The boilers provided for these engines were generally standard with the 2-6-0 tender locomotives built previously, somewhat modified by the addition of a self cleaning smokebox, rocking firegrate and self emptying ashpan. The boiler also incorporated top feed apparatus, unusual on the LMS for a parallel boiler, as was the circular handwheel in the centre of the smokebox door, a relic of BNCR locomotive practice. The livery, as turned out, was black with straw lining and maroon edging, and the number was displayed on a cast plate on the bunker sides, the side tanks carrying the letters "NCC".

In order to despatch these from Derby the completed locomotives had to be partially dismantled, the boiler side-tanks and bunker went in three wagons and the main frames went on a special flat vehicle. Upon arrival in Ireland the main frames were placed on the leading and trailing driving wheels and hauled to the NCC shops for the remainder of the locomotive to be re-assembled. The first was delivered to Belfast on August 6, 1946, the remainder following at fortnightly intervals.

One further event needs to be recorded before we close this chapter and the record of locomotive building at Derby under the LMS and pass into the short steam era of British Railways. This was the emergence from the No 10A Diesel Shop on December 5, 1947, of No 10000, the first main line diesel-electric locomotive to run in Britain on revenue earning service (*see Plate 96*).

The story began, as E. S. Cox has recorded*, at a meeting at Stafford on May 20, 1946, between representatives of the LMS and English Electric Companies an agreement was reached to proceed with the construction of two prototypes, each of 1,600hp and capable of working as a coupled unit of 3,200hp. The mechanical parts were designed in the Derby locomotive drawing office along with all the installation drawings, under the direct control of T. F. Coleman, and construction of No 10000 commenced in the works in the summer of 1947 to order 2510, the locomotive being completed in six months. The diesel engine, supplied by the English Electric Co, was their 16SVT unit with 16 cylinders of 10in bore and 12in stroke, running at a maximum speed of 750rpm and having a continuous rating of 1,600hp. The generator continuous rating was 1,500 amps 727 volts, and each traction motor, with 55/18 gear ratio, had a continuous rating of 178hp at 500 amps, 300 volts. The locomotive, mounted on two six wheeled bogies at 35ft 6in centres and on wheelbases of 8ft + 7ft 8in, with 3ft 6in diameter wheels, weighed 127 tons 13cwt in working order.

No 10000 made its first run to London on December 16, 1947, the second unit No 10001, went into service on July 10, 1948, and after an extensive trial period the two made an inaugural run on "The Royal Scot" train from Euston to Glasgow, non-stop, on June 1, 1949. The original livery for 10000 was black bodywork with silver roof and a wide polished aluminium band down each side of the body above the aluminium numbers 10000 (on the cab side at each end) and letters LMS. The appearance was further enhanced by the aluminium painting of the bogie frames and spring gear. Both locomotives were later re-painted in BR green livery lined out in orange and black.

There is no doubt that these units were a great tribute to the craftsmanship and know-how of both English Electric and the designers and workshop staff at Derby, and they gave many years of reliable service before being withdrawn for scrap. It seems a great pity that one of these

Locomotive Panorama Vol. I by E. S. Cox. Ian Allan Ltd, 1965.

locomotives was not preserved rather than the Deltic now reposing in a place of honour in the Science Museum in London.

To cope with the expected expansion of the diesel fleet on the LMS one bay of the former paint shop, some 450ft long and 45ft wide, was converted into a special diesel shop and numbered "10A". Three engines roads with pits ran the length of the shop and lifting facilities were provided by the installation of a new overhead crane gantry carrying two 50 ton travelling cranes. The system provided for general, service and casual repairs. A general repair, undertaken after 60,000 miles on shunters and representing seven or eight years in service, required complete stripping, rebuilding and repainting, whilst a service repair after three or four years in service, following a 25,000 to 30,000 miles run concerned mainly the diesel engine itself, this being stripped for attention to bearings, pistons, valve gear and fuel injection equipment. Other work done involved checking auxiliaries and electrical equipment, checking and testing air reservoirs and brake gear, and necessary attention to axleboxes, tyre turning etc. The casual repair was for rectification of faults developing in service, repair to collision damage, etc, where these were beyond the capabilities of the running depots.

At the end of October, 1947, A. E. Robson was succeeded as Works Superintendent by T. F. B. Simpson, undoubtedly one of the most popular persons ever to fill that post, who arrived on November 1, from the post of Assistant for water supplies and water softening in the CME Department at Derby having previously been with the CME Department at Manchester where he had been District Outdoor Machinery Assistant from December, 1943. "Freddie" was a pupil of D. L. Rutherford the Locomotive, Carriage and Wagon Superintendent of the Furness Railway Company, Barrow, and by 1925 had become Assistant Works Superintendent of the Barrow shops, later moving to Horwich and Euston. He was a man with a natural flair for organisation and an excellent manager of men, knowing a large proportion by name. His conversation was always enlightening and usually contained those quick flashes of perceptive wit that endeared him to every member of his staff.

Before closing this chapter, mention must be made of the opening of the Locomotive Works Apprentice Training School at Derby in 1947, the forerunner of similar Works Training Schools at other main works throughout the country. On the Midland Company apprentices had for many years been taken on, after suitable family references had been provided, and almost immediately allocated to a chosen trade, serving their time usually from 14 years of age to their twenty-first birthday. Their remuneration was not paid out of the contract price awarded to the group of workmen with which they worked but by the company itself, and the apprentice scale in the 1880s was as follows:

14 years	5s 7½d per week
15 years	6s 9d per week
16 years	7s 10½d per week
17 years	9s 0d per week
18 years	11s 3d per week
19 years	13s 6d per week
20 years	15s 9d per week
21 years	21s 0d per week

After age 21 the apprentice was in due course handed his indentures of apprenticeship and set on as a craftsman.

By 1943 the disposition of the various apprentices in the various shops was as shown in Table II.

The engineering apprentice differed from the trade apprentice in that he was drawn from secondary and public schools, holding a matriculation or school certificate and being over sixteen but under eighteen years of age, although the promotion of a trade apprentice to this grade was possible on the basis of outstanding progress in the shops, at technical studies and on his personality. The same wage rates applied.

The Progressive System of Workshop Training for apprentices was introduced by the LMS into the Derby Locomotive Works in 1932, later being extended to the other main works of the company. Then, shortly after the outbreak of war in 1939, the LMS management began to consider one particular aspect of apprentice training, namely that boys were being placed in the various workshops without much attention being paid to their natural ability or to which trade they were best suited.

As a result of an interim report submitted by E. J. Larkin in June, 1941 a remit was given him to devise a training scheme for all apprentices and all boy machinists to follow before being placed in the general workshops. His report, of March, 1943, advocated the setting up of apprentice training schools in the seven main works of the LMSR, but due to the possibility of the war effort being disrupted by the implementation of his proposals, action was deferred until the cessation of hostilities.

In April, 1946, approval was given for the setting up of the first Works Training School in Derby Locomotive Works, and space was allocated, adjacent to the main office buildings and behind the general stores, for the erection of classrooms, gymnasium and a large training workshop together with office accommodation. The school was com-

TABLE II.

ALLOCATION OF TRADE APPRENTICES ACCORDING TO SHOP—DERBY LOCOMOTIVE WORKS 1943.

Age Group	Shop															
Years of age	Boiler	Boiler mounting	Brass foundry	Copper-smiths'	Erecting	Iron foundry	Machine	Mill-wrights'	Paint	Pattern	Smiths	Tin-smiths'	Tube	Weld-ing	Wheel	Total
15–16	28	—	—	3	—	—	47	—	1	—	—	—	2	—	5	86
16–17	15	5	—	—	7	—	30	2	1	1	1	1	3	—	3	69
17–18	12	2	—	1	24	—	11	—	1	2	—	2	1	—	1	57
18–19	17	3	1	1	15	—	18	2	—	2	1	1	—	—	2	63
19–20	12	4	1	1	16	1	17	2	1	1	1	2	—	1	3	62
20–21	16	6	1	2	27	—	18	1	1	1	1	1	—	1	2	78
All ages	100	20	3	8	89	1	141	7	4	7	4	7	6	2	16	415

Special Note In addition to the above, there were 39 Engineering Apprentices, 3 Foundry Boys, 11 Hammer Drivers and 40 sundry staff and Shop Office Boys, making a grand total of 508.

pleted by Easter 1947, at a cost of £49,000. The first intake of thirty 14 year olds was taken on, and activities commenced under the direction of the Chief Instructor, H. J. Thomas. A further thirty boys were taken on in August, and on December 4, 1947, Sir Robert Burrows, then Chairman of the LMS accompanied by the Vice Chairman, Sir Harold Hartley, who had been largely instrumental in getting the scheme off the ground, performed the official opening ceremony.

A further thirty boys were taken on after the 1947 Christmas holiday, but the following year the school leaving age was raised to 15 years, and in order to keep the school functioning to quota, some trade apprentices were brought back from the workshops, to give them the benefit of training in basic workshop practice.

After completion of the 12 month course in the school, the apprentice trainee was transferred to the main workshops to progress round those shops connected with the trade to which he had been found most suited and in which he was to specialise, by spending a definite time on each section. At the age of 18 a report showing progress in practical ability and educational successes was submitted, and young men showing outstanding ability were considered for promotion as Engineering Apprentice whose training covered a much wider field including administration. I am indebted to Mr H. J. Thomas, now Training Officer for British Railways Workshops for his valued assistance in the compilation of these notes, which, the author appreciates, do scant justice to this great model scheme for apprentice training, and which has now been adopted by the Engineering Industry Training Board in their recommendations for all apprentice training schemes.

One further trainee grade was that of pupil, a limited number of whom were accepted for a pupilage of two years duration without premium. These were admitted entirely on merit, normally being in possession of an engineering degree, and were usually over 21 and under 24 years of age. Their course covered every important section of workshop practice including the running department, planning and drawing offices and experimental and dynamometer car work. A very limited number of such pupils of outstanding promise were promoted to engineer pupils, with a course extending over three years, covering further areas of training, those chosen being definitely destined for the corridors of managerial power.

CHAPTER FIFTEEN

The Steam Age Closes
(1948-1963)

ON THE FIRST DAY of January, 1948, the four main line groups of railways in Britain became "nationalised", and the Derby Works found itself now in competition with other works scattered throughout the length and breadth of the new British Railways system. Little did anyone realise at that time that within the space of some 20 years the steam locomotive would be a thing of the past.

At first the change of ownership meant little to the men in the shops, for the former designs of the old LMS Company continued to be produced, and the first design to be perpetuated was the 2-6-4T, the building of which must, by now, have become almost second nature to the men of the new work section in the erecting shop.

Forty more Fairburn pattern tanks were produced to O/2420 between April, 1948, and February, 1949, these being given the numbers 42147-86, and this design was chosen as an initial standard for BR, batches being built also at the Brighton Works of the former Southern Railway Company. The others built at Derby were:

Order	Locomotive Nos	Year built
O/3282	42107-46	1949-50
O/4310	42050-65	1950

As may be observed 40000 had been added to the running numbers of the original 2000 number series. This was to avoid duplication of engine numbers with locomotives absorbed from the other three companies. The majority of LMS locomotives had their numbers similarly altered, except for those in the 20000 series which were renumbered in the range 58000 upwards with a few exceptions.

At the end of 1948 the first of a further batch of 0-6-0 diesel shunting locomotives, No 12049, emerged from the diesel shop, having been built to O/2437, and the remainder of the batch of ten followed in sequence. The original shunters, numbered 7080-99 and 7110-31 were renumbered 12003-12044 in sequence, thus removing all diesel locomotives into a separate number sequence 10000 upwards.

Further shunters were built in large numbers, and the list opposite gives the remainder of this type built to the end of 1952.

Order	Locomotive Nos	Year built
O/3285	12059–68	1949–50
O/4311	12069–87	1950
O/5127	12088–12102	1951–2

In 1952 the Derby Works turned out the first of a long string of orders for the new BR standard design of shunter, based on the old LMS design but with 4ft 6in diameter driving wheels, these being 13000–24 built to O/6232 between October, 1952 and June, 1953, No 13000 being put into traffic on October 8, 1952. Up to 1960, when the building of this type ceased at Derby, no less than 474 of these locomotives had been built in the shops there.

The final two orders of steam locomotives for the NCC were built during 1949–50, these being for eight more 2-6-4 tank engines, Nos 50–53 built to O/3283 and 54–57 built to O/4332 (see Plate 90).

In a works as large as that at Derby it is not surprising that among the workmen in the various shops there are those who stand out as characters in their own right, and also some who draw attention to themselves by their eccentricities, nevertheless being excellent workmen. Most of those to be mentioned in this chapter are now deceased, but should there be one or two still alive I hope they will accept the mention of their names in this book as a compliment to the fact that they were so individual as to stand out from the crowd and make life in the workshop more interesting at times for the rest of the staff.

Perhaps the most well known of all the characters of recent years was Samuel Jennison or "Noggin" as he was known to friends and antagonist alike. His somewhat unkempt bewhiskered appearance belied his reputed private wealth. He was a labourer in the No 9 machine shop, and boasted a vintage Midland Railway barrow, with solid cast iron wheels, which he trundled about the shop and the yards with his various loads. The shout of his nickname was guaranteed to stop him in his tracks and cause him to spin round to seek out his tormentor. Many were the unkind pranks played upon him, such as drilling through the bottom of his tea or "mashing" can and screwing it inside a cupboard, also the hoisting of his barrow up high on a pillar crane, which was of course unattended when he came to get it down! Collections of washers or white metal "coins" were often given to him, and his proudest moment came when the shop foreman and his assistant personally presented him with a brass medal for the tidiest shop on the grounds!

Fellow labourer with Sam was Percy Oakley or "Little Percy" as he was fondly known. Because he insisted having his barrow handle attached upside down, he and his loads were instantly recognisable, even at a distance, on account of his permanent stoop when pushing his barrow. He was very small, but wiry, in build. He always smoked a straight stemmed ancient clay pipe, and had the most unusual habit of removing his wooden clogs in frosty weather, "to get a better grip" with assistance from his thick woollen socks. He was immensely strong for his size, and is said to have served on a minesweeper during World War I. Some of the loads moved by Percy would, I believe, have defeated larger men. In fact he often had to swing on the end of his barrow handle to raise its body clear of the floor and get it moving. One morning he arrived to find his barrow wheels missing but, unlike Sam, he did not complain vociferously, but merely searched until he found the various parts secured in the vaults beneath the shop floor. He then patiently reassembled his vehicle before commencing the morning's work.

Harold Walker was another labouring character who always insisted on altering the name on his weekly clock card to "Merryweather", much to the annoyance of the clerical staff. His quiet periods, when he would stand deep in thought in the middle of some shop or yard, were viewed quizically by his workmates.

Many more characters could be mentioned, Ernest Woodward the No 9 shop crane driver, affectionately christened "Merrylegs" on account of his rather peculiar walk; Sammy Collis, nicknamed Mr So-So on account of his use of the phrase while instructing in the making of some particular item prior to machining thus: "Well you measure up so-so, then along so-so and across the centres so-so".

A well loved foreman was Tommy Ison, caught one day with a tinned penny made to look like a half crown, but soldered to a nail and driven hard into the wooden shop floor. William Mark Anthony Draicy (or Draisey), known to all and sundry as "Spider", was a bachelor with an enormous thirst, who "swam in it" as the saying goes, and who always claimed to be the first one to see the lights on the Chaddesden sidings go out, warning of an approaching air raid, during the last war, he relaying the news from his airy rooftop perch to the staff below. "Sludgie" Jack, onetime leading hand at Firth Brown's machine shop at Sheffield, who married twice and amazed allcomers with a cherished photograph of his 18-stone second wife in a swimsuit, was another character of note.

There was also William Peat, "grease corner Billy", always in wooden clogs, who presided over the apprentices in the corner of the machine shop reserved for the manufacture of nuts and bolts and who called all the boys "Willie", whatever their real names. Naturally when he called one boy to him, all came up together. Tommy Foreman took his place when he retired.

"Noisy" Bill Hithersay was another character who worked his quick cylinder boring machine accompanied by a choking cloud of smoke pouring from a pipe stuffed with "Railway" twist, a unique local tobacco mixture very popular with many of the old timers. He it was who always wore a starched shirt front complete with dickey bow which he would remove in hot weather, leaving his chest naked and his starched front heavily marked with greasy fingerprints.

The last No 9 shop "character" to be mentioned here is "Bandy" the ghost, erected in the vaults by one Harold Lawton, and which consisted of a skull lit from within by a small electric bulb.

One particular workman was the victim of this joke, having indicated his interest in the subject of "spirits". On being led down into the vaults in total darkness he was suddenly confronted with the glowing skull and doused from behind with a bucket of water, which presumably dampened his enthusiasm for the spirit world.

In the No 8 erecting shop were to be found other like characters, "Snobby" Bentley on injectors, who wore starched shirt cuffs and just a shirt front with collar over his vest. Being a bachelor this saved him a tremendous amount of laundry. "Cabbie" Eric Ashworth, on gland packing was another whose nickname was passed onto him from his father. There was Frank Wilson, "Nigger" as he was known, now retired, who could do the work of two men in half the time, such was his strength. Unique perhaps was Horace Bancroft, the lunchtime orator who swayed crowds of a hundred or more with his views on politics until work began again after the break. Ted Foley, with the drooping moustache, was the expert on injector assembling. He carried on his hat a collection of candle stubs, all lit and ready to be placed at suitable points on the engine to assist in the erection of the various pipes. He was a pigeon fancier in his spare time and was always sent for when "strays" turned up in the Works. Bill Grudgins was the expert in marking out valves, whose favourite phrase when referring to these to apprentices was "push it in lad and mark it once more for luck". His two recipes for a long life were a peculiar mixture of the holy and the profane, these being "Trust in the Lord" and the second "Keep your bowels open". "Togger" Hines was well known for his expert knowledge on cactii, which the presentation and acceptance of a suitably planted pineapple top one day did nothing to assuage.

George Wesley was the chief foreman, formerly in No 9 shop and was feared by all, a firm disciplinarian who would brook no slacking or horseplay in the shop, yet who was very good company when away from work. He expected, and got, 100 per cent from his workmen, giving advice once only, after which the storm clouds broke!

There were many like characters in the other shops, but lack of space

o

forbids the mention of these. Apprentices passing into the shops for the first time were the target for the usual jokes played on the inexperienced, being sent to the shop stores for a "long wait (weight)" or a "long stand", "a rubber hammer", a "bucket of blue steam" or "red oil for tail lamps". The favourite joke played on newcomers into the loco-motive drawing office, chiefly office boys, was to ask the person con-cerned to find the "stationary boiler mileage book". In an office of that size the seeker would be sent to see persons situated at the opposite ends of it, the searcher himself doing some "mileage" in his vain search.

Such is the stuff of the lighter moments of shop and office life, the rare exception rather than the rule, but such events and persons added to an often otherwise monotonous routine a few odd moments of light relief from the daily task.

One amusing story is told of evenings after work spent in the *Railway Tavern* at the bottom of High Street, where would gather in the bar five drinking companions from the Works. The signal for action would be the arrival of an old driver who, settling down with his "half" could be easily induced to recount the run down through the Peak, nursing a compound across the wind and rain swept Derbyshire hills, while the five, seated on a long low bar seat, would simulate the action of the train, all swaying in concert to the left as the train ran through Amber-gate curve, and then later standing up and reaching for their luggage as the "train" reached Derby! This performance was repeated time and time again, the participants never tiring of this comical pantomime.

Throughout its chequered history there had been no really serious fire in the works but on April 19, 1950, the old general stores, one of the original North Midland buildings to the right of the clock tower, caught fire. The fire began in a lift shaft and quickly spread through the whole building, setting fire to the adjacent offices and spreading along the top floor almost as far as the clock tower. This and the old No 1 roundhouse were only saved after a long battle in which the works brigade and the Derby Borough brigade made heroic efforts to prevent the fire from spreading any further (*see Plate 97*). When the smoke cleared the store lay in ruins, the right wing of the offices was severely damaged, the top floor including the roof being completely gutted; only four chimney stacks stood like stark sentinels amid the rubble. Fortunately No 1 shed was only slightly damaged but the end of the training school workshop was badly damaged and had to be rebuilt.

Opportunity was taken, with the demolition of the ruined stores, to extend the school workshop and add more classroom space and administrative offices, bringing the covered area to 4,720sq ft. Accom-modation was now available for 100 trainee apprentices with a standard intake of 30 per quarter. Of the $38\frac{3}{4}$ hours in the working week it was now possible for 27 hours to be spent on practical workshop training.

The office block itself was rebuilt and modernised, whilst a new site was chosen for a replacement general and locomotive stores building occupying part of the site of the old No 3 shed, adjacent to the pattern shop. Pile driving for this new store began in May, 1952 and the building was completed towards the end of August, 1953.

In 1951 H. G. Ivatt retired from his position as the last of the CMEs having taken on the position for the London Midland Region when the Transport Act brought about the 1948 unification into British Railways, but shortly before he left his staff were involved in yet another pioneering venture. This was the experimental "Fell" diesel mechanical locomotive, an attempt to develop 2,000hp at the rails through a mechanical transmission utilising four Paxman 12-cylinder supercharged engines, two at each end of the locomotive, rated at 500hp each, with blowers driven by auxiliary diesel engines of 150hp each which also provided power for the radiator fans, exhausters etc. The four driving shafts were carried through fluid couplings into a common gearbox. The engines could be brought into use one at a time thus providing four stages of power output, and the drive was onto the two middle pairs of the four axles coupled on crank pins by an outside coupling rod. Initially there was a single coupling rod joining all four axles but to relieve undue strain being placed on the gearbox this was later split into two driving two axles each, giving the appearance of a 4-4-4-4. Leading and trailing bogies made up the 4-8-4 wheel arrangement and 10100, as it was numbered, was completed to O/3610 in mid-January, 1952, a joint venture by BR and Fell Developments Ltd. Numerous modifications were made to this novel locomotive, the brain child of Lt Col L. F. R. Fell, the major alterations being in the cooling radiator area which had to be increased considerably, but the design acquitted itself reasonably well. Following a 16 month withdrawal for a number of modifications chiefly involving the radiators, its career was brought to an untimely end in 1958 when a nut became detached from the inside of the gearbox and fell amongst the gears, damaging them beyond repair. The locomotive was officially withdrawn on November 22, 1958.

With the nationalisation of the four main railway companies in 1948 overall responsibility for design passed to R. A. Riddles, the member of the Railway Executive responsible for Mechanical & Electrical Engineering, and it was from him and his Locomotive Standards Committee that the last designs for steam locomotive classes on the BR system emanated.

The Derby design office was responsible for the design of the largest passenger classes of the 4-6-2 type, the 2-6-0 Class 2 tender engines and the Class 2 2-6-2 tank engines. None of these was built in the Derby Works however, but the works did turn out the first of the Class 5 4-6-0 mixed traffic locomotives No 73000 which was put into traffic on April 12, 1951, the first of 30 built to O/5122.

These locomotives were designed at the former LNER design office at Doncaster and in common with all other classes in the standard fleet, there were four main reasons behind the decision to adopt a new series of locomotives.

Firstly a wide range of standard fittings could be completely standardised on a new range of locomotives whilst the introduction of these would have involved considerable alterations to existing locomotives.

Secondly so narrowly balanced were the design aspects of the up to date regional locomotives that the Locomotive Standards Committee were unable to recommend the adoption of any one particular type over another.

Further the interchange trials of 1948, specially instigated for the purpose, confirmed the committee's findings in (ii) above, locomotives working well anywhere in Britain irrespective of railway of origin.

Finally there were severe weight and loading gauge restrictions preventing wide-user classification, a good example being that of ex-GWR locomotives which were prohibited from working over the ex-LMS system due to the width over their cylinders being excessive, a relic of broad gauge days.

Six new types were therefore evolved for construction in 1951, followed by four further types of lower classification and still later two further designs; a heavy freight and a heavy passenger locomotive. All except the latter two were to be mixed traffic locomotives.

The new standard two cylinder 4-6-0s built at Derby had 6ft 2in diameter driving wheels at 7ft + 8ft 6in centres and a leading bogie on 3ft diameter wheels at 6ft 3in centres pivoted 8ft 7½in in front of the leading driver. Length over buffers was 62ft 7in. The outside cylinders were 19in diameter and 28in stroke driven through Walschaerts valve gear by 11in diameter piston valves. The BR Type 3 taper boiler pressed to 225psi carried 28 large superheater flues of 5⅛in diameter and 151 small tubes of 1⅞in outside diameter totalling 1,479sq ft of heating surface to which the superheater tubes added a further 358sq ft and the firebox a further 171sq ft. Grate area was 28.7sq ft. This boiler was adapted from the Stanier Class 5 4-6-0 boiler of the LMS modified to take the standard fittings. A standard BR 1 tender was fitted having 7 tons of coal space and capacity for 4,250gal of water. Working weights were: engine 76 tons, tender 49 tons 3cwt, totalling 125 tons 3cwt. The designed driving axleload was originally to have been 19 tons, but this came out at 18 tons 16cwt, 19 tons 14cwt, and 19 tons 11cwt respectively.

The tractive effort was calculated to be 26,120lb at 85 per cent boiler pressure. The remainder of this first batch of locomotives were 73001–29, put into traffic between May, 1951 and January, 1952 (*see Plate 101*).

Also in 1952 the works turned out their first batch of ten standard Class 4MT 2-6-4 tank engines, Nos 80000–9, built to O/5124. These particular locomotives owed their origins to the LMS 2-6-4T more than to any other class and were made the design responsibility of the Brighton drawing office, a number of standard parts being designed elsewhere, the Derby office for instance being generally responsible for the design of all bogies and pony trucks, tenders, wheels, tyres, axles and spring gear.

These new 2-6-4 tank engines had to pass the restrictive L1 loading gauge requirements and the cylinders were therefore reduced in diameter from 19⅝in to 18in, the stroke being lengthened by 2in to ensure a similar tractive effort to the former LMS design. 5ft 8in diameter driving wheels at 7ft 7in + 7ft 9in centres were provided, the leading pony truck axle being centred 9ft in front of the leading driver, and carried on 3ft diameter wheels as was the trailing bogie centred 9ft 4½in to the rear of the trailing driver the axles being at 6ft 3in centres. Length over buffers was 44ft 9⅞in. A BR 5 boiler, pressed to 225psi, was fitted carrying 21 superheater flues of 5⅛in outside diameter and 157 small tubes of 1¾in outside diameter providing 1,223sq ft of heating surface to which the superheater tubes added a further 240sq ft. Grate area was 26.7sq ft. The side and back tanks provided space for 2,000gal of water and the bunker 3½ tons of coal. Weight in working order was 86 tons 13cwt, and the tractive effort calculated at 85 per cent boiler pressure, was 25,515lb.

Nothing further need be said on these two designs, their whole history having been admirably covered by E. S. Cox in the book *British Standard Steam Locomotives*, along with the remainder of this last steam generation.

One further order for five 2-6-4 tanks Nos 80054–58 built to O/6231 was filled in December, 1954 and January, 1955, and these were to be the last tank engines to be built in the Derby Works.

Preceding them was the only Derby order for the Ivatt 1200 Class 2-6-2 tank engines designed by him way back in 1946. The Crewe shops constructed all but the last batch of ten locomotives Nos 41320–29 built to O/5125 at Derby between January and May, 1952. The engines, classed 2MT, had two outside cylinders originally 16in diameter × 24in stroke, altered to 16¾in diameter for the later engines including the Derby batch. The 5ft diameter driving wheels were on a 6ft 9in + 7ft wheelbase, the leading pony truck axle carried on 3ft wheels, being

8ft 6in in front of the leading driver, and the trailing pony truck axle being 8ft behind the trailing driver. The taper boiler pressed to 200psi carried 162 small tubes of 1⅝in outside diameter and 12 large superheater flues of 5⅛in outside diameter. Heating surfaces were: tubes 924sq ft, superheater 124sq ft, firebox 101sq ft, totalling 1,149sq ft. Grate area was 17.5sq ft and tractive effort, at 85 per cent boiler pressure, was 18,500lb (with the larger cylinders). Working weights were: leading 13 tons, driving 13 tons 5cwt, trailing 13 tons, totalling 63 tons 5cwt, with 1,350gal of water in the tanks and 3 tons of coal in the bunker. These Derby engines and some of the earlier Crewe built locomotives (Nos 41210—29 & 41270–89) had vacuum controlled regulator gear fitted for use when working motor trains on branch lines.

In mid-1952 it became necessary to renumber the various shops in the works to simplify shop documentation and the following changes were made:

Old Shop Number	Description	New Shop Number
1	Millwrights	1
2	Millwrights (building)	2
—	Works Training School	3
4	Electrical	4
5	Coppersmiths	5
6	Brass Foundry	12
7	Iron Foundry (Loco and C&W)	15
8	Erecting (Steam) (incorporating existing 11 and 12 shops)	8
9M	Machine (Machining)	9
9F	Machine (Fitting)	10
9B	Machine (Heat Treatment)	11
10	Paint	24
10A	Erecting (diesel)	7
11	Bogie and Cab Repair	Now incorporated in 8 shop
14	Pattern making and joinery	14
15	Wheel	16
15A	Firebox stays (turning)	17
18	Boiler	18
18B	Boiler mounting	23

19	Smiths (general and springs)	19
19A	Forging	21
19B	Nut and bolt forge	20
20	Stores (concentration depot)	Now incorporated in 30 shop
21	Yard	27
22	Tube	22
25	Sheet metal work	6
26	Hot brass pressing	13
—	Stores – general	29
—	Stores – locomotive	30

Nos 25, 26 and 28 were spare numbers retained against future requirements.

At the beginning of 1952, when your author entered employment as an engineering apprentice in No 9 machine shop, steam was still very much to the fore, and the wide variety of locomotives to be found in the erecting shop bore evidence to this, as will be seen from the shopping list for the week ended June 12, 1951, here given as a fairly typical example of a week's work load for repairs:

For general repair:
43956, boiler 13917 (G7s) new, tender 3045
40059, boiler 11941 (G6s) ex-40050
58248, boiler 11957 (G6) ex-22926, tender 2005
42347, boiler 12584 (G8as) ex-42403
47558, boiler 7810 (G5½) ex-47632
58288, boiler 7424 (G6) ex-23006, tender 2327
64750, boiler 8589 ex-64907, tender 5538
                 (boiler to be renumbered 27671*)

Intermediate repair
40486 Tender 2028
44084 Tender 3218
58040
44229 Tender 3363
64724 Tender 5540
42384
42391
47611

*Boilers were only normally changed at general repair.

Casual repair

42361   Attention to header
(4)1856   For special exam
44501   Tender 3695. Frame for welding
40444   Tender 1941. For examination
12012   Attention to big end bearings (Costs to O/6467)

Supplementary list (published the following week)

44501   Tender 3695. Now to have intermediate repairs
40444   Tender 1941 boiler 7460 G7s ex-40633, now to have a general repair
41005   Tender 2804, to be cut up to code 230/33
58285   Tender 1563, to be cut up to code 230/33
44533   To have boiler 7721 G7s ex-44534
64724   Tender 5540 to have a general repair, boiler 825 renumbered 27673 ex-64713

Perhaps the most unusual visitor ever to visit the Derby shops was Stanier 4-6-2 No 46203 *Princess Margaret Rose* which arrived under her own steam in November, 1951, for a general repair, having cracked frames and loose cylinders. She was given a place of honour in the middle road of 3 bay in the erecting shop, and received the full Derby treatment, being given new front end frames during her two months stay, emerging in excellent condition and repainted from blue to the new BR green livery. There is a story that on her return to the Western Division lines she was hauled into Crewe shops for a "going over" before being put back into traffic, but this seems rather unlikely.

As can be seen from the above shopping list ex-London and North Eastern Railway J39 Class 0-6-0 tender engines were also being repaired at Derby around this time, and a shocking state some of them were in too. Also under repair were a number of ex-GWR pannier tank engines. In addition to these five Stanier 2-8-0 tender locomotives of LMS design but belonging to the War Department, were put into good repair, after being returned in various conditions, from the Middle East. These locomotives, after being given thorough overhauls in the Derby shops, were despatched to the Royal Engineers Transport Unit at Longmoor.

The fact that Derby shops could cope with this additional workload bore testimony to the excellent functioning of the progressive system of workshop organisation brought in as mentioned previously, but the end of the steam era was already in sight.

The last steam locomotives to be built at Derby were further standard Class 5 4-6-0 locomotives still under construction while those in authority planned the future for their modern successors, and these are listed below:

Order No	Locomotive Nos	Year built
O/6230	73030–49	1953
O/6735	73050–59	1954
O/8035	73060–64	1954
O/8025	73065–74	1954
N8241	73075–89	1955
N8845	73090–99	1955
N9247	73125–54	1956–7

The last order for steam locomotives to be built at Derby were somewhat different to the rest of the class in that they incorporated British-Caprotti valve gear, a final refinement. Of that order No 73154 holds the honour of being the last new steam locomotive ever to be built in the Derby shops, being put into traffic on June 14, 1957 (see Plate 98).

Thus the long cavalcade of 2,941 new steam locomotives built at Derby came to an end. It had begun, as we have seen, way back in September, 1851, with 147, a 0-6-0 goods tender engine, which surprisingly enough lasted in service some 15 years as against the nine and a half accorded to Derby's last steam product!

One ray of sunshine in these dark days was the restoration to Midland livery of Midland Compound No 1000, built way back in 1901 as 2631 by Johnson. She had been withdrawn in September, 1951, but languished in BR livery at Derby and Crewe until early in 1959 when she was hauled back to Derby again and put under general repair in order to bring her to her 1914 pristine condition (as first superheated) again. By June 15, she was ready in "shop grey" (more correctly "shop pink") for steaming trials between Derby and Trent and by the end of the month she was once again in her crimson lake livery, lined out, with converted tender 4298 attached, ready to work specials. This she did for a fair period until eventually delivered to the Museum of British Transport at Clapham on December 9, 1962.

This was quite a period for restored locomotives for in 1956 the ex-LT&SR 4-4-2 tank locomotive No 41966, was shopped at Derby to be renovated to its pre-grouping livery as LT&SR No 80 Thundersley for that line's centenary celebrations, although having Midland extended smokebox and Stanier chimney.

Some eight years earlier, as previously mentioned, the Kirtley double framed 2-4-0 No 20002 withdrawn in July, 1947, had also been restored to Midland Railway crimson lake livery and renumbered 158A. It was fortunate that this engine was preserved indeed knowing the fate of her sister 156A cruelly despatched by Stanier, but 158A has a stronger connection with the past for she was the 1866 replacement of the first new locomotive ever built at Derby Locomotive Works and so deserves a special place of honour in the Leicester Railway Museum where she now resides, as previously mentioned.

However steam locomotives continued to grace the erecting shops with their presence for a few more years, until, with proper ceremony, 75042, the last steam locomotive to be repaired "officially" left the shops, amid speeches from T. F. B. Simpson, then restyled Works Manager, and the then lady Mayor of Derby (see Plate 99).

Thus September 20, 1963, became a red letter day in the annals of the Derby Works, notwithstanding the fact that one or two further steam locomotives were later repaired in the works, the last actually occupying space in the erecting shop being BR standard Class 9 2-10-0 No 92102, brought in early in 1964 for repair to the front end damaged in a collision locally (see Plate 100).

So ended the steam age at Derby, and the men of the various shops and offices now turned their full attentions on the diesel locomotives of the new age. Inevitably there were to be many alterations in a few short years. Shops were reorganised, progress systems revised, shopping procedures amended and some of the old shops renovated or demolished to make way for the new scheme of things.

Of the old parts of the works, No 2 roundhouse, formerly the home of the few locomotives preserved at Derby, was emptied and demolished during the summer of 1966. The No 3 shed had long been swept away as previously recorded, and in the spring of 1969 No 4 shed shared a similar fate, only a few offices remaining temporarily as a signing on point, whilst the bright modern brick and concrete diesel depot in Etches Park took over all maintenance and stabling functions.

Only the historic No 1 roundhouse remains, (see Plate 58) now inevitably showing signs of wear and tear after 130 years of existence, and this is at the time of writing receiving urgent attention to its roof beams. It is still in use incidentally as a brakedown crane repair shop.

Although outside the province of this book the old trijunct station ought to be briefly mentioned. Since the addition of platforms 4, 5 and 6 complete with luggage lifts, footbridge and waiting rooms in June, 1881, for the Royal Agricultural show of that year which was held at Derby, little work of a major nature was done to the platforms until in 1952 a £200,000 modernisation plan was put into operation involving the demolition of the train shed, footbridge, etc and their replacement with individual roofing for each island platform of reinforced concrete construction together with a new footbridge opened in July, 1954.

In September, 1958, the first main line diesel-electric locomotive of the new generation emerged from the erecting shop. This was an 1,160 hp Bo-Bo Type 2 Sulzer engined locomotive No D5000 built to order No D251, the overall designing of which was undertaken in the Derby Locomotive Drawing Office (*see Plate 103*).

The following year the first of the new 2,300hp "Peak" Class 1Co-Co1 Type 4 Sulzer engined locomotives No D1 *Scafell Pike* emerged from the works and 105 of these were to be built at Derby over the next six years (*see Plate 102*).

By January, 1967, the works had turned out its 1,000th diesel locomotive, a Sulzer engined Bo-Bo Type 2 diesel-electric locomotive of 1,250hp, proudly bearing a plaque on the assistant's side of the cab at each end "D7667. This is the 1,000th diesel locomotive to be built at Derby Locomotive Works" (*see Plate 105*). The various orders for these locomotives summarised in Appendix IV, along with all orders for diesel locomotives built from 1953 to 1967 when the last of the Type 2 Bo-Bo locomotives, No D7677, was built. This was also incidentally the last locomotive built in the works at the time of writing.

Since then two changes in organisation within BR have resulted first in the Derby Works coming under the British Railways Workshops organisation and then, from January 1, 1970, under the newly formed company "British Rail Engineering Ltd."

What of the future? At the present time, apart from their normal function of repairing main line and shunting diesel locomotives, the Derby shops are undertaking some work for private industry during one of those inevitable lulls between generations of diesel and electric locomotives. The design work for the next generation of motive power is already well advanced, although it is understood that the building of prototype locomotives is likely to be undertaken at Crewe.

One hopes that the traditions of craftsmanship built up in the Derby Works for well over a century will continue unbated, and that eventually further new locomotives will emerge once more from its venerable precincts when production quantities are required.

Appendices

Birmingham & Derby Junction Railway

Locomotive Foreman, Hampton-in-Arden Shops
Matthew Kirtley, May 1839–June 1842.

Locomotive Superintendent
Matthew Kirtley, June 1842–June 12, 1844.

Midland Counties Railway

Locomotive Superintendent
Josiah Kearsley, January 14, 1839–June 11, 1844.

North Midland Railway

Manager of Motive Power
Robert Stephenson, January 1839–August 21, 1842.
Thomas Cabrey, January 1843–May 1844.

Chief Assistant & Locomotive Superintendent
William Prime Marshall, March 27, 1840–April 4, 1843.
Thomas Kirtley, April 5, 1843–June 11, 1844.

Foreman of Repair Shops, Derby
Mr Dobson, March 1840–May 1844.

Superintendent of the Line
Robert Stephenson, March 2, 1840–December 10, 1840.
Mr Hanson, December 11, 1840–February 29, 1843.

Midland Railway Company

Locomotive Superintendent
Matthew Kirtley (also Carriage & Wagon Superintendent), June 13, 1844–May 24, 1873.
Samuel Waite Johnson, July 1, 1873–December 31, 1903.
Richard Mountford Deeley, January 1, 1904–August 13, 1909.

Chief Mechanical Engineer
Henry Fowler, January 1, 1910–December 31, 1922. (Absent on Government Service as Director of Production – Ministry of Munitions – June 12, 1915–May 31, 1919.)

Assistant Chief Mechanical Engineer
James Edward Anderson, May 1, 1919–December 31, 1922. (Anderson was acting CME from June 13, 1915–April 30, 1919).

General Superintendent
Cecil Walter Paget, April 5, 1907–April, 1919.

General Foreman of Workshops
John Fernie, April 17, 1855–December 31, 1863.

Workshop Superintendent (re-styled)
William Kirtley, January 1, 1864–March 31, 1874.
Francis Holt, May 5, 1874–January 7, 1893.

Works Manager (re-styled)
John Lane, February 16, 1893–December 31, 1901.
Richard Mountford Deeley, January 1, 1902–June 18, 1903 (also appointed Electrical Engineer, January 1, 1903).
Cecil Walter Paget, June 19, 1903–April 4, 1907 (also appointed Assistant Locomotive Supt., November 1, 1905).
Henry Fowler, May 3, 1907–December 31, 1909.
James Edward Anderson, August 2, 1907 (temporary), January 1, 1910–July 24, 1913.

Works Assistant (re-styled)
James Edward Anderson, July 25, 1913–December 31, 1922 (also appointed Assistant CME, May 1, 1919).

General Chief Draughtsman
Charles Little, June 1, 1854–November 20, 1860.

Chief Stationary Draughtsman (re-styled)
James Newbould, December 30, 1860–January 31, 1898.
William James Newbould, April 1, 1898–June 30, 1905.

Chief Outdoor Draughtsman (re-styled)
George William Woolliscroft, July 1, 1905–May 14, 1908 (became Supt. of Apprentices on May 15, 1908).

Chief Locomotive Draughtsman
Robert John Billinton, November 21, 1874–January 31, 1890.
Thomas Gill Iveson, February 1, 1890–January 31, 1901.
John William Smith, January 1, 1901–August 18, 1906.*
James Edward Anderson, August 20, 1906–July 25, 1913.
Sandham John Symes, July 25, 1913–December 31, 1922.

London Midland & Scottish Railway Company

Works Manager
Sandham John Symes, January 1, 1923–April 30, 1928.

*Official records must be in error here, for the date should surely be February 1st.

Works Superintendent (re-styled)
  H. G. Ivatt, May 1, 1928–October 31, 1932.
  G. S. Bellamy, November 1, 1932–April 30, 1941.
  J. Rankin, May 1, 1941–January 31, 1946.
  A. E. Robson, February 1, 1946–October 31, 1947.
  T. F. B. Simpson, November 1, 1947–December 31, 1947.

Chief Locomotive Draughtsman
  H. G. Chambers, February 1, 1923–September 30, 1934.
  D. W. Sandford, October 1, 1934–October 5, 1937.
  A. E. Owen, October 6, 1937–November 22, 1942.
  G. R. Nicholson, November 23, 1942–March 25, 1945.
  E. A. Langridge, March 26, 1945–September 30, 1945.
  J. W. Caldwell, October 1, 1945–December 31, 1947.

Technical Assistant & Chief Draughtsman
  H. G. Chambers, October 1, 1934–March 17, 1935.
  T. F. Coleman, March 18, 1935– July 30, 1949 (from January 1,
  1948 under British Railways).

British Railways

Works Superintendent
  T. F. B. Simpson, January 1, 1948–December 31, 1952.

Works Manager (re-styled)
  T. F. B. Simpson, January 1, 1953–February 28, 1965.
  P. Gray, March 1, 1965–still in office.

ORIGINAL FORM · **REBUILD**

Date built	First Midland Number	Maker	Maker's No.	Type as built	Renumberings while in original form	Date rebuilt as tank	Midland Number at rebuild	Dia and stro... of c...
June 1845	276	Birmingham & Gloucester Railway	38 (Engine No.)	0-6-0ST	105 (6/52)	Jan. 1853	300	16″
Aug. 1848	215	Kitson & Co.	183	0-6-0	224 (/51)	June 1857	224	17″
						*June 1875	1092	16½
Oct. 1848	216	Kitson & Co.	185	0-6-0	225 (/51)	Dec. 1857	225	17″
						†June 1875	1094	16″

BROMSGROVE BANKERS

Date built	First Midland Number	Maker	Maker's No.	Type as built	Renumberings while in original form	Date rebuilt as tank	Midland Number at rebuild	Dia and stro... of c...
Dec. 1860	222	M.R.Co.	—	0-6-0WT		New	—	16½
Dec. 1860	320	M.R.Co.	—	0-6-0WT		New	—	16½
Dec. 1862	223	M.R.Co.	—	0-6-0WT		New	—	16½
Dec. 1863	221	M.R.Co.	—	0-6-0WT		New	—	16½
Dec. 1851	146	M.R.Co.	—	0-6-0	165 (6/52), 169 (8/62)	Aug. 1862	318	16″
Aug. 1848	206	Stephenson	607	0-6-0	201 (1/51), 212 (5/66)	Dec. 1862	201	15″
Sept. 1848	101	Kitson & Co.	130	2-2-2-0	221 (/49), 230 (by 9/51), 218 (6/55)	Dec. 1862	218	16½
Oct. 1848	102	Kitson & Co.	131	2-2-2-0	222 (/49), 231 (by 9/51), 219 (6/55)	Dec. 1862	219	16½
						Nov. 1875	200	17″
June 1857	172	M.R.Co.	—	0-6-0	181 (5/66)	Mar. 1867	213	16″ ;
Dec. 1860	179	M.R.Co.	—	0-6-0	188 (5/66), 700 (3/67)	Nov.(?) 1867	214	16½
June 1857	175	M.R.Co.	—	0-6-0	184 (5/66)	Mar.(?) 1867	215	16½
June 1859	198	M.R.Co.	—	0-6-0	703 (3/67)	Nov. 1867	216	16½
Dec. 1859	216	M.R.Co.	—	0-6-0	702 (3/67), 248 (8/67)	Dec. 1867	217	16½″

Date built	First Midland Number	Maker	Maker's No.	Type as built	Renumberings in original form	Date rebuilt as tank	Rebuild No.	No. alloc...
July 1848	80	E. B. Wilson & Co.	—	2-2-2	102 (2/62), 722 (3/67), 1000 (9/68)	‡Apr. 1872	2000	4/72
July 1855	16	M.R.Co.	—	2-2-2	103 (2/62), 723 (3/67), 1001 (5/69)	‡Jan. 1872	2001	1/72
Nov. 1855	104	M.R.Co.	—	2-2-2	724 (12/67), 1002 (9/68)	Dec. 1872 (?)	2002	12/7
June 1853	105	M.R.Co./ E. B. Wilson	—	2-2-2	725 (4/67), 1003 (9/68)	1871	2003	5/72
Dec. 1855	106	M.R.Co.	—	2-2-2	726 (3/67), 1004 (9/68)	Mar 1871	2004	12/7
Aug. 1854	3	M.R.Co.	—	2-2-2	35 (1/62), 107 (12/63), 727 (3/67), 1005 (9/68)	‡Mar. 1871	2005	12/7
May 1855	8	M.R.Co.	—	2-2-2	85 (2/62), 36 (5/62), 108 (12/63), 728 (9/67), 1006 (9/68)	Jan. 1872(?)	2006	1/72
May 1856	110	M.R.Co.	—	2-2-2	730 (9/67), 1008 (9/68)	Mar. 1871	2008	3/72
May 1856	111	M.R.Co.	—	2-2-2	731 (9/67), 1009 (5/69)	1872	2009	12/72
May 1856	114	M.R.Co.	—	2-2-2	734 (3/68), 1012 (6/69)	1872	2012	11/7
July 1855	10	M.R.Co.	—	2-2-2	88 (2/62), 116 (/62), 736 (3/68), 1013 (3/69)	‡Feb. 1872	2013	2/72
Feb. 1848	37	E. B. Wilson & Co.	—	2-2-2	637 (12/65), 737 (9/67), 1014 (9/68)	Apr. 1872	2014	4/72

(a) There is some evidence that further Stephenson and Kitson 0-6-0 Tender Engines were converted, but since ... records are lacking in this period they have been omitted.

of ...s	Coupled wheelbase	Subsequent renumberings	Date broken up	Notes
	6' 9¾" + 6' 11"	221 (6/55), taken out of service 10/61	July 1862	Bromsgrove Banker, for replacement see 221 of Dec. 1863.
	7' 9" + 7' 9"	1034 (8/71), 2034 (3/73)	*Jan. 1875	*Taken out of service for rebuilding. See below Bromsgrove Banking Engine.
	7' 9" + 8' 6"	1092A (12/84)	Aug. 1898	
	7' 9" + 7' 9"	1035 (11/71), 2035 (8/72)	†Jan. 1875	†Taken out of service for rebuilding, See below Bromsgrove Banking Engine.
	7' 9" + 8' 6"	1094A (11/84)	Mar. 1903	
	8' 3" + 8' 3"	222A (3/90)	Feb. 1894	
	8' 3" + 8' 3"	220 (5/66), 220A (9/79)	Nov. 1899	Rebuilt as Tender Engine 5' 2½" driving wheels & same cyls. Dec. 1883.
	8' 3" + 8' 6"	223A (2/90), 1604 (5/07), 1607 (/24)	July 1928	
	8' 3" + 8' 6"	221A (9/79), 1431 6/87), 1431A (6/90)	May, 1901	
	8' 0" + 8' 0"(?)	217 (5/66)	Mar. 1867	
		212 (5/66), 1038 (11/69)	Mar. 1870	See note (a) below.
	8' 3" + 8' 6"	1016 (11/71), 2016 (6/72)	Nov. 1873	Previously converted to 0-6-0 Tender Engine 5' 0" driving wheels 16" × 24" cyls. 1849–50.
	8' 3" + 8' 6"	1028 (11/71), 2028 (3/74)	Rebuilt	
	8' 3" + 8' 6"	203A (1/90), 1600 (11/07)	July 1921	Bromsgrove Banking Engine.
	8' 0" + 8' 3"	213A (11/75)	Sept. 1899	Rebuilt as 0-6-0 tender eng. on standard wheelbase 17" × 24" cyls. Oct. 1879.
	8' 0" + 8' 3"	214A (11/75), 322 (6/90)	Feb. 1897	Rebuilt as 0-6-0 tender eng. on standard wheelbase 17" × 24" cyls. Nov. 1881.
	8' 0" + 8' 6"	2038 (3/73), 2038A (2/92)	Feb. 1906	
	8' 0" + 8' 3"	318 (8/77), 2350 (8/07)	June 1920	Rebuilt as 0-6-0 tender eng. on standard wheelbase 17" × 24" cyls. Dec. 1871.
	8' 0" + 8' 3"	217A (11/75) 332 (6/90)	Mar. 1905	Rebuilt as 0-6-0 Tender engine on standard wheelbase 17" × 24" cyls. Aug. 1881.

e ...ls	Dia of driving wheels	Coupled wheelbase	Reboilered by Johnson	See note (c)	Subsequent renumberings	Date broken up	Notes
×22"	4' 2"	7' 3" + 6' 9"	Nov. 1875	213 (11/75)	205A (1/90), 201A (10/97), 1601 (12/07), 1605 (/23)	Jan. 1924	Out of use 1868–71.
×22"	4' 2"	7' 3" + 6' 9"	Feb. 1876	214 (11/75)	206A (12/89), 214A (11/97)	June 1898	
×22"	4' 2"	7' 3" + 6' 9"	June 1877	216 (6/77)	216A (4/83)	Feb. 1897	Out of use Dec. 1869 —Dec. 1870.
×22"	4' 2"	7' 3" + 6' 9"	June 1877	210 (6/77)	210A (4/83)	Sept. 1899	Out of use 1868–71.
×22"	4' 2"	7' 3" + 6' 9"	Oct. 1878	219 (11/78)	219A (6/83)	Aug. 1904	
×22"	4' 2"	7' 3" + 6' 9"	May 1876	217 (11/75)	207A (1/90), 216A (12/97)	June 1904	Out of use Dec. 1869 —Dec. 1870.
×22"	4' 2"	7' 3" + 6' 9"	Sept. 1875	1095 (1/76)	1095A (11/84), 1603 (11/07)	Sept. 1920	
×22"	4' 2"	7' 3" + 6' 9"	Dec. 1876	266 (11/76)	218 (7/77), 218A (6/83)	Mar. 1904	
×22"	4' 2"	7' 3" + 6' 9"	June 1877	211 (6/77)	211A (5/83)	Oct. 1899	
×22"	4' 2"	7' 3" + 6' 9"	June 1877	212 (6/77)	212A (5/83)	Nov. 1899	
×22"	4' 2"	7' 3" + 6' 9"	June 1877	215 (6/77)	215A (5/83)	Feb. 1898	Out of use 1870–71.
×22"	4' 2"	7' 3" + 6' 9"	Oct. 1876	1093 (9/76)	208A (6/90), 222A (12/97), 1602 (8/07)	July 1921	

(c) Date No allocated only in this column.

‡According to F. H. Clarke these four locomotives were Saddle Tanks at this rebuilding, but there are no known photographs of them in this form.

BOILERS

Class	*Max. Wkg. Press Lb/Sq. In*	**Typical heating surfaces* Firebox Sq. Ft.	*Tubes No.*	*O.D.*	*Sq. Ft*	*Total H.S. F'box & Tubes Sq. Ft.*	*Super-Heater Sq. Ft.*	*Grand Total Sq. Ft.*	*Grate Area Sq. Ft.*	*Type of Firebox*
A	160	91.00	196	1¾"	944	1035	—	—	14.5	Round to
A1	160	96.00	213	1¾"	1024	1120	—	—	14.5	Round to
B	160	110.00	244	1⅝"	1142	1252	—	—	17.5	Round to
C	160	104.00	246	1⅝"	1150	1254	—	—	16	Round to
C1	160	110.00	244	1⅝"	1142	1252	—	—	16	Round to
D	160	117.00	240	1⅝"	1106	1223	—	—	19.5	Round to
E	170	128.00	236	1⅝"	1105	1233	—	—	21.3	Round to
F	180	147.00	228	1⅝"	1070	1217	—	—	24.5	Round to
H	175	125.00	258	1¾"	1303	1428	—	—	21.1	Round to
Hx & H1	175	125.00	242	1¾"	1222	1347	—	—	21.1	Round to
J	140	44.00	110	1¾"	480	524	—	—	8	Round to (Raised)
J1	150	64.00	141	1¾"	700	764	—	—	10.5	Round to
J2	160	64.00	141	1¾"	700	764	—	—	10.5	Round to
P	160	110.00	246	1⅝"	1134	1244	—	—	17.5	Round to
G5	160	85.00	196	1¾"	932.5	1017.5	—	—	14.5	Belpaire
G5½	160	97.00	196	1¾"	977.5	1074.5	—	—	16	Belpaire
G6	160	104.00	196	1¾"	967	1071	—	—	17.5	Belpaire
G7	175	127.00	254	1¾"	1283	1410	—	—	21.1	Belpaire
G7s	180	125.00	148 21	1¾" 5⅛"	1045	1170	313	1483	21.1	Belpaire
G8	180	145.00	262	1¾"	1383	1528	—	—	25	Belpaire
G8A	200	145.00	251	1¾"	1327	1472	—	—	25	Belpaire
G8AS	200	137.25	148 21	1¾" 5⅛"	1092.75	1230	266.25	1496.25	25	Belpaire
G8½	200	150.00	261	1¾"	1448	1598	—	—	26	Belpaire
G9	220	153.00	216	1⅞"	1320	1473	—	—	28.4	Belpaire
G9A	220	153.00	216	1⅞"	1320	1473	—	—	28.4	Belpaire
G9AS	200	151.00	148 21	1¾" 5⅛"	1170	1321	360	1681	28.4	Belpaire
G9BS	200	148.00	145 27	1⅞" 5⅛"	1323	1471	374	1845	28.4	Belpaire
G9½S	200	183.00	140 24	2⅛" 5¼"	1552	1735	365	2100	30.5	Belpaire
G10S	200	158.25	147 27	1⅞" 5⅛"	1560	1718.25	445	2163.25	31.5	Belpaire
GX	180	145.00	272	1¾"	1374	1519	—	—	25	Belpaire
G6S	200	104.00	92 16	1¾" 5⅛"	691	795	186	981	17.5	Belpaire

There were considerable variations in heating surface values both in the number and size of tubes and also in method of calculation.

Main boiler dimensions

	B	C	D	E	F	G	H	*Loco. types to which fitted*
″	2′ 5¼″	4′ 1″	10′ 4⅝″	10′ 0″	5′ 0″	4′ 9½″	4′ 2½″	880 class reb, 0-6-0T, Johnson 0-6-0T with 17″ cylinders as built.
″	2′ 5¼″	4′ 1″	10′ 4⅝″	10′ 0″	5′ 0″	5′ 1⅛″	4′ 6½″	Later Johnson 0-6-0T and rebuilds with 17″ cyl.
″	2′ 5¼″	4′ 1″	10′ 10⅝″	10′ 6″	5′ 11″	5′ 1½″	4′ 6″½	Kirtley 2-2-2 & 2-4-0s as rebuilt, 4-4-0, 0-6-0 & 0-6-0T; Kirtley 0-6-0 reb.
″	2′ 5¼″	4′ 1″	10′ 10⅝″	10′ 6″	5′ 6″	5′ 1½″	4′ 6½″	Rebuilt Kirtley 0-4-4T, Johnson 0-4-4T, Kirtley 2-2-2s & 2-4-0s reb.
″	2′ 5¼″	4′ 1″	10′ 10⅝″	10′ 6″	5′ 6″	5′ 5½″	4′ 10½″	Johnson 0-4-4T and larger 0-6-0T.
″	2′ 5¼″	4′ 1″	10′ 8⅝″	10′ 4″	6′ 6″	5′ 2½″	4′ 7½″	First Johnson 4-2-2, 4-4-0. Kirtley 0-6-0 reb.
″	2′ 5¼″	4′ 1″	10′ 10⅝″	10′ 6″	7′ 0″	5′ 6½″	4′ 7½″	Middle group Johnson 4-2-2, 4-4-0, some Kirtley 0-6-0 reb.
	2′ 5¼″	4′ 1⅞″	10′ 10 11/16″	10′ 6″	8′ 0″	5′ 9½″	4′ 10½″	Later Johnson 4-2-2.
	2′ 9¼″	4′ 8″	10′ 10⅝″	10′ 5 15/16″	7′ 0″	5′ 6″	3′ 10½″	Johnson & Deeley 0-6-0, Johnson 4-4-0 and 0-6-0 reb, Deeley 0-6-4T and Kirtley 0-6-0 reb.
	2′ 9¼″	4′ 8″	10′ 10⅝″	10′ 5 15/16″	7′ 0″	5′ 6″	3′ 10½″	Deeley 0-6-4T & 0-6-0 as built, Johnson 4-4-0 & 0-6-0 rebuilds.
	1′ 10″	3′ 0″	9′ 4 7/16″	9′ 0″	3′ 0″	3′ 8″	3′ 8″	Small Johnson 0-4-0ST.
″	2′ 2 11/16″	3′ 8″	10′ 8⅝″	10′ 4″	4′ 0″	4′ 1½″	3′ 8″	Larger Johnson 0-4-0ST
	2′ 2 11/16″	3′ 8″	10′ 8⅝″	10′ 4″	4′ 0″	4′ 1½″	3′ 8″	Deeley 0-4-0T.
″	2′ 5¼″	4′ 1″	10′ 8⅝″	10′ 4″	5′ 11″	5′ 1½″	4′ 6½″	Kirtley 2-4-0 & 2-2-2 reb. Johnson 2-4-0s as built.
″	2′ 5¼″	4′ 1″	10′ 4⅝″	10′ 0 1/16″	4′ 11 15/16″	4′ 9½″	4′ 2½″	Johnson 0-6-0T rebuilds (17″ cyls) LMS. Class 2 0-6-0T.
″	2′ 5¼″	4′ 1″	10′ 10⅝″	10′ 6 1/16″	5′ 5 15/16″	5′ 1½″	4′ 6½″	Johnson 18″ cyl 0-6-0 T & 0-4-4T reb. LMS Class 3 0-6-0T.
″	2′ 5¼″	4′ 1″	10′ 10 11/16″	10′ 6 1/16″	5′ 10 15/16″	5′ 1½″	4′ 6½″	Kirtley 0-6-0 reb; Johnson 0-6-0 & 2-4-0 reb, LMS Class 2 0-4-4T.
	2′ 9¼″	4′ 8″	10′ 10⅝″	10′ 5 15/16″	7′ 0″	5′ 6″	3′ 10½″	Johnson 4-4-0s & 0-6-0s reb. Deeley 0-6-0 reb.
	2′ 9¼″	4′ 8″	10′ 10⅝″	10′ 5 15/16″	7′ 0″	5′ 6″	3′ 10½″	Johnson 4-4-0 reb, Deeley 0-6-4T & three 0-6-0 reb, & Fowler 0-6-0, LMS 2P 4-4-0s.
⅞″	2′ 9¼″	4′ 8″	11′ 4¾″	11′ 0″	8′ 0″	5′ 6½″	3′ 9″	Johnson Belpaire class 4-4-0s (1902–5).
⅞″	2′ 9¼″	4′ 8″	11′ 4¾″	11′ 0″	8′ 0″	5′ 6½″	3′ 9″	Johnson Belpaire class 4-4-0s (last 20).
⅞″	2′ 9¼″	4′ 8″	11′ 4¾″	11′ 0″	8′ 0″	5′ 6½″	3′ 9″	Johnson 700 class 4-4-0 rebuilt Fowler 2-6-4Ts.
″	2′ 9¼″	4′ 8″	11′ 11¾″	11′ 7″	8′ 6″	5′ 6½″	3′ 9″	First Five Johnson compound 4-4-0s as built.
″	2′ 9¼″	4′ 7⅞″	12′ 3¾″	11′ 11″	9′ 0″	5′ 6½″	3′ 9″	Deeley compound 4-4-0s as built.
″	2′ 9¼″	4′ 7⅞″	12′ 3¾″	11′ 11″	9′ 0″	5′ 6½″	3′ 9″	Deeley 990 class 4-4-0s as built.
″	2′ 9¼″	4′ 7⅞″	12′ 3¾″	11′ 11″	9′ 0″	5′ 6½″	3′ 9″	Deeley 990 class 4-4-0 rebuilds. LMS Compounds & MR rebuilds, First S&DJR 2-8-0s.
″	2′ 9¼″	5′ 3″	12′ 3¾″	11′ 11″	9′ 0″	5′ 6½″	3′ 9″	Last Five S&DJR 2-8-0s.
	3′ 0⅝″	5′ 3 11/16″	14′ 0″	14′ 5⅞″	9′ 6″	5′ 6⅝″	4′ 0½″	Patriot class 4-6-0s as built LNWR Claughtons as reb.
3 15/16″	3′ 0 13/16″	5′ 3″	14′ 4¾″	14′ 0″	10′ 0″	5′ 6¼″	3′ 11¾″	Fowler 0-10-0 Banker.
⅜″	2′ 9¼″	4′ 8″	10′ 10¾″	10′ 6″	8′ 0″	5′ 6¼″	3′ 9″	First ten 700 class 4-4-0s.
⅝″	2′ 5¼″	4′ 1″	10′ 10 11/16″	10′ 6 1/16″	5′ 10 15/16″	5′ 1½″	4′ 6½″	LMS Fowler Class 3 2-6-2T.

n boiler dimensions:
- Centre-line of dome to tubeplate.
- Radius of front tube plate.
- Barrel diameter (outside) first ring.
- Between tubeplates.

E — Firebox to tubeplate.
F — Firebox length.
G — Bottom of box to centre-line of boiler.
H — Back of box to centre-line of boiler.

*Appendix IV Summary of Diesel Locomotives
built at Derby for British Railways, 1953 to 1967*

Year	Running Numbers	Qty	Type	Order No.	Renumberings
1953	13015–24	10	0-6-0 Diesel Electric Shunter	O/6232	D3015–24 then 3015–24
	13025–33	9	0-6-0 Diesel Electric Shunter	O/6739	D3025–33 then 3025–33
	13034–9	6	0-6-0 Diesel Electric Shunter	Part O/6839	D3034–9 then 3034–9
1954	13040–59	20	0-6-0 Diesel Electric Shunter	Part O/6839	D3040–59 then 3040–59
	13082–96	15	0-6-0 Diesel Electric Shunter	O/8240	D3082–96 then 3082–96
1955	13097–116	20	0-6-0 Diesel Electric Shunter	O/8340	D3097–116 then 3097–116
	13117–24	8	0-6-0 Diesel Electric Shunter	Part D8350	D3117–24 then 3117–24
	13167–91	25	0-6-0 Diesel Electric Shunter	Part D9244	D3167–91 then 3167–91
	13192–206	15	0-6-0 Diesel Electric Shunter	Part D9245	D3192–206 then 3192–206
1956	13207–16	10	0-6-0 Diesel Electric Shunter	Part D9245	D3207–16 then 3207–16
	13245–94	50	0-6-0 Diesel Electric Shunter	Part D9248	D3245–94 then 3245–94
1957	13295–7	3	0-6-0 Diesel Electric Shunter	Part D9248	D3295–7 then 3295–7
	13125–6	2	0-6-0 Diesel Electric Shunter	Part D8350	D3125–6 then 3125–6
	D3337–3407	71	0-6-0 Diesel Electric Shunter	Part D252	3337–3407
1958	D3408–18	11	0-6-0 Diesel Electric Shunter	Part D252	3408–18
	D3503–72	70	0-6-0 Diesel Electric Shunter	D658	3503–72
	D5000–6	7	1160hp Bo-Bo Main Line D.E.	Part D251	5000–6
1959	D5007–19	13	1160hp Bo-Bo Main Line D.E.	Part D251	5007–19

*NOTE: in consequence of the withdrawal of the last steam locomotives on British Railways the 'D' prefix for diesel locomotives was dispensed with from August 1968.

Year	Running Numbers	Qty	Type	Order No.	Renumberings
	D5020-9	10	116ohp Bo-Bo Main Line D.E.	D861	5020-9
	D5066-9	4	116ohp Bo-Bo Main Line D.E.	Part D1410	5066-9
	D1-9	9	2300hp 1Co-Co1 Main Line D.E.	Part D9650	1-9
	D3763-3802	40	0-6-0 Diesel Electric Shunter	D1400	3763-3802
1960	D3937-4010	74	0-6-0 Diesel Electric Shunter	D2277	3937-4010
	D5070-5	6	116ohp Bo-Bo Main Line D.E.	Part D1410	5070-5
	D5114-48	35	116ohp Bo-Bo Main Line D.E.	Part D2276	5114-48
	D10	1	2300hp 1Co-Co1 Main Line D.E.	Part D9650	10
	D11-9	9	2500hp 1Co-Co1 Main Line D.E.	D2275	11-9
1961	D20-30	11	2500hp 1Co-Co1 Main Line D.E.	Part D2275	20-30
	D31-49	19	2500hp 1Co-Co1 Main Line D.E.	Part D2278	31-49
	D138-47	10	2500hp 1Co-Co1 Main Line D.E.	Part D2278	138-47
	D148-50	3	2500hp 1Co-Co1 Main Line D. E.	Part N3290	148-50
	D5149-50	2	116ohp Bo-Bo Main Line D.E.	Part D2276	5149-50
1962	D151-7	7	2500hp 1Co-Co1 Main Line D.E.	Part N3290	151-7
	D158-65	8	2500hp 1Co-Co1 Main Line D.E.	Part N3291	158-65
	D166-88	23	2500hp 1Co-Co1 Main Line D.E.	Part N3892	166-88
1963	D189-93	5	2500hp 1Co-Co1 Main Line D.E.	Part N3892	189-93
	D5186-5222	37	1250hp Bo-Bo Main Line D.E.	Part N4600	5186-5222
	D7568-77	10	1250hp Bo-Bo Main Line D.E.	Part N4600	7568-77
	D5233-7	5	1250hp Bo-Bo Main Line D.E.	Part N5701	5233-7
	D5238-42	5	1250hp Bo-Bo Main Line D.E.	Part N5702	5238-42

Year	Running Numbers	Qty	Type	Order No.	Renumberings
1964	D5243–57	15	1250hp Bo-Bo Main Line D.E.	Part N5702	5243–57
	D5258–97	40	1250hp Bo-Bo Main Line D.E.	N5703	5258–97
	D5298 D7500–18 & D7520	21	1250hp Bo-Bo Main Line D.E.	Part N5704	5298, 7500–18 & 7520
1965	D5299, D7519, D7521–37	19	1250hp Bo-Bo Main Line D.E.	Part N5704	5299, 7519, 7521–37
	D7538–65	28	1250hp Bo-Bo Main Line D.E.	Part N5705	7538–65
1966	D7566–7	2	1250hp Bo-Bo Main Line D.E.	Part N5705	7566–7
	D7598–7623	26	1250hp Bo-Bo Main Line D.E.	O/10001	7598–7623
	D7660–6	7	1250hp Bo-Bo Main Line D.E.	Part O/11001	7660–6
1967	D7667–77	11	1250hp Bo-Bo Main Line D.E.	Part O/11001	7667–77

List correct to December 31, 1970

Summary of Locomotives Built

Steam	2941
Battery Electric	1
Diesel	1010
	3952

Bibliography

BRITISH TRANSPORT HISTORICAL RECORDS
including minutes of the various committees, locomotive registers
and diagram books, staff registers and miscellaneous records of the
various railway companies involved.

JOURNALS
The Journal of the Institution of Locomotive Engineers
The Journal of the Institution of Mechanical Engineers
The Journal of the Stephenson Locomotive Society
The Railway Gazette
The Railway Engineer
The Railway Magazine
The Locomotive and Carriage and Wagon Review

MISCELLANEOUS
The Development of British Locomotive Design (E. L. Ahrons)
The British Steam Railway Locomotive (1825–1925) (E. L. Ahrons)
*Locomotive and Train Working in the latter part of the Nineteenth Century
Vol. 2* (E. L. Ahrons)
The Midland Railway (C. Hamilton Ellis)
Locomotive Panorama. Vol. 1 (E. S. Cox)
Chronicles of Steam (E. S. Cox)
The Fowler and Stanier Locomotives of the LMS (C. Langley Aldrich)
The Midlands Compounds (D. F. Tee)
Midland Railway Memories (G. J. Pratt)
St Andrew's Church, Derby (Rev. M. R. Austin)

Index

235